Three Months in the Southern States

THREE MONTHS IN THE SOUTHERN STATES:

APRIL – JUNE, 1863.

by
Lt. Col. Arthur James Lyon Fremantle
COLDSTREAM GUARDS

Introduction by Gary W. Gallagher

University of Nebraska Press
Lincoln and London

First Bison Book printing: 1991
Most recent printing indicated by the last digit below:
10   9   8   7   6   5   4   3   2   1

Library of Congress Cataloging-in-Publication Data
Fremantle, Arthur James Lyon, Sir. 1835–1901.
Three months in the Southern states: April–June, 1863 /
by Lieut.-Col. Fremantle; introduction by Gary W. Gallagher.
p. cm.
"Bison book"—T.p. verso.
Reprint, with new introd. and index. Originally published: New York: J. Bradburn, 1864.
Includes bibliographical references and index.
ISBN 0-8032-6875-0 (paper)
1. Confederate States of America—Description and
travel. 2. Fremantle, Arthur James Lyon, Sir, 1835–
1901—Journeys—Confederate States of America. 3.
United States—History—Civil War, 1861–1865—Personal narratives, British. 4. British—Confederate States
of America. I. Title.
E487.F863   1991
973.7'692—dc20
90-46246   CIP

Reprinted from the 1864 edition published in New York
by John Bradburn

♾

CONTENTS.

Introduction...................................... vii

Preface 5

Three Months in the Southern States....... 7

Postscript 305

Index...311

INTRODUCTION
By Gary W. Gallager

Foreign observers left some of the most vivid accounts of society and military affairs in the Confederacy. William Howard Russell painted an unforgettable picture of the South during the early days of the war, while Thomas Conolly, a member of Parliament, sketched the dramatic closing scenes in the southern capital at Richmond. Garnot Wolseley's brief trip to Virginia in the fall of 1862 inspired a famous—and unabashedly sympathetic—description of the southern people at war. Francis Charles Lawley, who covered the Confederacy for the *Times* of London from October 1862 to April 1865, echoed Wolseley's enthusiasm for the Confederate cause in his detailed reports. Heros von Borcke's stirring tale of his service with the cavalry of Lee's army reflected its author's exuberance, passionate devotion to the Confederacy, and occasional willingness to opt for drama over strict accuracy. Among several excellent eyewitnesses who wrote books about the pivotal year of 1863 were Captain Justus Scheibert, a Prussian engineer who observed Lee's army and joined his countryman von Borcke on "Jeb"

Stuart's staff for a time; Captain Fitzgerald Ross of the Austrian cavalry, who traveled across much of the Confederacy in 1863 and early 1864; and French scientist Charles F. Girard, who addressed a memoir of his time in the Confederacy to Napoleon III.[1]

Arthur James Lyon Fremantle also traveled through the Confederacy in 1863. A twenty-eight-year-old graduate of Sandhurst and son of an English major general, Fremantle held the rank of captain in the Coldstream Guards and lieutenant colonel in the British army. He had been assigned in 1860 to the post of military secretary at Gibraltar, whence he read avidly about the mushrooming war in North America. Initial sympathy for the North, which Fremantle attributed to his own dislike of slavery, quickly gave way to open support for the South. He admired the "gallantry and determination of the Southerners" and disapproved of what he termed the "foolish, bullying conduct of the Northerners."[2] In January 1862 he met the Confederate naval Captain Raphael Semmes, whose *C.S.S. Sumter* had put in at Gibraltar. Semmes recalled shortly after the war: "I found Freemantle [sic] to be an ardent Confederate, expressing himself without any reserve, and lauding in the highest terms our people and cause." After a pleasant discussion with the inquisitive young British officer, Semmes accepted Fremantle's invitation to tour the British holdings at Gibraltar. In all, it was a cordial acquaintanceship that did nothing to dim Fremantle's growing southern sympathies. He eventually decided that he must see "something of this wonderful struggle" himself, secured a leave of six months, and made his way to the Confederacy via Mexico.[3]

Fremantle entered Texas at Brownsville in early April and set off on a remarkable three-month odyssey that took him to nine of the eleven Confederate states and many of the principal southern cities.[4] Along the way he managed to meet such prominent figures as Jefferson Davis, Robert E. Lee, James Longstreet, Braxton Bragg, Joseph E. Johnston, and P. G. T. Beauregard. He kept a diary in which he recorded perceptive observations not only about these famous men but also about the countryside and common folk of the Confederacy from the Texas frontier to the northern stretches of Virginia. No foreigner grasped more fully the South's immense size and diversity, none possessed a keener eye or greater facility in committing to paper what he had seen.

Nor did any other European visitor impress more favorably his Confederate hosts. The Prussian observer Scheibert spoke of the Englishman's ability "to win the hearts of everyone with his open, candid behavior" and remarked fur-

ther that he "was respected by all."[5] Fremantle
spent perhaps his most exciting days with the
First Corps headquarters of Lieutenant General
James Longstreet, joining the general and his
staff as the Army of Northern Virginia marched
toward its fateful rendezvous with the Army of
the Potomac at Gettysburg. Armed with letters
of introduction from Secretary of War James E.
Seddon, Fremantle explained that he wished to
observe the coming campaign as a noncomba-
tant and, in the words of Fitzgerald Ross, quickly
became "a great favourite" of the taciturn
Longstreet.[6]

In his postwar memoir, Longstreet remembered that the Englishman "travelled with us,
divided his time between general head-quarters
and head-quarters of the First Corps, cheerfully
adapted his tastes to the rough ways of Confederate soldiers, and proved to be an interesting
companion." Longstreet especially recalled Fremantle's colorful stories of his trek across Texas
in a "two-horse hack"; the drivers of the hack,
one of whom was a judge, were familiar to
Longstreet from his antebellum service in Texas
with the United States army. "In England there
are few judges comparatively, and those of high
estate," remarked Longstreet in reference to his
English visitor's reaction to the absence of strict
class distinction in Texas. "To find an American
judge playing assistant to a hack-driver was re-

freshing, and Colonel Fremantle thoroughly enjoyed it." Fitzgerald Ross noted that Longstreet disagreed with members of his staff who doubted the Englishman could pass safely through the Federal lines when he left the Army of Northern Virginia: "A man who has travelled all through Texas as successfully as the Colonel, is safe to get through Yankee lines all right."[7]

Gilbert Moxley Sorrel, Longstreet's urbane chief of staff, shared his superior's view of Fremantle as a "fine officer and friend of ours." The Englishman "roughed it with the hardest, and took everything as it came," thought Sorrel. "A quick, observant eye and indefatigable sightseer, apparently nothing escaped him." Published several decades after Appomattox, Sorrel's recollections applauded Fremantle's successful postwar career and continued sympathy with the Confederate cause: "[He] successively obtained rank as major general, lieutenant general, and general, with several military orders of coveted distinction. He is now Sir Arthur Lyon-Fremantle, K.C.M.G., and of other good-service orders. He commanded the brigade of guards in Egypt, and has just finished . . . his four years's tour of duty as Governor of Malta, one of the greatest of the British military posts. He is delightful to every Confederate he can put his hands upon."[8]

Officers in the western armies of the Confederacy seconded the opinions of their eastern comrades. W. N. Mercer Otey, a member of Lieutenant General Leonidas Polk's staff, described Fremantle as one of "the most agreeable" of the many foreigners who visited the Army of Tennessee. "He was a most pleasant companion and seemed to enjoy our table d'hote with as much zest as any of us, " stated Otey, who hinted that Fremantle's hosts indulged in light sport with their good-natured guest: "Our gumbo fillet was quite *au fait,* and he could hardly credit our chef's remark that it was made from the tender twigs of the young sassafras bush that grows so lavishly in the South, with the photograph of a chicken that had done service in the days gone by." Charles Todd Quintard, a well-educated man who served as a chaplain and surgeon with the Army of Tennessee, remembered Fremantle's arrival at General Polk's headquarters as "a very agreeable addition to our party." Quintard pronounced the colonel a "very intelligent and very companionable" officer of ancient and honorable lineage who seemed "worthy to wear his ancestral honors."[9]

Fremantle's personal appearance probably impressed Confederates almost as much as his geniality and sympathy for the South. Sorrel described him as "a very small, slight man, wiry, and much enduring," adding, "I don't believe he changed his clothing or boots while he was with us." A photograph taken of Fremantle in the clothing he wore on his trip confirms Sorrel's general description and also illuminates Fremantle's comment to Fitzgerald Ross about "the invariable custom of the Confederate soldiers, of never allowing the smallest peculiarity of dress or appearance to pass without a torrent of jokes, which, however good-humored, ended in becoming rather monotonous." The photograph reveals a diminutive Ichabod Crane who must have inspired untold gibes as he passed within sight of sardonic southern infantrymen. A rail-thin figure in wide corduroy pants and boots that reached mid-calf, Fremantle affected a tartan shawl or throw worn casually across one shoulder. Long sidewhiskers accentuated his already elongated face; drooping eyes peered from beneath a high-crowned hat set at a jaunty angle. With his head cocked slightly in the direction his hat pointed, the colonel seemed to list precariously to his right. Extreme good humor, which Fremantle habitually exhibited, would have been essential for any visitor to the Confederate armies who dressed in this way.[10]

Fremantle returned to England after his sojourn in the Confederacy and soon prepared his diary from America for publication. An excerpt embracing Lee's march into Maryland and the battle of Gettysburg appeared in the September 1863 number of *Blackwood's Magazine,* fol-

lowed later that year by the first English edition
of the entire diary titled *Three Months in the
Southern States: April– June, 1863*.[11] American
publishers soon brought Fremantle's work to
northern and southern audiences. The New York
version of Edward A. Pollard's *Southern History
of the War: The Second Year of the War* included
Fremantle's passages on Gettysburg, and houses
in New York and Mobile printed full editions of
the work.[12] Southerners applauded the book's
warm support for their cause at a time when
fortunes on the battlefield had begun to mock
Fremantle's prediction of Confederate victory.
Constance Cary Harrison, wife of Jefferson
Davis's closest aide, subsequently asserted that
when the English edition of *Three Months in
the Southern States* came through the blockade
"its charming spirit and interesting present-
ment of the situation was greatly welcomed."
Moxley Sorrel marveled at Fremantle's preci-
sion in depicting events: "I never saw him use
a notebook or any scrap of paper as an aid to
memory, and yet his book put down things with
such accuracy." For many years after the war,
southern writers continued to quote approv-
ingly from their staunch English friend's book.[13]

Three Months in the Southern States eventually earned a reputation as one of the best
personal accounts of the war. Douglas Southall
Freeman considered Fremantle's treatment of

the campaign into Pennsylvania the "classic 'foreign observer's' account of Gettysburg"; as for the book as a whole, Freeman believed that a "more dignified picture of the Confederate cause could not have been presented." James I. Robertson, Jr., agreed that the diary fully deserved "its reputation as the best commentary on the wartime South by an English visitor." Acknowledging Fremantle's general identification with the South, E. Merton Coulter pointed out that he nonetheless recorded "some uncomplimentary observations." Overall, Coulter, who assessed the works of hundreds of eyewitnesses in the Confederacy, considered Fremantle "intelligent and observant" and his account "reliable and incisive." *Three Months in the Southern States* occupies a place on Richard B. Harwell's roster of two hundred essential books on the Confederacy and surely would win a position on even a much more selective list.[14]

Fremantle's book remains a superior source on the Confederacy. Its most quoted pages pertain to Gettysburg, where the colonel managed to participate in a number of dramatic scenes. His innocent comment to Longstreet that he would not miss the assault on July 3 for anything, and Longstreet's grimly humorous response that the attack already had failed and he "*would like to have missed it very much,*" form one of the best military anecdotes from the

Civil War. Equally famous are Fremantle's passages on Lee's calm attempts to rally the sur-
vivors of the assault and his willingness to take
full responsibility for its failure. "Never mind,
General," Fremantle quotes Lee in conversation
with Cadmus Wilcox, "*all this has been MY
fault*—it is *I* that have lost this fight, and you
must help me out of it in the best way you can."
Defenders of Lee often cite this passage as evidence of his humility, implying that he did not
really consider himself to blame. But if the general is taken at his word in this crucial moment
(and there is no reason to doubt Fremantle's
veracity in reporting the exchange), the passionate appeals of postwar apologists and later
generations of historians ill-disposed to criticize
Lee lose most of their force.[15]

A great strength of the book lies in its bio-
graphical vignettes. For example, Fremantle
captures much of Sam Houston's complex character, as well as a frontier roughness that years
in state and national office had not dispelled,
in just two sentences: "Though evidently a remarkable and clever man, he is extremely egotistical and vain, and much disappointed at
having to subside from his former grandeur.
. . . In appearance he is a tall, handsome old
man, much given to chewing tobacco, and blowing his nose with his fingers." In his portrait of
Mr. Sargent, the "professor" of mule-skinning,

Fremantle sometimes approaches Mark Twain's ability to sketch outlandish characters, while his sensitive observations about Jefferson Davis suggest warm humanity behind a brittle public exterior. Fremantle sometimes allowed a subject's courtly facade to warp his judgment, as with Leonidas Polk, a seriously flawed military commander characterized as "a sincere patriot, a gallant soldier, and a perfect gentleman." Far more often, however, the glimpses of men such as Joseph Johnston, Beauregard, John Bankhead Magruder, Braxton Bragg, and Judah P. Benjamin include useful insights.[16]

The diary offers ample evidence for those who seek to understand the relative reputations of Jackson, Longstreet, and Lee. Stories about Jackson's prewar career, his peculiar notions about health, and other facets of his life and personality greeted Fremantle in all parts of the South—surely an indication of national interest and acclaim. In the lower Shenandoah Valley, where Jackson performed magnificently in the spring of 1862, Fremantle thought the citizens considered him "a regular demigod." But other entries underscore that in both the army and the government Jackson was viewed as Longstreet's peer and Lee's lieutenant, not as a semi-independent hero who rivaled Lee and dwarfed Longstreet. Secretary of State Benjamin pointed out the fallacy of according too much credit to

Jackson for Lee's strategic successes at Second Manassas and Chancellorsville (as British newspapers had done), and Fremantle correctly observed that Jackson was third in command of the army behind Lee and Longstreet. As for Longstreet, he emerges as a man upon whom Lee relied for counsel and friendship, and an accomplished soldier "invariably spoken of as 'the best fighter in the whole army.' "[17]

Lee towers above both his great lietuenants and all other Confederate commanders in Fremantle's pages. At Joseph Johnston's headquarters in Mississippi, several officers somewhat defensively insisted that they considered their chief to be the equal of "Lee or any one else." It is difficult to imagine Lee's officers feeling the need to make such a statement; Johnston's subordinates almost certainly reacted to a public perception of Lee as the South's preeminent general. After meeting all of the full generals then in active field command, Fremantle concluded that Lee "is a perfect gentleman in every respect. I imagine no man has so few enemies, or is so universally esteemed. Throughout the South, all agree in pronouncing him to be as near perfection as a man can be." On this point, Fremantle's testimony serves as strong counterpoint to studies that argue Lee did not achieve his position in the forefront of the Confederate pantheon until the postwar mythmaking of the Lost Cause.[18]

Successful Confederate generals such as Lee and Longstreet understood their men, Fremantle believed, and thereby elicited from them magnificent performances on the battlefield. Individually courageous, adept with weapons, and confident in themselves, southern soldiers demanded personal bravery on the part of their officers. From Colonel George St. Leger Grenfel, a British soldier of fortune who served with the western Confederate armies, Fremantle heard that Confederate soldiers demanded their their officers *lead* them in combat. Any commander who demonstrated the least reluctance to face danger immediately lost influence over his men: "Colonel Grenfell's expression was, 'every atom of authority has to be purchased by a drop of your blood.'" Students of the Civil War who wonder why southern generals and field grade officers seem to have exposed themselves needlessly might ponder Fremantle's discussion of the relationship between Confederate commanders and their men.[19]

Fremantle's wide travels make his diary a good source for information on the Confederate home front, though his pro-Confederate feelings probably led him to overlook evidence of antiwar sentiment. He generally found strong civilian support for the war, even among poorer families who suffered economic distress. From central Mississippi, Fremantle observed that "it is impossible to exaggerate the unfortunate condition of the women left behind in these farmhouses; they have scarcely any clothes, and nothing but the coarsest bacon to eat, and are in miserable uncertainty as to the fate of their relations, whom they hardly ever communicate with." Yet despite their hardship, these people "were red-hot in favor of fighting for their independence to the last, and I constantly hear the words, 'This is the most unjust war ever waged upon a people by mortal man.' " He did report that many southern men sought to evade the draft through government employment, and he quoted two conscripts who confessed "their extreme dislike of the military profession." However, Fremantle added that even the two conscripts "acknowledged the enthusiasm of the masses for the war."[20]

Wherever he traveled in the Confederacy, white southerners sought to convince Fremantle that the institution of slavery imposed few hardships on blacks. They admitted "many instances of cruelty," but blamed Yankees who settled in the South for perpetrating the worst outrages (Fremantle stated in a footnote that Mr. Sargent, who described an instance in which he beat a female slave, "is a Northerner by birth"). They said most educated southerners once viewed slavery as "a misfortune and not justifiable, though necessary under the circumstances," until abolitionist agitation "had caused the bonds to be drawn much tighter." Fremantle's hosts insisted that slave traders remained anathema, that the vast majority of slaves were perfectly happy, and that any owner who beat a slave incurred the contempt of the rest of the community. In sum, Fremantle heard the classic defense of slavery as refined over the decades preceding the war. He took these arguments to heart, as evidenced by his opinion that "if the Confederate States were *left alone,* the system would be much modified and amended, although complete emancipation cannot be expected." Indeed, the colonel went so far as to predict that southern slaves would readily fight for their Confederate masters, though he doubted that whites would conduct such an experiment except in extreme circumstances. Fremantle's unsparing description of northern racism during the New York draft rioting, although certainly accurate, contrasts sharply with his usually gentle treatment of southern whites and slavery.[21]

Fremantle's own cultural assumptions understandably colored many of his entries. As an upper-class Englishman he noted with approval similarities between southerners and aristo-

crats in England. He especially praised Leonidas Polk's principal aides: "Highly educated,
wealthy, and prosperous before the war, they
have abandoned all for their country. They, and
all other Southern gentlemen of the same rank,
are proud of their descent from Englishmen.
They glory in speaking English as we do, and
that their manners and feelings resemble those
of the upper classes in the old country." Anyone
wondering how seriously to take the cavalier
image of antebellum southern males should heed
Fremantle's claim that "all wellbred" southern
men spoke English "exactly like an English
gentleman." Other groups fared less well at Fremantle's hands. He considered the Mexicans a
brutal people, mocked their Catholic religion,
and disparaged their style of dress. Germans,
Irish, Poles, and other ethnic members of southern and northern society received similar criticism.[22]

A careful reading of *Three Months in the
Southern States* reveals a kaleidoscopic view of
the Confederacy at floodtide. From the primitive backcountry of Texas to the sedate drawing
rooms of Richmond, Colonel Fremantle trained
his lens on a people whose hopes for independence remained vital. If he missed certain facets
of southern society and misinterpreted others,
his roving eye nonetheless captured a bountiful
slice of United States history. Few books in all

the vast literature on the Civil War have proved
to be more durable, fewer still have supplied
historians and other students with more drama
and insight. This new edition of Fremantle's
diary, now indexed for the first time, makes
available to another generation of readers a
classic account of Americans at war.

NOTES

1. For the observations of these European visitors, see
William Howard Russell, *My Diary North and South,* ed.
Fletcher Pratt (New York: Harper and Brothers, 1954 [an
expanded reprint of the original 1863 edition]); Nelson D.
Lankford, ed., *An Irishman in Dixie: Thomas Conolly's
Diary of the Fall of the Confederacy* (Columbia: University
of South Carolina Press, 1988); Field Marshall Viscount
Wolseley, *The American Civil War: An English View,* ed.
James A. Rawley (Charlottesville: University Press of Vir-
ginia, 1964 [a collection of Wolseley's writings that in-
cludes "A Month's Visit to the Confederate Headquarters,"
first published in *Blackwood's Magazine* in January 1863]);
William Stanley Hoole, *Lawley Covers the Confederacy*
(Tuscaloosa, Ala: Confederate Publishing Company, 1964);
Heros von Borcke, *Memoirs of the Confederate War for
Independence,* 2 vols. (Edinburgh and London: W. Blackwood and Sons, 1866 [these *Memoirs* have been reprinted
in the United States several times]); Justus Scheibert,
*Seven Months in the Rebel States during the North Amer-
ican War, 1863,* trans. from the German by Joseph C. Hayes
and ed. by William Stanley Hoole (Tuscaloosa, Ala: Confederate Publishing Company, 1958 [reprint of original
German edition published in 1868]); Fitzgerald Ross, *Cit-*

ies and Camps of the Confederate States, ed. Richard B. Harwell (Urbana: University of Illinois Press, 1958 [reprint of original edition published in 1865]); Charles F. Girard, *A Visit to the Confederate States of America in 1863: Memoir Addressed to His Majesty Napoleon III,* translated and ed. by William Stanley Hoole (Tuscaloosa, Ala: Confederate Publishing Company, 1962 [reprint of original French edition published in 1864]).

2. The outline of Fremantle's life may be traced in his obituary in the *Times* of September 26, 1901. The quotations are on page 5 in the text.

3. Raphael Semmes, *Memoirs of Service Afloat, During the War Between the States* (Baltimore: Kelly, Piet and Company, 1869), p. 315. Fremantle's quotation is on page 5 in the text.

4. Fremantle's journeys excluded only Arkansas and Florida.

5. Scheibert, *Seven Months in the Rebel States,* pp. 104, 121. Scheibert and Fremantle saw each other frequently during the Gettysburg campaign. Early on the morning of July 2, Confederate divisional commander John Bell Hood saw Fremantle "ensconced in the forks of a tree . . . with glass in constant use, examining the lofty position of the Federal army." Scheibert testified that he joined Fremantle: "From here the battlefield lay before us like a panorama. On July 2 and 3, therefore, I did not move a step from the tree, from where I frequently had to report what I saw" (pp. 112–13); John Bell Hood, "Letter from General John B. Hood," in J. William Jones and others, eds., *The Southern Historical Society Papers,* 52 vols. and 2-vol. index (1876–1959; reprint, Millwood, N.Y.: Kraus Reprint Company, 1977–80), 4:147. See also Justus Scheibert, "Letter from Maj. Scheibert, of the Prussian Royal Engineers," in *Southern Historical Society Papers,* 5:90.

Fremantle's discussion of his climbing the tree is on pages 257–59 in the text.

6. Ross, *Cities and Camps,* p. 75.

7. James Longstreet, *From Manassas to Appomattox: Memoirs of the Civil War in America* (Philadelphia: J. B. Lippincott Company, 1896), pp. 343–44; Ross, *Cities and Camps,* p. 74.

8. Gilbert Moxley Sorrel, *Recollections of a Confederate Staff Officer* (1905; reprint, ed. Bell I. Wiley, Jackson, Tenn.: McCowat-Mercer Press, 1959), pp. 160–61. Sorrel mentioned only the most important features of Fremantle's career after 1863 and was mistaken about some details. Commander of a battalion in the Coldstream Guards from 1877 to 1880, Fremantle served as aide-de-camp on the staff of the Duke of Cambridge in 1881–82. Promoted to major general in April 1882, he led a brigade in the Sudan expedition of 1884. Over the next two years he held various posts, including governor of Suakim, commander of the Brigade of Guards, and Chief of the Staff. Named Deputy Adjutant-General for Militia, Yeomanry, and Volunteers in 1886, he remained at Army Headquarters until 1892. February 1893 brought transfer to the Scottish District, which he commanded until appointed governor of Malta the following January. After a five-year term on Malta, he returned to England and settled in Brighton. He died on September 25, 1901, at the Royal Yacht Squadron Castle, Cowes. The recipient of many honors, Fremantle was created a K.C.M.G in 1894 and a G.C.M.G in 1898.

9. W. N. Mercer Otey, "Operations of the Signal Corps," in *Confederate Veteran* 8 (March 1900): 129; Arthur Howard Stoll, ed., *Doctor Quintard, Chaplain C.S.A. and Second Bishop of Louisiana* (Sewanee, Tenn.: The University Press, 1905), pp. 76–77.

10. Sorrel, *Recollections,* p. 170. Fremantle's quotation is on page 244 in the text. The photograph, sent to Longstreet as a token of thanks, was taken when Fremantle returned to London. In his novel *The Killer Angels* (New York: David McKay Company, 1975, p. 56), Michael Shaara describes Fremantle in a memorable passage: "He was a scrawny man, toothy, with a pipelike neck and monstrous Adam's apple. He looked like a popeyed bird who had just swallowed something large and sticky and triangular. He was wearing a tall gray hat and a remarkable coat with very wide shoulders, like wings." Shaara merged the tartan throw and Fremantle's coat to come up with a winged garment.

11. W. Blackwood and Sons of Edinburgh and London published the diary.

12. Edward A. Pollard, *Southern History of the War: The Second Year of the War* (New York: Charles B. Richardson, 1864); A. J. L. Fremantle, *Three Months in the Southern States: April–June, 1863* (New York: John Bradburn, 1864; Mobile, Ala.: S. H. Goetzel, 1864). A shortage of paper in the Confederacy obliged the publisher of the Mobile edition to use wallpaper wrappers. The book was reprinted in somewhat altered form, with an introduction and notes by Walter Lord, under the title *The Fremantle Diary: Being the Journal of Lieutenant Colonel Arthur James Lyon Fremantle, Coldstream Guards, on His Three Months in the Southern States* (Boston: Little, Brown and Company, 1954). A decade later, Richard B. Harwell included the chapters on Gettysburg, together with an excellent introduction on Fremantle and his book, in *Two Views of Gettysburg* (Chicago: R. R. Donnelley and Sons Company, 1964 [the other "view" was that of Union officer Frank A. Haskell]). See also Morgan Peoples, ed., "An Excursion across North Louisiana: Excerpts from the Di-

ary of British Lieutenant Colonel Thomas [sic] Fremantle (May 8 to May 15, 1863)," *North Louisiana Historical Association Journal* 8 (Summer 1977); 159–69.

13. Constance Cary Harrison, *Recollections Grave and Gay* (New York: Charles Scribner's Sons, 1911), p. 133; Sorrel, *Recollections,* p. 171. For examples of southern authors who quoted Fremantle, see Randolph McKim, "The Gettysburg Campaign," in *Southern Historical Society Papers* 40:256; *Confederate Veteran* 24 (August 1916): 357–58; and *Confederate Veteran* 39 (October 1931): 372–74.

14. Douglas Southall Freeman, *R. E. Lee: A Biography,* 4 vols. (New York: Charles Scribner's Sons, 1934–35), 4:562; Freeman, *The South to Posterity: An Introduction to the Writing of Confederate History* (New York: Charles Scribner's Sons, 1939), p. 19; Allan Nevins, et al., eds., *Civil War Books: A Criitical Bibliography,* 2 vols. (Baton Rouge: Louisiana State University Press, 1967, 1969), 1:91; E. Merton Coulter, *Travels in the Confederate States: A Bibliography* (Norman: University of Oklahoma Press, 1948), p. 101; Richard B. Harwell, *In Tall Cotton: The 200 Most Important Confederate Books for the Reader, Researcher and Collector* (Austin, Tex.: Jenkins Publishing Company, 1978), p. 22.

15. The quotations are on pages 266 and 269 in the text. For a discussion of the postwar effort to absolve Lee of all responsibility for the defeat at Gettysburg, see Thomas L. Connelly, *The Marble Man: Robert E. Lee and His Image in American Society* (New York: Alfred A. Knopf, 1977), chapters 2–3; and Glenn Tucker, *Lee and Longstreet at Gettysburg* (Indianapolis: Bobbs-Merrill Company, 1968).

16. The quotations are on pages 69 and 171–72 in the text. Edward Porter Alexander offered a more realistic evaluation of General Polk: "Now Gen. Polk graduated at West Point . . . & went into the ministry about 1832. The

Lord had made him a splendid bishop & a great & good man. So all our pious people with one consent & with secret conviction that the Lord would surely favor a bishop turned in & made him a lieut. gen., which the Lord had not." Gary W. Gallagher, ed., *Fighting for the Confederacy: The Personal Recollections of General Edward Porter Alexander* (Chapel Hill: University of North Carolina Press, 1989), pp. 288–89.

17. The quotations are on pages 225 and 237 in the text. On the tendency to elevate Jackson at Longstreet's expense, see William Garrett Piston, *Lee's Tarnished Lieutenant: James Longstreet and His Place in Southern History* (Athens: University of Georgia Press, 1987), chapters 6–8.

18. The quotations are on pages 118 and 248 in the text. In *The Marble Man,* Thomas L. Connelly sought to demonstrate that during and immediately after the war Beauregard, Joseph E. Johnston, Albert Sidney Johnston, and Jackson rivaled Lee as popular southern heroes. Mark E. Neely, Jr., Harold Holzer, and Gabor S. Boritt, *The Confederate Image: Prints of the Lost Cause* (Chapel Hill: University of North Carolina Press, 1987), demonstrated that in terms of pictoral representation Jackson and others preceded Lee as southern icons.

19. The quotation is on page 159 in the text. Douglas Southall Freeman addressed the problem of heavy casualties among officers in the Army of Northern Virginia in *Lee's Lieutenants: A Study in Command,* 3 vols. (New York: Charles Scribner's Sons, 1942–44). See especially chapter 16 of colume 2 and chapters 10 and 25 of volume 3.

20. The quotations are on pages 102 and 99 in the text. An excellent treatment of southern women that details significant opposition to the Confederate war effort is

George C. Rable, *Civil Wars: Women and the Crisis of Southern Nationalism* (Champaign: University of Illinois Press, 1989). On the southern home front as a whole, see Richard E. Beringer, et al., *Why the South Lost the Civil War* (Athens, Ga.: University of Georgia Press, 1986).

21. The quotations are on pages 82, 52, 81, and 191 in the text. Two useful studies of slavery and the Confederacy are Robert F. Durden, *The Gray and the Black: The Confederate Debate on Emancipation* (Baton Rouge: Louisiana State University Press, 1972), and Clarence L. Mohr, *On the Threshold of Freedom: Masters and Slaves in Civil War Georgia* (Athens: University of Georgia Press, 1986).

22. The quotations are on pages 172 and 140 in the text.

Three Months in the Southern States

PREFACE.

AT the outbreak of the American war, in common with many of my countrymen, I felt very indifferent as to which side might win; but if I had any bias, my sympathies were rather in favor of the North, on account of the dislike which an Englishman naturally feels at the idea of slavery. But soon a sentiment of great admiration for the gallantry and determination of the Southerners, together with the unhappy contrast afforded by the foolish bullying conduct of the Northerners, caused a complete revulsion in my feelings, and I was unable to repress a strong wish to go to America and see something of this wonderful struggle.

Having successfully accomplished my design, I returned to England, and found amongst all my friends an extreme desire to know the truth of what was going on in the South; for, in consequence of the blockade, the truth can with difficulty be arrived at, as intelligence coming mainly through Northern sources is not believed; and, in fact, nowhere is the ignorance of what is passing in the South more profound than it is in the Northern States.

In consequence of a desire often expressed, I now publish the Diary which I endeavored, as well as I could, to keep up day by day during my travels throughout the Confederate States.

I have not attempted to conceal any of the peculiarities or defects of the Southern people. Many persons will doubtless highly disapprove of some of their customs and habits in the wilder portion of the country; but I think no generous man, whatever may be his political opinions, can do otherwise than admire the courage, energy, and patriotism of the whole population, and the skill of its leaders, in this struggle against great odds. And I am also of opinion that many will agree with me in thinking that a people in which all ranks and both sexes display a unanimity and a heroism which can never have been surpassed in the history of the world, is destined, sooner or later, to become a great and independent nation.

THREE MONTHS

IN

THE SOUTHERN STATES.

APRIL, MAY, JUNE, 1863.

2d March, 1863.—I left England in the royal mail steamer Atrato, and arrived at St. Thomas on the 17th.

22d March.—Anchored at Havana at 6.15 A. M., where I fell in with my old friend, H. M.'s frigate Immortalité.   Captain Hancock not only volunteered to take me as his guest to Matamoros, but also to take a Texan merchant, whose acquaintance I had made in the Atrato.   This gentleman's name is M'Carthy.   He is of Irish birth—an excellent fellow, and a good companion; and when he understood my wish to see the "South," he had most good-naturedly volunteered to pilot me over part of the Texan deserts.   I owe much to Captain Hancock's kindness.

23d March.—Left Havana in H. M. S. Immortalité, at 11 A. M. Knocked off steam when outside the harbor.

1st April.—Anchored at 8.30 P. M., three miles from the mouth of the Rio Grande, or Rio Bravo del Norte, which is, I believe, its more correct name, in the midst of about seventy merchant vessels.

2d April.—The Texan and I left the Immortalité, in her cutter, at 10 A. M., and crossed the bar in fine style. The cutter was steered by Mr. Johnston, the master, and having a fair wind, we passed in like a flash of lightning, and landed at the miserable village of Bagdad, on the Mexican bank of the Rio Grande.

The bar was luckily in capital order—3½ feet of water, and smooth. It is often impassable for ten or twelve days together: the depth of water varying from 2 to 5 feet. It is very dangerous, from the heavy surf and under-current; sharks also abound. Boats are frequently capsized in crossing it, and the Orlando lost a man on it about a month ago.

Seventy vessels are constantly at anchor outside the bar; their cotton cargoes being brought to them, with very great delays, by two small steamers from Bagdad. These steamers draw only 3 feet of water, and realize an enormous profit.

Bagdad consists of a few miserable wooden shanties, which have sprung into existence since the war began. For an immense distance endless bales of cotton are to be seen.

Immediately we landed, M'Carthy was greeted by his brother merchants. He introduced me to Mr. Ituria, a Mexican, who promised to take me in his buggy to Brownsville, on the Texan bank of the river opposite Matamoros. M'Carthy was to follow in the evening to Matamoros.

The Rio Grande is very tortuous and shallow; the distance by river to Matamoros is sixty-five miles, and it is navigated by steamers, which sometimes perform the trip in twelve hours, but more often take twenty-four, so constantly do they get aground.

The distance from Bagdad to Matamoros by land is thirty-five miles; on the Texan side to Brownsville, twenty-six miles.

I crossed the river from Bagdad with Mr. Ituria, at 11 o'clock; and as I had no pass, I was taken before half-a-dozen Confederate officers, who were seated round a fire contemplating a tin of potatoes. These officers belonged to Duff's cavalry (Duff being my Texan's partner). Their dress consisted simply of flannel shirts, very ancient trousers, jack-boots with enormous spurs, and black felt hats, ornamented with the "lone star of Texas." They looked rough and dirty, but were extremely civil to me.

The captain was rather a boaster, and kept on

1*

remarking, "We've given 'em h—ll on the Mississippi, h—ll on the Sabine" (pronounced Sabeen),
" and h—ll in various other places."

He explained to me that he couldn't cross the river
to see M'Carthy, as he with some of his men had
made a raid over there three weeks ago, and carried
away some "renegadoes," one of whom, named Mongomery, they had *left* on the road to Brownsville;
by the smiles of the other officers, I could easily guess
that something very disagreeable must have happened to Mongomery. He introduced me to a skipper
who had just run his schooner, laden with cotton,
from Galveston, and who was much elated in consequence. The cotton had cost 6 cents a pound in
Galveston, and is worth 36 here.

Mr. Ituria and I left for Brownsville at noon. A
buggy is a light gig on four high wheels.

The road is a natural one—the country quite flat,
and much covered with mosquite-trees, very like pep-
per-trees. Every person we met carried a six-shooter,
although it is very seldom necessary to use them.

After we had proceeded about nine miles we met
General Bee, who commands the troops at Brownsville. He was travelling to Boca del Rio in an ambulance,* with his quartermaster-general, Major Rus-

* An ambulance is a light wagon, and generally has two springs
behind, and one transverse one in front. The seats can be so arranged that two or even three persons may lie at full length.

sell.   I gave him my letter of introduction to General
Magruder, and told him who I was.

He thereupon descended from his ambulance, and
regaled me with beef and beer in the open.   He is
brother to the General Bee who was killed at Manassas.   We talked politics and fraternized very ami-
cably for more than an hour.   He said the Mongomery affair was against his sanction and he was sorry
for it.   He said that Davis, another renegado, would
also have been put to death, had it not been for the
intercession of his wife.   General Bee had restored
Davis to the Mexicans.

Half an hour after parting company with General
Bee, we came to the spot where Mongomery had been
left; and sure enough, about two hundred yards to
the left of the road, we found him.

He had been slightly buried, but his head and arms
were above the ground, his arms tied together, the
rope still round his neck, but part of it still dangling
from quite a small mosquite-tree.   Dogs or wolves had
probably scraped the earth from the body, and there
was no flesh on the bones.   I obtained this my first
experience of Lynch law within three hours of landing in America.

I understand that this Mongomery was a man of
very bad character, and that, confiding in the neutrality of the Mexican soil, he was in the habit of calling
the Confederates all sorts of insulting epithets from

the Bagdad bank of the river; and a party of his
"renegadoes" had also crossed over and killed some
unarmed cotton teamsters, which had roused the fury
of the Confederates.

About three miles beyond this we came to Colonel
Duff's encampment.   He is a fine looking, handsome
Scotchman, and received me with much hospitality.
His regiment consisted of newly raised volunteers—
a very fine body of young men, who were drilling in
squads.   They were dressed in every variety of costume, many of them without coats, but all wore the
high black felt hat.   Notwithstanding the peculiarity
of their attire, there was nothing ridiculous or con-
temptible in the appearance of these men, who all
looked thoroughly like "business."   Colonel Duff
told me that many of the privates owned vast tracts
of country, with above a hundred slaves, and were
extremely well off.   They were all most civil to me.

Their horses were rather raw-boned animals, but
hardy and fast.   The saddles they used were nearly
like the Mexican.   Colonel Duff confessed that the
Mongomery affair was wrong, but he added that his
boys "*meant well.*"

We reached Brownsville at 5.30 P. M., and Mr. Ituria
kindly insisted on my sleeping at his house, instead
of going to the crowded hotel.

3d April (Good Friday).—At 8 A. M. I got a military pass to cross the Rio Grande into Mexico, which I presented to the sentry, who then allowed me to cross in the ferry-boat.

Carriages are not permitted to run on Good Friday in Mexico, so I had a hot dusty walk of more than a mile into Matamoros.

Mr. Zorn, the acting British Consul, and Mr. Behnsen, his partner, invited me to live at the Consulate during my stay at Matamoros, and I accepted their offer with much gratitude.

I was introduced to Mr. Colville, a Manchester man; to Mr. Maloney, one of the principal merchants; to Mr. Bennet, an Englishman, one of the owners of the Peterhoff, who seemed rather elated than otherwise when he heard of the capture of his vessel, as he said the case was such a gross one that our government would be obliged to take it up. I was also presented to the gobernador, rather a rough.

After dining with Mr. Zorn I walked back to the Rio Grande, which I was allowed to cross on presenting Mr. Colville's pass to the Mexican soldiers, and I slept at Mr. Ituria's again.

Brownsville is a straggling town of about 3,000 inhabitants; most of its houses are wooden ones, and its streets are long, broad, and straight. There are about 4,000 troops under General Bee in its immediate vicinity. Its prosperity was much injured when Matamoros was declared a free port.

After crossing the Rio Grande, a wide dusty road, about a mile in length, leads to Matamoros, which is a Mexican city of about 9,000 inhabitants. Its houses are not much better than those at Brownsville, and they bear many marks of the numerous revolutions which are continually taking place there. Even the British Consulate is riddled with the bullets fired in 1861–2.

The Mexicans look very much like their Indian forefathers, their faces being extremely dark, and their hair black and straight. They wear hats with the most enormous brims, and delight in covering their jackets and leather breeches with embroidery.

Some of the women are rather good-looking, but they plaster their heads with grease, and paint their faces too much. Their dress is rather like the Andalusian. When I went to the cathedral, I found it crammed with kneeling women; an effigy of our Saviour was being taken down from the cross and put into a golden coffin, the priest haranguing all the time about His sufferings, and all the women howling most dismally as if they were being beaten.

Matamoros is now infested with numbers of Jews, whose industry spoils the trade of the established merchants, to the great rage of the latter.

It suffers much from drought, and there had been no rain to speak of for eleven months.

I am told that it is a common thing in Mexico for

the diligence to arrive at its destination with the blinds down. This is a sure sign that the travellers, both male and female, have been stripped by robbers nearly to the skin. A certain quantity of clothing is then, as a matter of course, thrown in at the window, to enable them to descend. Mr. Behnsen and Mr. Maloney told me they had seen this happen several times; and Mr. Oetling declared that he himself, with three ladies, arrived at the city of Mexico in this predicament.

4th April (Saturday).—I crossed the river at 9 A. M., and got a carriage at the Mexican side to take my baggage and myself to the Consulate at Matamoros. The driver ill-treated his half-starved animals most cruelly. The Mexicans are even worse than the Spaniards in this respect.

I called on Mr. Oetling, the Prussian Consul, who is one of the richest and most prosperous merchants in Matamoros, and a very nice fellow.

After dinner we went to a *fandango*, or open-air fête. About 1500 people were gambling, and dancing bad imitations of European dances.

5th April (Sunday).—Mr. Zorn, or Don Pablo as he is called here, Her Majesty's acting Vice-Consul, is a quaint and most good-natured little man—a Prussian by birth. He is overwhelmed by the sudden importance he has acquired from his office, and by the amount of work (for which he gets no pay) entailed by it,—the office of British Consul having been a comparative sinecure before the war.

Mr. Behnsen is head of the firm. The principal place of business is at San Luis Potosi, a considerable city in the interior of Mexico. All these foreign merchants complain bitterly of the persecutions and extortion they have to endure from the Government, which are, doubtless, most annoying; but nevertheless they appear to fatten on the Mexican soil.

I crossed to Brownsville to see General Bee, but he had not returned from Boca del Rio.

I dined with Mr. Oetling. We were about fourteen at dinner, principally Germans, a very merry party. Mr. Oetling is supposed to have made a million of dollars for his firm, by bold cotton speculations, since the war.

We all went to the theatre afterwards. The piece was an attack upon the French and upon Southern institutions.

6th April (Monday).—Mr. Behnsen and Mr. Colville left for Bagdad this morning, in a very swell ambulance drawn by four gay mules.

At noon I crossed to Brownsville, and visited Captain Lynch, a quartermaster, who broke open a great box, and presented me with a Confederate felt hat to travel in. He then took me to the garrison, and introduced me to Colonel Buchel of the 3d Texas regiment, who is by birth a German, but had served in the French army; and he prepared cocktails in the most scientific manner. I returned to Matamoros at 2.30 P. M.

Captain Hancock and Mr. Anderson (the paymaster) arrived from Bagdad in a most miserable vehicle, at 4 P. M. They were a mass of dust, and had been seven hours on the road, after having been very nearly capsized on the bar.

There was a great firing of guns and squibs in the afternoon, in consequence of the news of a total defeat of the French at Puebla, with a loss of 8,000 prisoners and 70 pieces of cannon.

Don Pablo, who had innocently hoisted his British flag in honor of Captain Hancock, was accused by his brother merchants of making a demonstration against the French.

After dinner we called on Mr. Maloney, whose house is gorgeously furnished, and who has a pretty wife.

7th April (Tuesday).—Mr. Maloney sent us his carriage to conduct Captain Hancock, Mr. Anderson, and myself to Brownsville.

We first called on Colonels Luckett and Buchel; the former is a handsome man, a doctor by profession, well informed and agreeable, but most bitter against the Yankees.

We sat for an hour and a half talking with these officers and drinking endless cocktails, which were rather good, and required five or six different liquids to make them.

We then adjourned to General Bee's, with whom we had another long talk, and with whom we discussed more cocktails.

At the General's we were introduced to a well-dressed good-looking Englishman, Mr. ——, who, however, announced to us that he had abjured his nationality until Great Britain rendered justice to the South.* Two years since, this individual had his house burnt down; and a few days ago, happening to hear that one of the incendiaries was on the Mexican bank of the river, boasting of the exploit, he rowed himself across, shot his man, and then rowed back.

I was told afterwards that, notwithstanding the sentiments he had given out before us, Mr. —— is a stanch Britisher, always ready to produce his six-shooter at a moment's notice, at any insult to the Queen or to England.

We were afterwards presented to ——, rather a sinister-looking party, with long yellow hair down to

* It seems he has been dreadfully "riled" by the late Peterhoff affair.

his shoulders. This is the man who is supposed to have hanged Mongomery.

We were treated by all the officers with the greatest consideration, and conducted to the place of embarkation with much ceremony. Colonel Luckett leclared I should not leave Brownsville until General Magruder arrives. He is expected every day.

Mr. Maloney afterwards told us that these officers, having given up every thing for their country, were many of them in great poverty. He doubted whether —— had a second pair of boots in the world; but he added that, to do honor to British officers, they would scour Brownsville for the materials for cocktails.

At 3 P. M. we dined with Mr. Maloney, who is one of the principal and most enterprising British merchants at Matamoros, and enjoyed his hospitality till 9.30. His wine was good, and he made us drink a good deal of it. Mr. Oetling was there, and his stories of highway robberies, and of his journeys *en chemise*, were most amusing.

At 10 P. M. Mr. Oetling conducted us to the grand faudango given in honor of the reported victory over the French.

A Mexican fandango resembles a French *ducasse*, with the additional excitement of gambling. It commences at 9.30, and continues till daylight. The scene is lit up by numerous paper lanterns of various colors.

A number of benches are placed so as to form a large quare, in the centre of which the dancing goes on, the men and women gravely smoking all the time. Outside the benches is the promenade bounded by the gambling-tables and drinking-booths. On this occasion there must have been thirty or forty gambling-tables, some of the smaller ones presided over by old women, and others by small boys.

Monte is the favorite game, and the smallest silver coin can be staked, or a handful of doubloons. Most of these tables were patronized by crowds of all classes intent on gambling, with grave, serious faces under their enormous hats. They never moved a muscle, whether they won or lost.

Although the number of people at these fandangos is very great, yet the whole affair is conducted with an order and regularity not to be equalled in an assembly of a much higher class in Europe. If there ever is a row, it is invariably caused by Texans from Brownsville. These turbulent spirits are at once seized and cooled in the calaboose.

8th April (Wednesday).—Poor Don Pablo was " taken ill" at breakfast, and was obliged to go to bed. We were all much distressed at his illness, which was brought on by over-anxiety connected with his official duties ; and the way he is bothered by

English and "Blue-nose"* skippers is enough to try any one.

Mr. Behnsen and Mr. Colville returned from Bagdad this afternoon, much disgusted with the attractions of that city.

General Bee's orderly was assaulted in Matamoros yesterday by a renegado with a six-shooter. This circumstance prevented the General from coming to Matamoros as he had intended.

At 5 p. m. Captain Hancock and I crossed over to Brownsville, and were conducted in a very smart ambulance to General Bee's quarters, and afterwards to see a dress parade of the 3d Texas infantry.

Lieutenant-colonel Buchel is the *working man* of the corps, as he is a professional soldier. The men were well clothed, though great variety existed in their uniforms. Some companies wore blue, some gray, some had French *képis*, others wide-awakes and Mexican hats. They were a fine body of men, and really drilled uncommonly well. They went through a sort of guard-mounting parade in a most creditable manner. About a hundred out of a thousand were conscripts.†

* Nova-Scotian.

† During all my travels in the South I never saw a regiment so well clothed or so well drilled as this one, which has never been in action, or been exposed to much hardship.

After the parade, we adjourned to Colonel Luckett's to drink prosperity to the 3d regiment.

We afterwards had a very agreeable dinner with General Bee; Colonels Luckett and Buchel dined also. The latter is a regular soldier of fortune. He served in the French and Turkish armies, as also in the Carlist and the Mexican wars, and I was told he had been a principal in many affairs of honor; but he is a quiet and unassuming little man, and although a sincere Southerner, is not nearly so violent against the Yankees as Luckett.

At 10 P. M. Captain Hancock and myself went to a ball given by the authorities of the *"Heroica y invicta ciudad de Matamoros"* (as they choose to call it), in honor of the French defeat. General Bee and Colonel Luckett also went to this fete, the invitation being the first civility they had received since the violation of the Mexican soil in the Davis-Montgomery affair. They were dressed in plain clothes, and carried pistols concealed in case of accidents.

We all drove together from Brownsville to the Consulate, and entered the ball-room *en masse*.

The outside of the municipal hall was lit up with some splendor, and it was graced by a big placard, on which was written the amiable sentiment, *" Muera Napoleon—viva Méjico !"* Semi-successful squibs and crackers were let off at intervals. In the square also was a triumphal arch, with an in-scription to the effect that "the effete nations of Europe might tremble." I made great friends with the gobernador and administrador, who endeavored to entice me into dancing, but I excused myself by saying that Europeans were unable to dance in the graceful Mexican fashion. Captain Hancock was much horrified when this greasy-faced gobernador (who keeps a small shop) stated his intention of visiting the Immortalité with six of his friends, and sleeping on board for a night or two.

The dances were a sort of slow valse, and between the dances the girls were planted up against the wall, and not allowed to be spoken to by any one. They were mostly a plain-headed, badly-painted lot, and ridiculously dressed.

9th April (Thursday).—Captain Hancock and Mr. Anderson left for Bagdad in Mr. Behnsen's carriage at noon.

I crossed over to Brownsville at 11.30, and dined with Colonels Luckett, Buchel, and Duff, at about one o'clock. As we were all colonels, and as every one called the other colonel *tout court*, it was difficult to make out which was meant. They were obliged to confess that Brownsville was about the rowdiest town of Texas, which was the most lawless State in the Confederacy; but they declared they had never seen an inoffensive man subjected to insult

or annoyance, although the shooting-down and
stringing-up systems are much in vogue, being almost a necessity in a thinly-populated State, much
frequented by desperadoes driven away from more
civilized countries.

Colonel Luckett gave me a letter to General Van
Dorn, whom they consider the *beau ideal* of a cav
alry soldier. They said from time immemorial the
Yankees had been despised by the Southerners, as a
race inferior to themselves in courage and in honorable sentiments.

At 3 P. M. Colonel Buchel and I rode to Colonel
Duff's camp, distant about thirteen miles. I was
given a Mexican saddle, in which one is forced to sit
almost in a standing position. The stirrups are very
long, and right underneath you, which throws back
the feet.

Duff's regiment is called the Partisan Rangers.
Although a fine lot of men, they don't look well at a
foot parade, on account of the small amount of drill
they have undergone, and the extreme disorder of
their clothing. They are armed with carbines and
six-shooters.

I saw some men come in from a scouting expedition against the Indians, 300 miles off. They told
me they were usually in the habit of scalping an Indian when they caught him, and that they never
spared one, as they were such an untamable and fe-

rocious race. Another habit which they have learned from the Indians is, to squat on their heels in a most peculiar manner. It has an absurd and extraordinary effect to see a quantity of them so squatting in a row or in a circle.

The regiment had been employed in quelling a counter-revolution of Unionists in Texas. Nothing could exceed the rancor with which they spoke of these renegadoes, as they called them, who were principally Germans.

When I suggested to some of the Texans that they might as well bury the body of Mongomery a little better, they did not at all agree with me, but said it ought not to have been buried at all, but left hanging as a warning to other evil-doers.

With regard to the contentment of their slaves, Colonel Duff pointed out a good number they had with them, who had only to cross the river for freedom if they wished it.

Colonel Buchel and I slept in Colonel Duff's tent, and at night we were *serenaded*. The officers and men really sang uncommonly well, and they finished with " God save the Queen !"

Colonel Duff comes from Perth. He was one of the leading characters in the secession of Texas ; and he said his brother was a banker in Dunkeld.

10th April (Friday).—We roused up at daylight,

and soon afterwards Colonel Duff paraded some of
his best men, to show off the Texan horsemanship, of
which they are very proud. I saw them lasso cattle,
and catch them by the tail at full gallop, and throw
them by slewing them around. This is called tailing. They pick small objects off the ground when
at full tilt, and, in their peculiar fashion, are beautiful riders; but they confessed to me they could not
ride in an English saddle, and Colonel Duff told me
that they could not jump a fence at all. They were
all extremely anxious to hear what I thought of the
performance, and their thorough good opinion of
themselves was most amusing.

At 9 o'clock Colonel Buchel and I rode back to
Brownsville; but as we lost our way twice, and were
enveloped in clouds of dust, it was not a very satisfactory ride. Poor Captain Hancock must be lux-
uriating at Bagdad; for with this wind the bar must
be impassable to the boldest mariner.

In the evening, a Mr. ——, a Texan Unionist, or
renegado, gave us his sentiments at the Consulate,
and drank a deal of brandy. He finished, however,
by the toast, " Them as wants to fight, let 'em fight—
I don't."

11th April (Saturday).—Mr. ——, the Unionist,
came to me this morning, and said, in a contrite
manner, " I hope, Kernel, that in the fumes of brandy

I didn't say any thing offensive last night." I assured
him that he hadn't. I have now become comparatively accustomed and reconciled to the necessity of
shaking hands and drinking brandy with every one.*

The ambulance returned from Bagdad to-day.
Captain Hancock had managed to cross the bar in
Mr. Oetling's steamer or lighter, but was very nearly
capsized.

I went to a grand supper, given by Mr. Oetling in
honor of Mr. Hill's departure for the city of Mexico.
This, it appears, is the custom of the country.

12th April (Sunday).—I took an affectionate leave
of Don Pablo, Behnsen, Oetling & Co., all of whom
were in rather weak health on account of last night's
supper.

The excellent Maloney insisted on providing me
with preserved meats and brandy for my arduous
journey through Texas. I feel extremely grateful
for the kindness of all these gentlemen, who rendered
my stay in Matamoros very agreeable. The hotel
would have been intolerable.

I crossed to Brownsville at 3 P. M., where I was
hospitably received by my friend Ituria, who confesses to having made a deal of money lately by cotton speculations. I attended evening parade, and

* This necessity does not exist except in Texas.

saw General Bee, Colonels Luckett, Buchel, Duff, and ——. The latter (who hanged Mongomery) improves on acquaintance.

General Bee took me for a drive in his ambulance, and introduced me to Major Leon Smith, who captured the Harriet Lane. The latter pressed me most vehemently to wait until General Magruder's arrival, and he promised, if I did so, that I should be sent to San Antonio in a first-rate ambulance. Major Leon Smith is a seafaring man by profession, and was put by General Magruder in command of one of the small steamers which captured the Harriet Lane at Galveston, the crews of the steamers being composed of Texan cavalry soldiers. He told me that the resistance offered after boarding was feeble; and he declared that, had not the remainder of the Yankee vessels escaped unfairly under flag of truce, they would likewise have been taken.

After the Harriet Lane had been captured, she was fired into by the other ships; and Major Smith told me that, his blood being up, he sent the ex-master of the Harriet Lane to Commodore Renshaw, with a message that, unless the firing was stopped, he would *massa*CREE the captured crew. After hearing this, Commodore Renshaw blew up his ship, with himself in her, after having given an order to the remainder, *sauve qui peut.*

13*th April* (Monday).—I breakfasted with General Bee, and took leave of all my Brownsville friends.

M'Carthy is to give me four times the value of my gold in Confederate notes.*

We left Brownsville for San Antonio at 11 A. M. Our vehicle was a roomy, but rather overloaded, four-wheel carriage, with a canvas roof, and four mules. Besides M'Carthy, there was a third passenger, in the shape of a young merchant of the Hebrew persuasion. Two horses were to join us, to help us through the deep sand.

The country, on leaving Brownsville, is quite flat, the road, a natural one, sandy and very dusty, and there are many small trees, principally mosquites. After we had proceeded seven miles, we halted to water the mules.

At 2 P. M. a new character appeared upon the scene, in the shape of an elderly, rough-faced, dirty-looking man, who rode up, mounted on a sorry nag. To my surprise he was addressed by M'Carthy with the title of "Judge," and asked what he had done with our other horse. The Judge replied that it had already broken down, and had been left behind. M'Carthy informs me that this worthy really is a magistrate or sort of judge in his own district; but he

* The value of Confederate paper has since decreased. At Charleston I was offered six to one for my gold, and at Richmond eight to one.

now appears in the capacity of assistant mule-driver, and is to make himself generally useful.   I could not help feeling immensely amused at this specimen of a Texan judge.   We started again about 3 P. M., and soon emerged from the mosquite bushes into an open prairie eight miles long, quite desolate, and producing nothing but a sort of rush; after which we entered a chaparral, or thick covert of mosquite-trees and high prickly-pears.   These border the track, and are covered with bits of cotton torn from the endless trains of cotton wagons.   We met several of these wagons. Generally there were ten oxen or six mules to a wagon carrying ten bales, but in deep sand, more animals are necessary.   They journey very slowly towards Brownsville, from places in the interior of Texas at least five hundred miles distant.   Want of water and other causes make the drivers and animals undergo much hardship.

The Judge rides on in front of us on his "Rosinante," to encourage the mules.   His back view reminds one in a ludicrous manner of the pictures of Dr. Syntax.

Mr. Sargent, our portly driver, cheers his animals by the continual repetition of the sentence, " Get up, now, you great long-eared G—d d—d son of a ——."

At 5 P. M. we reached a well, with a farm or ranch close to it.   Here we halted for the night.   A cotton train was encamped close to us, and a lugubrious half-naked teamster informed us that three of his oxen had been stolen last night.

In order to make a fire, we were forced to enter the chaparral for wood, and in doing so, we ran many prickles into our legs, which caused us great annoyance afterwards, as they fester, if not immediately pulled out.

The water at this well was very salt, and made very indifferent coffee. M'Carthy called it the "meanest halting-place we shall have."

At 8 P. M. M'Carthy spread a bullock-rug on the sand near the carriage, on which we should have slept very comfortably, had it not been for the prickles, the activity of many fleas, and the incursions of wild hogs. Mr. Sargent and the Judge, with much presence of mind, had encamped seventy yards off, and left to us the duty of driving away these hogs. I was twice awoke by one of these unclean animals breathing in my face.

We did about twenty-one miles to-day.

14th April (Tuesday).—When we roused up at 4 A. M. we found our clothes saturated with the heavy dew; also that, notwithstanding our exertions, the hogs had devoured the greatest part of our pet kid, our only fresh meat.

After feeding our mules upon the Indian corn we had brought with us, and drinking a little more salt-water coffee, the Judge "hitched in," and we got under way at 5.30 A. M. The country just the same as yesterday—a dead level of sand, mosquite-trees, and prickly-pears.

At 7.30 A. M. we reached "Leatham's ranch," and watered our mules. As the water was tolerable, we refilled our water-barrels. I also washed my face, during which operation Mr. Sargent expressed great astonishment, not unmingled with contempt.

At Leatham's we met a wealthy Texan speculator and contractor, called Major or Judge Hart.

I find that *our* Judge is also an M. P., and that, in his capacity as a member of the Texan legislature, he is entitled to be styled the Honorable —— ——.

At 9 A. M. we halted in the middle of a prairie, on which there was a little grass for the mules, and we prepared to eat. In the midst of our cooking, two deer came up quite close to us, and could easily have been killed with rifles.

We saw quantities of rat-ranches, which are big sort of mole-hills, composed of cow-dung, sticks, and earth, built by the rats.

Mr. Sargent, our conductor, is a very rough cus-tomer—a fat, middle-aged man, who never opens his mouth without an oath, strictly American in its char-acter. He and the Judge are always snarling at one another, and both are much addicted to liquor.

We live principally on bacon and coffee, but as the

water and the bacon are both very salt, this is very inconvenient. We have, however, got some claret, and plenty of brandy.

During the mid-day halts, Mr. Sargent is in the habit of cooling himself by removing his trousers (or pants), and, having gorged himself, he lies down and issues his edicts to the Judge as to the treatment or the mules.

At 2.30 the M. P. hitched in again, and at 2.45 we reached a salt-water arm of the sea called the "Aroyo del Colorado," about eighty yards broad, which we crossed in a ferry-boat. Half an hour later we "struck water" again, which, being superior to Leatham's, we filled up.

We are continually passing cotton trains going to Brownsville, also government wagons with stores for the interior. Near every well is a small farm or ranch, a miserable little wooden edifice surrounded by a little cultivation. The natives all speak Spanish, and wear the Mexican dress.

M'Carthy is very proud of his knowledge of the country, in spite of which he is often out in his calculations. The different tracks are so similar to one another, they are easily mistaken.

At 4.45 p. m. we halted at a much better place than yesterday. We are obliged to halt where a little grass can be found for our mules.

Soon after we had unpacked for the night, six

2*

Texan Rangers, of "Wood's" regiment, rode up to us. They were very picturesque fellows; tall, thin, and ragged, but quite gentlemanlike in their manners.

We are always to sleep in the open until we arrive at San Antonio, and I find my Turkish lantern most useful at night.*

15th April (Wednesday).—I slept well last night in spite of the ticks and fleas, and we started at 5.30 P. M. After passing a dead rattlesnake eight feet long, we reached water at 7 A. M.

At 9 A. M. we espied the cavalcade of General Magruder passing us by a parallel track about half a mile distant. M'Carthy and I jumped out of the carriage, and I ran across the prairie to cut him off, which I just succeeded in doing by borrowing the spare horse of the last man in the train.

I galloped up to the front, and found the General riding with a lady who was introduced to me as Mrs. ——, an undeniably pretty woman, wife to an officer on Magruder's staff, and she is naturally the object of intense attention to all the good-looking officers who accompany the General through this desert.

General Magruder, who commands in Texas, is a fine soldierlike man, of about fifty-five, with broad

* A lantern for a candle, made of white linen and wire, which collapses when not in use. They are always used in the streets of Constantinople. The Texans admired it immensely.

shoulders, a florid complexion, and bright eyes. He wears his whiskers and mustaches in the English fashion, and he was dressed in the Confederate gray uniform. He was kind enough to beg that I would turn back and accompany him in his tour through Texas. He had heard of my arrival, and was fully determined I should do this. He asked after several officers of my regiment whom he had known when he was on the Canadian frontier. He is a Virginian, a great talker, and has always been a great ally of English officers.

He insisted that M'Carthy and I should turn and dine with him, promising to provide us with horses to catch up Mr. Sargent.

After we had agreed to do this, I had a long and agreeable conversation with the General, who spoke of the Puritans with intense disgust, and of the first importation of them as "*that pestiferous crew of the Mayflower;*" but he is by no means rancorous against individual Yankees. He spoke very favorably of M'Clellan, whom he knew to be a gentleman, clever, and personally brave, though he might lack moral courage to face responsibility. Magruder had commanded the Confederate troops at Yorktown which opposed M'Clellan's advance. He told me the different dodges he had resorted to, to blind and deceive the latter as to his (Magruder's) strength; and he spoke of the intense relief and amusement with which he had at length seen M'Clellan with his magnificent army begin to break ground before miserable earthworks, defended only by 8,000 men. Hooker was in his regiment, and was "essentially a mean man and a liar." Of Lee and Longstreet he spoke in terms of the highest admiration.

Magruder was an artilleryman, and has been a good deal in Europe; and having been much stationed on the Canadian frontier, he became acquainted with many British officers, particularly those in the 7th Hussars and Guards.

He had gained much credit from his recent successes at Galveston and Sabine Pass, in which he had the temerity to attack heavily-armed vessels of war with wretched river steamers manned by Texan cavalrymen.

His principal reason for visiting Brownsville was to settle about the cotton trade. He had issued an edict that half the value of cotton exported must be imported in goods for the benefit of the country (government stores). The President had condemned this order as illegal and despotic.

The officers on Magruder's Staff are a very good-looking, gentlemanlike set of men. Their names are—Major Pendleton, Major Wray, Captain De Ponté, Captain Alston, Captain Turner, Lieutenant-Colonel M'Neil, Captain Dwyer, Dr. Benien, Lieutenant Stanard, Lieutenant Yancy, and Major Ma-

gruder.   The latter is nephew to the General, and is
a particularly good-looking young fellow.   They all
live with their chief on an extremely agreeable foot-
ing, and form a very pleasant society.   At dinner I
was put in the post of honor, which is always fought
for with much acrimony—viz., the right of Mrs.
———.   After dinner we had numerous songs.   Both
the General and his nephew sang; so also did Captain Alston, whose corpulent frame, however, was
too much for the feeble camp-stool, which caused his
sudden disappearance in the midst of a song with a
loud crash.   Captain Dwyer played the fiddle very
well, and an aged and slightly elevated militia general brewed the punch and made several " elegant"
speeches.   The latter was a rough-faced old hero, and
gloried in the name of M'Guffin.   On these festive
occasions General Magruder wears a red woollen cap,
and fills the president's chair with great aptitude.

It was 11.30 before I could tear myself away from
this agreeable party; but at length I effected my exit
amidst a profusion of kind expressions, and laden
with heaps of letters of introduction.

16th April (Thursday).—Now our troubles commenced.   Seated in Mexican saddles, and mounted
on raw-boned mustangs, whose energy had been a
good deal impaired by a month's steady travelling on
bad food, M'Carthy and I left the hospitable mess-

tent about midnight, and started in search of Mr. Sargent and his vehicle. We were under the guidance of two Texan Rangers.

About daylight we hove in sight of "Los Animos," a desolate farm-house, in the neighborhood of which Mr. Sargent was supposed to be encamped; but nowhere could we find any traces of him.

We had now reached the confines of a dreary region, sixty miles in extent, called "The Sands," in comparison with which the prairie and chaparral were luxurious.

The sand being deep and the wind high, we could not trace the carriage; but we soon acquired a certainty that our perfidious Jehu had decamped, leaving us behind.

We floundered about in the sand, cursing our bad luck, cursing Mr. Sargent, and even the good Magruder, as the indirect cause of our wretchedness. Our situation, indeed, was sufficiently deplorable. We were without food or water in the midst of a desert: so were our horses, which were nearly done up. Our bones ached from the Mexican saddles; and, to complete our misery, the two Rangers began to turn restive and talk of returning with the horses. At this, the climax of our misfortunes, I luckily hit upon a Mexican, who gave us intelligence of our carriage; and with renewed spirits, but very groggy horses, we gave chase.

But never did Mr. Sargent's mules walk at such a pace; and it was 9 A. M. before we overtook them. My animal had been twice on his head, and M'Carthy was green in the face with fatigue and rage. Mr. Sargent received us with the greatest affability, and we were sensible enough not to quarrel with him, although M'Carthy had made many allusions as to the advisability of shooting him.

We had been nine and a half hours in the saddle, and were a good deal exhausted. Our sulky Texan guides were appeased with bacon, coffee, and $5 in coin.

We halted till 2 P. M., and then renewed our struggle through the deep sandy wilderness; but though the services of the Judge's horse were put into requisition, we couldn't progress faster than two miles an hour.

Mule driving is an art of itself, and Mr. Sargent is justly considered a *professor* at it.

He is always yelling—generally imprecations of a serio-comic character. He rarely flogs his mules; but when one of them rouses his indignation by extraordinary laziness, he roars out, " Come here, Judge, with a big club, and give him h—ll." While the animal is receiving such discipline as comes up to the Judge's idea of the infernal regions, Mr. Sargent generally remarks, "I wish you was Uncle Abe, I'd make you move, you G—d d—n son of a ——." His idea of perfect happiness seems to be to have Messrs. Lincoln and Seward in the shafts.   Mules travel much better when other mules are in front of them ; and another dodge to which Mr. Sargent continually resorts is, to beat the top of the carriage and kick the foot-board, which makes a noise, and gratifies the mules quite as much as licking them.   Mr. Sargent accounts for his humanity by saying, " It's the worst plan in the world licking niggers or mules, because the more you licks 'em, the more they wants it."

We reached or "struck" water at 5.30 P. M. ; but, in spite of its good reputation, it was so salt as to be scarcely drinkable.   A number of cotton wagons, and three carriages belonging to Mr. Ward, were also en-camped with us.

We have only made sixteen miles to-day.

17th April (Friday).—Having spent last night in a Mexican saddle, our bullock-rug in the sand ap-peared to me a most luxurious bed.

We hitched in at 5 A. M., and struck water at 9 A. M., which, though muddy in appearance, was not so bad to drink.

I walked ahead with the Judge, who, when sober, is a well-informed and sensible man.   Mr. Sargent and I are great friends, and, rough as he is, we get on capitally together.

A Mr. Ward, with three vehicles—a rival of Mr.

Sargent's—is travelling in our company. He drove his buggy against a tree and knocked its top off, to the intense delight of the latter.

We breakfasted under difficulties. The wind being high, it drove up the sand in clouds and spoiled our food.

Our travelling companion, Mr. ——, is a poor little weakly Israelite, but very inoffensive, although he speaks with a horrible Yankee twang, which Mr. Sargent and the Judge are singularly free from.

We went on again at 2 P. M. I had a long talk with a big mulatto slave woman, who was driving one of Ward's wagons. She told me she had been raised in Tennessee, and that three years ago she had been taken from her mistress for a bad debt, to their mutual sorrow. "Both," she said, "cried bitterly at parting." She doesn't like San Antonio at all, "too much hanging and murdering for me," she said. She had seen a man hanged in the middle of the day, just in front of her door.

Mr. Sargent bought two chickens and some eggs at a ranch, but one of the chickens got up a tree, and was caught and eaten by the Ward faction. Our camp to-night looks very pretty by the light of the fires.

18*th April* (Saturday).—At daylight we discovered, to our horror, that three of our mules were absent; but after an hour's search they were brought back in triumph by the Judge.

This delayed our start till 6.30 A. M.

I walked ahead again with the Judge, who explained to me that he was a "senator," or member of the Upper House of Texas—"just like your House of Lords," he said. He gets $5 a day whilst sitting, and is elected for four years.*

We struck water at 8.30 A. M., and bought a lamb for a dollar. We also bought some beef, which in this country is dried in strips by the sun, after being cut off the bullock, and it keeps good for any length of time. To cook it the strips are thrown for a few minutes on hot embers.

One of our mules was kicked last night. Mr. Sargent rubbed the wound with brandy, which did it much good.

Soon after leaving this well, Mr. Sargent discovered that, by following the track of Mr. Ward's wagons, he had lost the way. He swore dreadfully, and solaced himself with so much gin, that when we arrived at Sulphur Creek at 12.30, both he and the Judge were, by their own confession, *quite tight*.

We halted, ate some salt meat, and bathed in this creek, which is about forty yards broad and three feet deep.

---

* I was afterwards told that the Judge's term of service had expired. El Paso was his district.

Mr. Sargent's extreme "tightness" caused him to fall asleep on the box when we started again, but the more seasoned Judge drove the mules.

The signs of getting out of the sands now began to be apparent; and at 5 P. M. we were able to halt at a very decent place with grass, but *no* water. We suffered here for want of water, our stock being very nearly expended.

Mr. Sargent, who was now comparatively sober, killed the sheep most scientifically at 5.30 P. M.; and at 6.30 we were actually devouring it, and found it very good. Mr. Sargent cooked it by the simple process of stewing junks of it in a frying-pan, but we had only just enough water to do this.

19th April (Sunday).—At 1 A. M. this morning our slumbers on the bullock-rug were disturbed by a sudden and most violent thunder-storm. M'Carthy and I had only just time to rush into the carriage, and hustle our traps underneath it, when the rain began to descend in torrents.

We got inside with the little Jew (who was much alarmed by the thunder); whilst Mr. Sargent and the Judge crept underneath.

The rain lasted two hours; and at daylight we were able to refresh ourselves by drinking the water from the puddles, and effect a start.

But fate seemed adverse to our progress. No

sooner had we escaped from the sand than we fell into the mud, which was still worse.

We toiled on till 11.30 A. M., at which hour we reached " *King's Ranch*," which for several days I had heard spoken of as a sort of Elysium, marking as it does the termination of the sands, and the commencement of comparative civilization.

We halted in front of the house, and after cooking and eating, I walked up to the "ranch," which is a comfortable, well-furnished wooden building.

Mr. and Mrs. King had gone to Brownsville; but we were received by Mrs. Bee, the wife of the Brownsville general, who had heard I was on the road.

She is a nice lively little woman, a red-hot Southerner, glorying in the facts that she has no Northern relations or friends, and that she is a member of the Church of England.

Mr. King first came to Texas as a steamboat captain, but now owns an immense tract of country, with 16,000 head of cattle, situated, however, in a wild and almost uninhabited district. King's Ranch is distant from Brownsville only 125 miles, and we have been six days in reaching it.

After drying our clothes and our food after the rain of last night, we started again at 2.30 P. M.

We now entered a boundless and most fertile

prairie, upon which, as far as the eye could reach, cattle were feeding.

Bulls and cows, horses and mares, came to stare at us as we passed. They all seemed sleek and in good condition, yet they get nothing but what they can pick up on the prairie.

I saw a man on horseback kill a rabbit with his revolver. I also saw a scorpion for the first time.

We halted at 5.30 P. M., and had to make our fire principally of cow-dung, as wood is very scarce on this prairie.

We gave up the Judge's horse at King's Ranch. The lawgiver now rides on the box with Mr. Sargent.

20th April (Monday).—I slept well last night in spite of the numerous prairie-wolves which surrounded us, making a most dismal noise.

The Jew was ill again, but both Mr. Sargent and the Judge were very kind to him; so also was M'Carthy, who declared that a person incapable of protecting himself, and sickly, such as this little Jew, is always sure of kind treatment and compassion, even from the wildest Texans.

We started at 5 A. M., and had to get through some dreadful mud—Mr. Sargent in an awful bad humor, and using terrific language.

We were much delayed by this unfortunate rain,

which had converted a good road into a quagmire. We detected a rattlesnake crawling along this morning, but there are not nearly so many of them in this country as there used to be.

We halted at 9 A. M., and, to make a fire for cooking, we set a rat-ranch alight, which answered very well; but one big rat, annoyed by our proceedings, emerged hastily from his den, and very nearly jumped into the frying-pan.

Two Texan Rangers, belonging to Taylor's regiment, rode up to us whilst we were at breakfast. These Rangers all wear the most enormous spurs I ever saw.

We resumed our journey at 12.30, and reached a creek* called "Agua Dulce" at 2 P. M. M'Carthy and I got out before crossing, to forage at some huts close by. We got two dozen eggs and some lard; but, on returning to the road, we found that Mr. Sargent had pursued his usual plan of leaving us in the lurch.

I luckily was able to get hold of a Mexican boy, and rode across the creek *en croupe*. M'Carthy dismounted a negro, and so got over.

We halted at 5 P. M.

After dark M'Carthy crossed the prairie to visit

* All streams or rivers are called creeks, and pronounced " criks."

some friends who were encamped half a mile distant. He lost his way in returning, and wandered about for several hours. The Judge, with great presence of mind, kept the fire up, and he found us at last.

The heat from nine to two is pretty severe; but in Texas there is generally a cool sea-breeze, which makes it bearable.

21st *April* (Tuesday).—We started at 5 A. M., and reached a hamlet called "Casa Blanca" at 6. We procured a kid, some Indian corn, and two fowls in this neighborhood.

We had now quitted the flat country, and entered an undulating or "rolling" country, full of live oaks of very respectable size, and we had also got out of the mud.

Mr. Sargent and the Judge got drunk again about 8 A. M., which, however, had a beneficial effect upon the speed. We descended the hills at a terrific pace —or, as Mr. Sargent expressed it, "*Going like h—ll a-beating tan bark.*"

We "nooned it" at a small creek; and after unhitching, Mr. Sargent and the Judge had a row with one another, after which Mr. Sargent killed and cooked the goat, using my knife for these operations. With all his faults he certainly is a capital butcher, cook, and mule-driver. He takes great care of his animals, and is careful to inform us that the increased pace we have been going at is not attributable to gin.

He was very complimentary to me, because I acted as assistant cook and butcher.

Mr. Ward's party passed us about 1 P. M. The front wheels of his buggy having now smashed, it is hitched in rear of one of the wagons.

We made a pretty good afternoon's drive through a wood of post oaks, where we saw another rattlesnake, which we tried to shoot.

We halted at Spring creek at 6.30 P. M.; water rather brackish, and no grass for the mules.

The Judge gave us some of his experiences as a filibuster. He declares that a well-cooked polecat is as good to eat as a pig, and that stewed rattlesnake is not so bad as might be supposed. The Texans call the Mexicans "greasers," the latter retort by the name "gringo."

We are now living luxuriously upon eggs and goat's flesh; and I think we have made about thirty-two miles to-day.

22d April (Wednesday).—We got under weigh at 5 A. M., the mules looking rather mean for want of grass.

At 8 A. M. we reached the Nueces river, the banks of which are very steep, and are bordered with a beautiful belt of live-oak trees, covered with mustang grapes.

On the other side of the Nueces is "Oakville," a miserable settlement, consisting of about twenty wooden huts. We bought some butter there, and caught up Ward's wagons. The women at Oakville were most anxious to buy snuff. It appears that the Texan females are in the habit of dipping snuff—which means, putting it into their mouths instead of their noses. They rub it against their teeth with a blunted stick.

We reached grass about 10 A. M., and "nooned it," the weather being very trying—very sultry, without sun or wind.

We hitched in at 1.15—Ward's wagons in our front, and a Frenchman's four-horse team in our rear. At 4 P. M. we reached the "Weedy," a creek which, to our sorrow, was perfectly dry. We drove on till 7 P. M., and halted at some good grass. There being a report of water in the neighborhood, Mr. Sargent, the Judge, Ward, and the Frenchman, started to explore; and when, at length, they did discover a wretched little mud-hole, it appears that a desperate conflict for the water ensued, for the Judge returned to us a mass of mud, and presenting a very crestfallen appearance. Shortly after, Mr. Sargent appeared, in such a bad humor that he declined to cook, to eat, to drink, or do any thing but swear vehemently.

Deprived by this *contretemps* of our goat's flesh, we had recourse to an old ham and very stale bread.

3

We met many cotton trains and government wag
ons to-day, and I think we have progressed about
thirty-four miles.

23d April (Thursday).—The wily Mr. Sargent
drove the animals down to the mud-hole in the
middle of last night, and so stole a march upon
Ward.

Our goat's flesh having spoiled, had to be thrown
away this morning. We started at 5.30 A. M., and
reached "Rocky" at 7.30; but before this two of
Ward's horses had "*caved in*," which completely
restored our driver's good humor.

Rocky consists of two huts in the midst of a stony
country; and about a mile beyond it we reached a
pond, watered our mules, and filled our barrels. The
water was very muddy to look at, but not bad to
drink.

The mules were lazy to-day; and Mr. Sargent was
forced to fill his bucket with stones, and pelt the
leaders occasionally.

At 8 A. M. we reached an open, undulating prairie,
and halted at 10.30. Mr. Sargent and I killed and
cooked the two chickens.

He has done me the honor to call me a "right
good companion for the road." He also told me that
at one time he kept an hotel at El Paso—a sort of
half-way house on the overland route to California—

and was rapidly making his fortune when the war totally ruined him. This accounts for his animosity to "Uncle Abe."*

We hitched in again at 3 P. M., and after pushing through some deepish sand, we halted for the night only twenty-four miles from San Antonio. No corn or water, but plenty of grass; our food, also, was now entirely expended. Mr. Ward struggled up at 8.15, making a desperate effort to keep up with us, and this rivalry between Sargent and him was of great service.

This was our last night of camping out, and I felt almost sorry for it, for I have enjoyed the journey in spite of the hardships. The country through which I have passed would be most fertile and productive (at least the last 150 miles), were it not for the great irregularity of the seasons. Sometimes there is hardly any rain for two and three years together.

24th April (Friday).—We made a start at 4.15 A.M., and with the assistance of M'Carthy, we managed to lose our way; but at 6.15 a loud cheer from the box, of "Hoorraw for h—ll! who's afraid of fire?" pro-

---

* General Longstreet remembered both Sargent and the Judge perfectly, and he was much amused by my experiences with these worthies. General Longstreet had been quartered on the Texan frontiers a long time when he was in the old army.—August, 1863.

claimed that Mr. Sargent had come in sight of Grey's ranch.

After buying some eggs and Indian corn there, we crossed the deep bed of the river San Antonio. Its banks are very steep and picturesque.

We halted immediately beyond, to allow the mules to feed for an hour. A woman was murdered at a ranch close by some time ago, and five bad characters were put to death at San Antonio by the vigilance committee on suspicion.

We crossed the Selado river at 11, and nooned it in its neighborhood.

Mr. Sargent and the Judge finished the gin; and the former, being rather drunk, entertained us with a detailed description of his treatment of a refractory negro girl, which, by his own account, must have been very severe. M'Carthy was much disgusted at the story.*

After bathing in the Selado, Mr. Sargent, being determined to beat Ward, pushed on for San Antonio; and we drew up before Menger's hotel at 3 P.M., our mules dead beat—our driver having fulfilled his promise of " making his long-eared horses howl."

---

* However happy and well off the slaves may be as a general rule, yet there must be many instances (like that of Mr. Sargent) of ill-treatment and cruelty. Mr. Sargent is a Northerner by birth, and is without any of the kind feeling which is nearly always felt by Southerners for negroes.—July, 1863.

Later in the day I walked through the streets with M'Carthy to his store, which is a very large building, but now desolate, every thing having been sold off. He was of course greeted by his numerous friends, and among others I saw a negro come up to him, shake hands, and welcome him back.

I was introduced to Colonel Duff's brother, who is also a very good-looking man; but he has not thrown off his British nationality and become a " citizen."

The distance from Brownsville to San Antonio is 330 miles, and we have been 11 days and 4 hours *en route*.

25th April (Saturday).—San Antonio is prettily situated on both banks of the river of the same name. It should contain about 10,000 inhabitants, and is the largest place in Texas, except Galveston.

The houses are well built of stone, and they are generally only one or two stories high. All have verandas in front.

Before the war San Antonio was very prosperous, and rapidly increasing in size; but trade is now almost at a complete stand-still. All the male population under forty are in the military service, and many necessary articles are at famine prices. Coffee costs $7 a pound.

Menger's hotel is a large and imposing edifice, but

its proprietor (a civil German) was on the point of shutting it up for the present.

During the morning I visited Colonel Bankhead, a tall, gentlemanlike Virginian, who was commanding officer of the troops here. He told me a great deal about the Texan history, the Jesuit missions, and the Louisiana purchase, &c.; and he alarmed me by doubting whether I should be able to cross the Mississippi if Banks had taken Alexandria.

I also made the acquaintance of Major Minter, another Virginian, who told me he had served in the 2d cavalry in the old United States army. The following officers in the Confederate army were in the same regiment—viz., General A. S. Johnson (killed at Shiloh), General Lee, General Van Dörn, General Hardee, General Kirby Smith, and General Hood.*

By the advice of M'Carthy, I sent my portmanteau and some of my heavy things to be sold by auction, as I could not possibly carry them with me.

I took my place by the stage for Alleyton (Houston): it cost $40; in old times it was $13.

I dined with M'Carthy and young Duff at 3 P. M. The latter would not hear of my paying my share of the expenses of the journey from Brownsville. Mrs. M'Carthy was thrown into a great state of agitation and delight by receiving a letter from her mother,

* Also the Federal Generals Thomas and Stoneman.

who is in Yankeedom. Texas is so cut off that she only hears once in many months.

Colonel and Mrs. Bankhead called for me in their ambulance at 5 p. m., and they drove me to see the source of the San Antonio, which is the most beautiful clear spring I ever saw. We also saw the extensive foundations for a tannery now being built by the Confederate government.

The country is very pretty, and is irrigated in an ingenious manner by ditches cut from the river in all directions. It is thus in a great degree rendered independent of rain.

At San Antonio spring we were entertained by a Major Young, a queer little naval officer,—why a major I couldn't discover.

Mrs. Bankhead is a violent Southerner. She was twice ordered out of Memphis by the Federals on account of her husband's principles; but she says that she was treated with courtesy and kindness by the Federal General Sherman, who carried out the orders of his government with regret.

None of the Southern people with whom I have spoken entertain any hopes of a speedy termination of the war. They say it must last all Lincoln's presidency, and perhaps a good deal longer.

In the neighborhood of San Antonio, one-third of the population is German, and many of them were at first by no means loyal to the Confederate cause.

They objected much to the conscription, and some even resisted by force of arms; but these were soon settled by Duff's regiment, and it is said they are now reconciled to the new regime.

My portmanteau, with what was in it—for I gave away part of my things—sold for $323. Its value in England couldn't have been more than £8 or £9. The portmanteau itself, which was an old one, fetched $51; a very old pair of butcher boots, $32; five shirts, $42; an old overcoat, $25.

26th April (Sunday).—At 11.30 A. M., M'Carthy drove me in his buggy to see the San Pedro spring, which is inferior in beauty to the San Antonio spring. A troop of Texan cavalry was bivouacked there.

We afterwards drove to the "*missions*" of San José and San Juan, six and nine miles from the town. These were fortified convents for the conversion of the Indians, and were built by the Jesuits about one hundred and seventy years ago. They are now ruins, and the architecture is of the heavy Castilian style, elaborately ornamented. These missions are very interesting, and there are two more of them, which I did not see.

In the afternoon I saw many negroes and negresses parading about in their Sunday clothes—silks and crinolines—much smarter than their mistresses.

At 5 P. M. I dined with Colonel Bankhead, who

gave an entertainment, which in these hard times must have cost a mint of money. About fourteen of the principal officers were invited; one of them was Captain Mason (cousin to the London commis sioner), who had served under Stonewall Jackson in Virginia. He said that officer was by no means popular *at first*. I spent a very agreeable evening, and heard many anecdotes of the war. One of the officers sang the abolition song, " John Brown," together with its parody, " I'm bound to be a soldier in the army of the South," a Confederate marching song, and another parody, which is a Yankee marching song, " We'll hang Jeff Davis on a sour-apple tree."

Whenever I have dined with Confederate officers, they have nearly always proposed the Queen's health, and never failed to pass the highest eulogiums upon her majesty.

27th April (Monday). — Colonel Bankhead has given me letters of introduction to General Bragg, to General Leonidas Polk, and several others.

At 2 P. M. I called on Mrs. Bankhead to say goodby. She told me that her husband had two brothers in the Northern service—one in the army and the other in the navy. The two army brothers were both in the battles of Shiloh and Perryville, on opposite sides. The naval Bankhead commanded the Monitor when she sank.

3*

—— introduced me to a German militia general in a beer-house this afternoon. These two had a slight dispute, as the latter spoke strongly in disapproval of "*secret or night lynching.*"

The recent escapade of Captain Peñaloso seems to have been much condemned in San Antonio. This individual (formerly a butcher) hanged one of his soldiers a short time ago, on his own responsibility, for desertion and stealing a musket. This event came off at 12 o'clock noon, in the principal plaza of the city. The tree has been cut down, to show the feelings of the citizens.

There can be no doubt that the enforcement of the conscription has, as a general rule, been extremely easy throughout the Confederacy (except among the Germans); but I hear of many persons evading it, by getting into some sort of government employment —such as contractors, agents, or teamsters to the Rio Grande. To my extreme regret, I took leave of my friend M'Carthy this evening, whose hospitality and kindness I shall never forget.

I left San Antonio by *stage* for Alleyton at 9 P. M. The stage was an old coach, into the interior of which nine persons were crammed on three transverse seats, besides many others on the roof. I was placed on the centre seat, which was extremely narrow, and I had nothing but a strap to support my back. An enormously fat German was my *vis-à-vis*, and a long-

legged Confederate officer was in my rear.   Our first
team consisted of four mules; we afterwards got
horses.

My fellow-travellers were all either military men,
r connected with the government.

Only five out of nine chewed tobacco during the
uight; but they aimed at the windows with great
iccuracy, and didn't *splash* me.   The amount of
sleep I got, however, was naturally very trifling.

28*th April* (Tuesday).—We crossed the river Gua-
dalupe at 5 A. M., and got a change of horses.

We got a very fair breakfast at Seguin, at 7 A. M.,
which was beginning to be a well-to-do little place
when the war dried it up.   It commenced to rain at
Seguin, which made the road very woolly, and an-
,noyed the outsiders a good deal.

The conversation turned a good deal upon military
subjects, and all agreed that the system of election
of officers had proved to be a great mistake.   According to their own accounts, discipline must have
been extremely lax at first, but was now improving.
They were most anxious to hear what was thought of
their cause in Europe; and none of them seemed
aware of the great sympathy which their gallantry
and determination had gained for them in England
in spite of slavery.   We dined at a little wooden hamlet called Belmont, and changed horses again there.

The country through which we had been travelling
was a good deal cultivated, and there were numerous
farms. I saw cotton-fields for the first time.

We amused ourselves by taking shots with our revolvers at the enormous jack-rabbits which came to
stare at the coach.

In the afternoon tobacco-chewing became universal, and the spitting was sometimes a little wild.

It was the custom for the outsiders to sit round the
top of the carriage, with their legs dangling over
(like mutes on a hearse returning from a funeral).
This practice rendered it dangerous to put one's head
out of the window, for fear of a back kick from the
heels, or of a shower of tobacco-juice from the mouths
of the Southern chivalry on the roof. In spite of
their peculiar habits of hanging, shooting, &c., which
seemed to be natural to people living in a wild and
thinly-populated country, there was much to like in
my fellow-travellers. They all had a sort of *bon-
hommie* honesty and straightforwardness, a natural
courtesy and extreme good-nature, which was very
agreeable. Although they were all very anxious to
talk to a European—who, in these blockaded times,
is a *rara avis*—yet their inquisitiveness was never
offensive or disagreeable.

Any doubts as to my personal safety, which may
have been roused by my early insight into Lynch
law, were soon completely set at rest; for I soon per-

ceived that if any one were to annoy me the remainder would stand by me as a point of honor.

We supped at a little town called Gonzales at 6 30.
We left it at 8 P. M. in another coach with six
horses—big, strong animals.

The roads being all natural ones, were much injured by the rains.

We were all rather disgusted by the bad news we
heard at Gonzales of the continued advance of Banks,
and of the probable fall of Alexandria.

The squeezing was really quite awful, but I did
not suffer so much as the fat or long-legged ones.
They all bore their trials in the most jovial good-
humored manner.

My fat *vis-à-vis* (in despair) changed places with
me, my two bench-fellows being rather thinner than
his, and I benefited much by the change into a back
seat.

29th April (Wednesday).—Exhausted as I was, I
managed to sleep wonderfully well last night. We
breakfasted at a place called Hallettsville at 7 A. M.,
and changed carriages again.

Here we took in four more Confederate soldiers as
outsiders, and we were now eighteen in all. Nowhere but in this country would such a thing be
permitted.

Owing to the great top-weight, the coach swayed

about like a ship in a heavy sea, and the escapes of a capsize were almost miraculous. It is said that at the end of a Texan journey the question asked is not, "Have you been upset?" but, "How many times have you been upset?"

The value of the negroes working in the fields was constantly appraised by my fellow-travellers; and it appeared that, in Texas, an able-bodied male fetched $2500, whilst a well-skilled seamstress was worth $3500.

Two of my companions served through the late severe campaign in New Mexico, but they considered forty-eight hours in a closely-packed stage a greater hardship than any of their military experiences.

We passed many cotton-fields and beautiful Indian corn, but much of the latter had been damaged by the hail.

I was told that one-third of the land formerly devoted to cotton is still sown with that article, the remainder being corn, &c.*

We also passed through some very pretty country, full of fine post-oak and cotton trees, and we met many Mexican cotton-teams—some of the wagons with fourteen oxen or twelve mules, which were being cruelly ill-treated by their drivers.

---

* It is only in Texas that so much cotton is still grown.

We crossed several rivers with steep and difficult banks, and dined at a farm-house at 2.30 P. M.

I have already discovered·that, directly the bell rings, it is necessary to rush at one's food and bolt it as quickly as possible, without any ceremony or delay, otherwise it all disappears, so rapacious and so voracious are the natives at their meals whilst travelling. Dinner, on such occasions, in no case lasts more than seven minutes.

We reached Columbus at 6 P. M., and got rid of half our passengers there. These Texan towns generally consist of one large plaza, with a well-built court-house on one side and an hotel opposite, the other two sides being filled up with wooden stores. All their budding prosperity has been completely checked by the war; but every one anticipates a great immigration into Texas after the peace.

We crossed the Colorado river, and reached Alleyton, our destination, at 7 P. M.

This little wooden village has sprung into existence during the last three years, owing to its being the present terminus to the railroad. It was crammed full of travellers and cotton speculators; but, as an especial favor, the fat German and I were given a bed *between us*. I threw myself on the bed with my clothes on (*bien entendu*), and was fast asleep in five minutes. In the same room there were three other beds, each with two occupants.

The distance from San Antonio to Alleyton is 140 miles—time, forty-six hours.

30th *April* (Thursday).—I have to-day acquired my first experience of Texan railroads.

In this country, where every white man is as good as another (by theory), and every white female is by courtesy a lady, there is only one class. The train from Alleyton consisted of two long cars, each holding about fifty persons. Their interior is like the aisle of a church, twelve seats on either side, each for two persons. ·The seats are comfortably stuffed, and seemed luxurious after the stage.

Before starting, the engine gives two preliminary snorts, which, with a yell from the official of "*all aboard*," warn the passengers to hold on; for they are closely followed by a tremendous jerk, which sets the cars in motion.

Every passenger is allowed to use his own discretion about breaking his arm, neck, or leg, without interference by the railway officials.

People are continually jumping on and off whilst the train is in motion, and larking from one car to the other. There is no sort of fence or other obstacle to prevent "humans" or cattle from getting on the line.

We left Alleyton at 8 A. M., and got a miserable meal at Richmond at 12.30. At this little town I was introduced to a seedy-looking man, in rusty black

clothes and a broken-down " stove-pipe" hat.   This
was Judge Stockdale, who will probably be the next
governor of Texas.   He is an agreeable man, and his
conversation is far superior to his clothing.   The rival candidate is General Chambers (I think), who
has become very popular by the following sentence
in his manifesto:—"I am of opinion that married
soldiers should be given the opportunity of embracing
their families at least once a year, their places in the
ranks being taken by unmarried men.   The population must not be allowed to suffer."

Richmond is on the Brazos river, which is crossed
in a peculiar manner.   A steep inclined plane leads
to a low, rickety, trestle bridge, and a similar inclined
plane is cut in the opposite bank.   The engine cracks
on all steam, and gets sufficient impetus in going
down the first incline to shoot across the bridge and
up the second incline.   But even in Texas this
method of crossing a river is considered rather unsafe.

After crossing the river in this manner, the rail
traverses some very fertile land, part of which forms
the estate of the late Colonel Terry.   There are more
than two hundred negroes on the plantation.   Some
of the fields were planted with cotton and Indian corn
mixed, three rows of the former between two of the
latter.   I saw also fields of cotton and sugar mixed.

We changed carriages at Harrisburg, and I completed my journey to Houston on a cotton truck.

The country near Houston is very pretty, and is studded with white wooden villas, which are raised off the ground on blocks like haystacks. I reached Houston at 4.30 p. m., and drove to the Fannin House hotel.

Houston is a much better place than I expected. The main street can boast of many well-built brick and iron houses. It was very full, as it now contained all the refugees from the deserted town of Galveston.

After an extremely mild supper, I was introduced to Lieutenant Lee, a wounded hero, who lost his leg at Shiloh; also to Colonel Pyron, a distinguished officer, who commands the regiment named after him.

The fat German, Mr. Lee, and myself, went to the theatre afterwards.

As a great favor, my British prejudices were respected, and I was allowed a bed to myself; but the four other beds in the room had two occupants each. A captain, whose acquaintance I had made in the cars, slept in the next bed to me. Directly after we had got into bed a negro came in, who, squatting down between our beds, began to clean our boots. The Southerner pointed at the slave, and thus held forth: —"Well, Kernel, I reckon you've got servants in your country, but not of that color. Now, sir, this is a real genuine African. He's as happy as the day's long; and if he was on a sugar plantation he'd be dancing half the night; but if you was to collect a thousand of them together, and fire one bomb in amongst them, they'd all run like h—ll." The negro grinned, and seemed quite flattered.

1st May (Friday).—I called on General Scurry, and found him suffering from severe ophthalmia. When I presented General Magruder's letter, he insisted that I should come and live with him so long as I remained here. He also telegraphed to Galveston for a steamer to take me there and back.

We dined at 4 P. M. : the party consisted of Colonel and Judge Terrill (a clever and agreeable man), Colonel Pyron, Captain Wharton, quartermaster-general, Major Watkins (a handsome fellow, and hero of the Sabine Pass affair), and Colonel Cook, commanding the artillery at Galveston (late of the U. S. navy, who enjoys the reputation of being a zealous Methodist preacher and a daring officer). The latter told me he could hardly understand how I could be an Englishman, as I pronounced my h's all right. General Scurry himself is very amusing, and is an admirable mimic. His numerous anecdotes of the war were very interesting. In peace times he is a lawyer. He was a volunteer major in the Mexican war, and distinguished himself very much in the late campaigns in New Mexico and Arizona, and at the recapture of Galveston.

After dinner, the Queen's health was proposed ; and

the party expressed the greatest admiration for Her
Majesty, and respect for the British Constitution.
They all said that universal suffrage did not produce
such deplorable results in the South as in the North;
because the population in the South is so very scattered, and the whites being the superior race, they
form a sort of aristocracy.

They all wanted me to put off going to Galveston
till Monday, in order that some ladies might go; but
I was inexorable, as it must now be my object to
cross the Mississippi without delay. All these officers despised sabres, and considered double-barrelled
shot-guns and revolvers the best arms for cavalry.

2d May (Saturday).—As the steamer had not arrived in the morning, I left by railroad for Galveston.
General Scurry insisted upon sending his servant to
wait upon me, in order that I might become acquainted with " an aristocratic negro." " John" was
a very smart fellow, and at first sight nearly as white
as myself.

In the cars I was introduced to General Samuel
Houston, the founder of Texan independence. He
told me he was born in Virginia seventy years ago,
that he was United States senator at thirty, and governor of Tennessee at thirty-six. He emigrated into
Texas in 1832 ; headed the revolt of Texas, and defeated the Mexicans at San Jacinto in 1836. He

then became President of the Republic of Texas, which he annexed to the United States in 1845. As Governor of the State in 1860, he had opposed the secession movement, and was *deposed*. Though evidently a remarkable and clever man, he is extremely egotistical and vain, and much disappointed at having to subside from his former grandeur. The town of Houston is named after him. In appearance he is a tall, handsome old man, much given to chewing tobacco, and blowing his nose with his fingers.*

I was also introduced to another " character," Captain Chubb, who told me he was a Yankee by birth, and served as coxswain to the United States ship Java in 1827. He was afterwards imprisoned at Boston on suspicion of being engaged in the slave trade; but he escaped. At the beginning of this war he was captured by the Yankees, when he was in command of the Confederate States steamer Royal Yacht, and taken to New York in chains, where he was condemned to be hung as a pirate; but he was eventually exchanged. I was afterwards told that the slave-trading escapade of which he was accused consisted in his having hired a colored crew at Boston, and then coolly *selling* them at Galveston.

At 1 p. m., we arrived at Virginia Point, a *tête-de-pont* at the extremity of the mainland. Here Bates's

---

* He is reported to have died in August, 1863.

battalion was encamped—called also the "swamp angels," on account of the marshy nature of their quarters, and of their predatory and irregular habits.

The railroad then traverses a shallow lagoon (called Galveston Bay) on a trestle-bridge two miles long; this leads to another *tête-de-pont* on Galveston island, and in a few mimutes the city is reached.

In the train I had received the following message by telegraph from Colonel Debray, who commands at Galveston : " Will Col. Fremantle sleep to-night at the house of a blockaded rebel ?" I answered:— "Delighted ;" and was received at the terminus by Captain Foster of the Staff, who conducted me in an ambulance to headquarters, which were at the house of the Roman Catholic bishop. I was received there by Colonel Debray and two very gentlemanlike French priests.

We sat down to dinner at 2 P. M., but were soon interrupted by an indignant drayman, who came to complain of a military outrage. It appeared that immediately after I had left the cars, a semi-drunken Texan of Pyron's regiment had desired this drayman to stop, and upon the latter declining to do so, the Texan fired five shots at him from his "six-shooter," and the last shot killed the drayman's horse. Captain Foster (who is a Louisianian, and very sarcastic about Texas) said that the regiment would probably hang the soldier for being such a *disgraceful bad shot*.

After dinner Colonel Debray took me into the observatory, which commands a good view of the city, bay, and gulf.

Galveston is situated near the eastern end of an island thirty miles long by three and a half wide. Its houses are well built; its streets are long, straight, and shaded with trees; but the city was now desolate, blockaded, and under military law. Most of the houses were empty, and bore many marks of the ill-directed fire of the Federal ships during the night of the 1st of January last.

The whole of Galveston Bay is very shallow, except a narrow channel of about a hundred yards immediately in front of the now deserted wharves. The entrance to this channel is at the northeastern extremity of the island, and is defended by the new works which are now in progress there. It is also blocked up with piles, torpedoes, and other obstacles.

The blockaders were plainly visible about four miles from land; they consisted of three gunboats and an ugly paddle steamer, also two supply-vessels.

The wreck of the Confederate cotton-steamer Neptune (destroyed in her attack on the Harriet Lane), was close off one of the wharves. That of the Westfield (blown up by the Yankee Commodore), was off Pelican Island.

In the night of the 1st January, General Magruder

suddenly entered Galveston, placed his field-pieces along the line of wharves, and unexpectedly opened fire in the dark upon the Yankee war vessels at a range of about one hundred yards; but so heavy (though badly directed) was the reply from the ships, that the field-pieces had to be withdrawn. The attack by Colonel Cook upon a Massachusetts regiment fortified at the end of a wharf, also failed, and the Confederates thought themselves "badly whipped." But after daylight the fortunate surrender of the Harriet Lane to the cotton-boat Bayou City, and the extraordinary conduct of Commodore Renshaw, converted a Confederate disaster into the recapture of Galveston. General Magruder certainly deserves immense credit for his boldness in attacking a heavily armed naval squadron with a few field-pieces and two river steamers protected with cotton bales and manned with Texan cavalry soldiers.

I rode with Colonel Debray to examine Forts Scurry, Magruder, Bankhead, and Point. These works have been ingeniously designed by Colonel Sulokowski (formerly in the Austrian army), and they were being very well constructed by one hundred and fifty whites and six hundred blacks under that officer's superintendence, the blacks being lent by the neighboring planters.

Although the blockaders can easily approach to within three miles of the works, and although one shell will always "stampede" the negroes, yet they have not thrown any for a long time.*

Colonel Debray is a broad-shouldered Frenchman, and is a very good fellow. He told me that he emigrated to America in 1848; he raised a company in 1861, in which he was only a private; he was next appointed aid-de-camp to the governor of Texas, with the rank of brigadier-general; he then descended to a major of infantry, afterwards rose to a lieutenant-colonel of cavalry, and is now colonel.

Captain Foster is properly on Magruder's Staff, and is very good company. His property at New Orleans had been destroyed by the Yankees.

In the evening we went to a dance given by Colonel Manly, which was great fun. I danced an American cotillion with Mrs. Manly; it was very violent exercise, and not the least like any thing I had seen before. A gentleman stands by shouting out the different figures to be performed, and every one obeys his orders with much gravity and energy. Colonel Manly is a very gentlemanlike Carolinian; the ladies were pretty, and, considering the blockade, they

---

* Such a stampede did occur when the blockaders threw two or three shells. All the negroes ran, showing every sign of great dismay, and two of them, in their terror, ran into the sea, and were unfortunately drowned. It is now, however, too late for the ships to try this experiment, as some heavy guns are in position. A description of the different works is of course omitted here.

4

were very well dressed. Six deserters from Banks'
army arrived here to-day. Banks seems to be advancing steadily, and overcoming the opposition
offered by the handful of Confederates in the Teche
country.

Banks himself is much despised as a soldier, and is
always called by the Confederates Mr. Commissary
Banks, on account of the efficient manner in which
he performed the duties of that office for "Stonewall"
Jackson in Virginia. The officer who is supposed
really to command the advancing Federals, is Weitzel; and he is acknowledged by all here to be an
able man, a good soldier, and well acquainted with
the country in which he is manœuvring.

3d May (Sunday).—I paid a long visit this morning to Mr. Lynn the British Consul, who told me
that he had great difficulty in communicating with
the outer world, and had seen no British man-of-war
since the Immortalité.

At 1.30 I saw Pyron's regiment embark for Niblitt's
Bluff to meet Banks. This corps is now dismounted
cavalry, and the procession was a droll one. First
came eight or ten instruments braying discordantly,
then an enormous Confederate flag, followed by about
four hundred men moving by fours—dressed in every
variety of costume, and armed with every variety of
weapon; about sixty had Enfield rifles; the remain-

der carried shot-guns (fowling-pieces), carbines, or long rifles of a peculiar and antiquated manufacture. None had swords or bayonets—all had six-shooters and bowie-knives. The men were a fine, determined-looking lot; and I saw among them a short stout boy of fourteen, who had served through the Arizona campaign. I saw many of the soldiers take off their hats to the French priests, who seemed much respected in Galveston. This regiment is considered down here to be a very good one, and its colonel is spoken of as one of the bravest officers in the army. The regiment was to be harangued by Old Houston before it embarked.*

In getting into the cars to return to Houston, I was nearly forced to step over the dead body of the horse shot by the soldier yesterday, and which the authorities had not thought necessary to remove.

I got back to General Scurry's house at Houston at 4.30 P. M. The general took me out for a drive in his ambulance, and I saw innumerable negroes and negresses parading about the streets in the most outrageously grand costumes—silks, satins, crinolines, hats with feathers, lace mantles, &c., forming an absurd contrast to the simple dresses of their mistresses.

---

* At the outbreak of the war it was found very difficult to raise infantry in Texas, as no Texan walks a yard if he can help it. Many mounted regiments were therefore organized, and afterwards dismounted.

Many were driving about in their master's carriages, or riding on horses which are often lent to them on Sunday afternoons; all seemed intensely happy and satisfied with themselves.

——— told me that old Sam Houston lived for several years amongst the Cherokee Indians, who used to call him "the Raven" or the "Big Drunk." He married an Indian squaw when he was with them.

Colonel Ives, aid-de-camp to the President, has just arrived from Richmond, and he seems a very well-informed and agreeable man.

I have settled to take the route to Shrieveport to-morrow, as it seems doubtful whether Alexandria will or will not fall.

4th May (Monday).—General Scurry's servant "John" had been most attentive since he had been told off to me. I made him a present of my evening clothes, which gratified him immensely; and I shook hands with him at parting, which seems to be quite the custom. The Southern gentlemen are certainly able to treat their slaves with extraordinary famil-iarity and kindness. John told me that the General would let him buy his freedom whenever he chose. He is a barber by trade, and was earning much money when he insisted on rejoining his master and going to the wars.

I left Houston by train for Navasoto at 10 A. M. A Captain Andrews accompanied me thus far: he was going with a troop of cavalry to impress one-fourth of the negroes on the plantations for the Government works at Galveston, the planters having been backward in coming forward with their darkies.

Arrived at Navasoto (70 miles) at 4 P. M., where I took a stage for Shrieveport (250 miles). I started at 4.30 P. M., after having had a little dispute with a man for a corner seat, and beating him.

It was the same sort of vehicle as the San Antonio one—eight people inside. During the night there was a thunderstorm.

5th May (Tuesday).—We breakfasted at Huntsville at 5.30 A. M. The Federal officers captured in the Harriet Lane are confined in the penitentiary there, and are not treated as prisoners of war. This seems to be the system now with regard to officers since the enlistment of negroes by the Northerners.

My fellow-travellers were mostly elderly planters or legislators, and there was one judge from Louisiana. One of them produced a pair of boots which had cost him $100; another showed me a common wide-awake hat which had cost him $40. In Houston, I myself saw an English regulation infantry sword exposed for sale for $225 (£45).

As the military element did not predominate, my companions united in speaking with horror of the depredations committed in this part of the country by their own troops on a line of march.

We passed through a well-wooded country—pines and post-oaks—the road bad: crossed the river Trinity at 12 noon, and dined at the house of a disreputable-looking individual, called a Campbellite minister, at 4.30 P. M. The food consisted almost invariably of bacon, corn bread, and buttermilk: a meal costing a dollar.

Arrived at Crockett at 9.30 P. M., where we halted for a few hours. A *filthy bed* was given to the Louisianian Judge and myself. The Judge, following my example, took to it boots and all, remarking, as he did so, to the attendant negro, that "they were a d——d sight cleaner than the bed."

Before reaching Crockett, we passed through the encampment of Phillipps's regiment of Texas Rangers, and we underwent much chaff. They were *en route* to resist Banks.

6th May (Wednesday).—We left all the passengers at Crockett except the Louisianian Judge, a Government agent, and the ex-boatswain of the Harriet Lane, which vessel had been manned by the Confederates after her capture; but she had since been dismantled, and her crew were being marched to Shrieveport to

man the iron-clad Missouri, which was being built
there.

The food we get on the road is sufficient, and good
enough to support life; it consists of pork or bacon,
bread made with Indian corn, and a peculiar mixture
called Confederate coffee, made of rye, meal, Indian
corn, or sweet potatoes. The loss of coffee afflicts the
Confederates even more than the loss of spirits; and
they exercise their ingenuity in devising substitutes,
which are not generally very successful.

The same sort of country as yesterday, viz.—large
forests of pines and post-oaks, and occasional Indian-
corn fields, the trees having been killed by cutting a
circle near the roots. At 3 p. m., we took in four
more passengers. One of them was a Major ———,
brother-in-law to ———, who hanged Mongomery at
Brownsville. He spoke of the exploit of his relative
with some pride. He told me that his three brothers
had lost an arm apiece in the war.

We arrived at Rusk at 6.30 p. m., and spent a few
hours there; but notwithstanding the boasted splendor of the beds at the Cherokee Hotel, and although
by Major ———'s influence I got one to myself, yet
I did not consider its aspect sufficiently inviting to
induce me to remove my clothes.

7th May (Thursday).—We started again at 1.30
A. M., in a smaller coach, but luckily with reduced

numbers,—viz., the Louisianian Judge (who is also a legislator), a Mississippi planter, the boatswain, the government agent, and a Captain Williams, of the Texas Rangers.

Before the day broke we reached a bridge over a stream called Mud Creek, which was in such a dilapidated condition that all hands had to get out and cover over the biggest holes with planks.

The government agent informed us that he still held a commission as adjutant-general to ——. The latter, it appears, is a cross between a guerilla and a horse thief, and, even by his adjutant-general's account, he seems to be an equal adept at both professions. The accounts of his forays in Arkansas were highly amusing, but rather strongly seasoned for a legitimate soldier.

The Judge was a very gentlemanlike nice old man. Both he and the adjutant-general were much knocked up by the journey; but I revived the former with the last of the Immortalité rum. The latter was in very weak health, and doesn't expect to live long; but he ardently hoped to destroy a few more " bluebellies"* before he " goes under."

The Mississippi planter had abandoned his estate near Vicksburg, and withdrawn with the remnant of his slaves into Texas. The Judge also had lost all his

---

* The Union soldiers are called " bluebellies" on account of their blue uniforms. These often call the Confederates " graybacks."

property in New Orleans. In fact, every other man one meets has been more or less ruined since the war, but all speak of their losses with the greatest equanimity. Captain Williams was a tall, cadaverous backwoodsman, who had lost his health in the war. He spoke of the Federal General Rosecrans with great respect, and he passed the following high encomium upon the Northwestern troops, under Rosecrans' command—

"They're reglar great big h—llsnorters, the same breed as ourselves. They don't want no running after,—they don't. They ain't no Dutch cavalry—* you bet!"

To my surprise all the party were willing to agree that, a few years ago, most educated men in the South regarded slavery as a misfortune and not justifiable, though necessary under the circumstances. But the meddling, coercive conduct of the detested and despised abolitionists had caused the bonds to be drawn much tighter.

My fellow-travellers of all classes are much given to talk to me about their "peculiar institution," and they are most anxious that I should see as much of it as possible, in order that I may be convinced that it is not so bad as has been represented, and that they are not all "Legrees," although they do not attempt

---

* German dragoons, much despised by the Texans on account of their style of riding.

4*

to deny that there are many instances of cruelty. But they say a man who is known to illtreat his negroes is hated by all the rest of the community. They declare that Yankees make the worst masters when they settle in the South; and all seem to be perfectly aware that slavery, which they did not invent, but which they inherited from us (English), is and always will be the great bar to the sympathy of the civilized world. I have heard these words used over and over again.

All the villages through which we passed were deserted except by women and very old men; their aspect was most melancholy. The country is sandy, and the land not fertile, but the timber is fine.

We met several planters on the road, who with their families and negroes were taking refuge in Texas, after having abandoned their plantations in Louisiana on the approach of Banks. One of them had as many as sixty slaves with him of all ages and sizes.

At 7 P. M. we received an unwelcome addition to our party, in the shape of three huge, long-legged, unwashed, odoriferous Texan soldiers, and we passed a wretched night in consequence. The Texans are certainly not prone to take offence where they see none is intended ; for when this irruption took place, I couldn't help remarking to the Judge, with regard to the most obnoxious man who was occupying the centre seat to our mutual discomfort,—" I say, Judge, this gentleman has got the longest legs I ever saw." "Has he?" replied the Judge; "and he has got the d—dest, longest, hardest back I ever felt." The Texan was highly amused by these remarks upon his personal appearance, and apologized for his peculiarities. Crossed the Sabine river at 11.30 P. M.

8th May (Friday).—We reached Marshall at 3 A. M., and got four hours' sleep there. We then got into a railroad for sixteen miles, after which we were crammed into another stage.

Crossed the frontier into Louisiana at 11 A. M. I have therefore been nearly a month getting through the single State of Texas. Reached Shrieveport at 3 P. M.; and, after washing for the first time in five days, I called on Gen. Kirby Smith, who commands the whole country on this side of the Mississippi.

He is a Floridian by birth, was educated at West Point, and served in the United States cavalry. He is only thirty-eight years old; and he owes his rapid rise to a lieutenant-general to the fortunate fact of his having fallen, just at the very nick of time, upon the Yankee flank at the first battle of Manassas.*

He is a remarkably active man, and of very agreeable manners; he wears big spectacles and a black beard.

* Called by the Yankees "Bull Run."

His wife is an extremely pretty woman, from Baltimore, but she had cut her hair quite short like a man's. In the evening she proposed that we should go down to the river and fish for cray-fish. We did so, and were most successful, the General displaying much energy on the occasion.

He told me that M'Clellan might probably have destroyed the Southern army with the greatest ease during the first winter, and without running much risk to himself, as the Southerners were so much over-elated by their easy triumph at Manassas, and their army had dwindled away.

I was introduced to Governor Moore, of Louisiana, to the Lieutenant-governor Hyams, and also to the exiled Governor of Missouri, Reynolds.

Governor Moore told me he had been on the Red River since 1824, from which date until 1840 it had been very unhealthy. He thinks that Dickens must have intended Shrieveport by "Eden."*

Governor Reynolds, of Missouri, told me he found himself in the unfortunate condition of a potentate exiled from his dominions; but he showed me an address which he had issued to his Missourians, promising to be with them at the head of an army to deliver them from their oppressors.

---

* I believe this is a mistake of Governor Moore. I have always understood Cairo was Eden.

Shrieveport is rather a decent-looking place on the Red River. It contains about 3,000 inhabitants, and is at present the seat of the Louisianian Legislature *vice* Baton Rouge. But only twenty-eight members of the Lower House had arrived as yet, and business could not be commenced with less than fifty.

The river now is broad and rapid, and it is navigated by large steamers; its banks are low and very fertile, but reputed to be very unhealthy.

General Kirby Smith advised me to go to Munroe, and try to cross the Mississippi from thence; he was so uncertain as to Alexandria that he was afraid to send a steamer so far.

I heard much talk at his house about the late Federal raid into the Mississippi,* which seems to be a copy of John Morgan's operations, except that the Federal raid was made in a thinly populated country, bereft of its male inhabitants.

9th May (Saturday).—Started again by stage for Munroe at 4.30 A. M. My companions were, the Mississippi planter, a mad dentist from New Orleans (called, by courtesy, doctor), an old man from Matagorda, buying slaves cheap in Louisiana, a wounded officer, and a wounded soldier.

The soldier was a very intelligent young Missourian,

---

* Grierson's raid.

who told me (as others have) that, at the commencement of these troubles, both he and his family were
strong Unionists.   But the Lincolnites, by using co-
ercion, had forced them to take one side or the other
—and there are now no more bitter Secessionists than
these people.   This soldier (Mr. Douglas) was on his
way to rejoin Bragg's army.   A Confederate soldier
when wounded is not given his discharge, but is employed at such work as he is competent to perform.
Mr. Douglas was quite lame; but will be employed
at mounted duties or at writing.

We passed several large and fertile plantations.
The negro quarters formed little villages, and seemed
comfortable : some of them held 150 or 200 hands.
We afterwards drove through some beautiful pine
forests, and were ferried across a beautiful shallow
lake full of cypresses, but not the least like European
cypress-trees.

We met a number more planters driving their families, their slaves, and furniture, towards Texas—in
fact, every thing that they could save from the ruin
that had befallen them on the approach of the Federal troops.

At 5 P. M. we reached a charming little town, called
Mindon, where I met an English mechanic who deplored to me that he had been such a fool as to natu-
ralize himself, as he was in hourly dread of the conscription.

I have at length become quite callous to many of
the horrors of stage travelling. I no longer shrink at
every random shower of tobacco-juice; nor do I shud-
der when good-naturedly offered a quid. I eat vo-
raciously of the bacon that is provided for my suste-
nance, and I am invariably treated by my fellow-
travellers of all grades with the greatest consideration
and kindness. Sometimes a man remarks that it is
rather "mean" of England not to recognize the South;
but I can always shut him up by saying, that a nation
which deserves its independence should fight and earn
it for itself—a sentiment which is invariably agreed
to by all.

10th *May* (Sunday).—I spent a very rough night
in consequence of the badness of the road, the jolting
of the carriage, and having to occupy a centre seat.

In the morning we received news from every one
we met of the fall of Alexandria.

The road to-day was alive with negroes, who are
being "run" into Texas out of Banks' way. We
must have met hundreds of them, and many families
of planters, who were much to be pitied, especially
the ladies.

On approaching Munroe, we passed through the
camp of Walker's division (8,000 strong), which was
on its march from Arkansas to meet Banks. The
division had embarked in steamers, and had already

started down the " Wachita" towards the Red River,
when the news arrived of the fall of Alexandria, and
of the presence of Federal gunboats in or near the
Wachita itself. This caused the precipitate return
and disembarkation of Walker's division. The men
were well armed with rifles and bayonets, but they
were dressed in ragged civilian clothes. The old
Matagorda man recognized his son in one of these
regiments—a perfect boy.

Munroe is on the " Wachita" (pronounced Wash-
taw), which is a very pretty and wide stream. After
crossing it we arrived at the hotel after dark.

Universal confusion reigned there; it was full of
officers and soldiers of Walker's division, and no person would take the slightest notice of us.

In desperation I called on General Hebert, who
commanded the post. I told him who I was, and
gave him a letter of introduction, which I had fortu-
nately brought from Kirby Smith. I stated my hard
case, and besought an asylum for the night, which he
immediately accorded me in his own house.

The difficulty of crossing the Mississippi appeared
to increase the nearer I got to it, and General Hebert
told me that it was very doubtful whether I could
cross at all at this point. The Yankee gunboats,
which had forced their way past Vicksburg and Port
Hudson, were roaming about the Mississippi and Red
River, and some of them were reported at the entrance

of the Wachita itself, a small fort at Harrisonburg being the only impediment to their appearance in front of Munroe.

On another side, the enemy's forces were close to Delhi, only forty miles distant.

There were forty or fifty Yankee deserters here from the army besieging Vicksburg. These Yankee deserters, on being asked their reasons for deserting, generally reply,—" Our government has broken faith with us. We enlisted to fight for the Union, and not to liberate the G—d d—d niggers." Vicksburg is distant from this place about eighty miles.

The news of General Lee's victory at Chancellorsville had just arrived here. Every one received it very coolly, and seemed to take it quite as a matter of course; but the wound of Stonewall Jackson was universally deplored.

11*th May* (Monday).—General Hebert is a good-looking creole.* He was a West-Pointer, and served in the old army, but afterwards became a wealthy sugar-planter. He used to hold Magruder's position as commander-in-chief in Texas, but he has now been shelved at Munroe, where he expects to be taken prisoner any day; and, from the present gloomy

* The descendants of the French colonists in Louisiana are called creoles; most of them talk French, and I have often met Louisianian regiments talking that language.

aspect of affairs about here, it seems extremely probable that he will not be disappointed in his expectations. He is extremely down upon England for not recognizing the South.*

He gave me a passage down the river in a steamer, which was to try to take provisions to Harrisonburg; but, at the same time, he informed me that she might very probably be captured by a Yankee gunboat.

At 1 p. m. I embarked for Harrisonburg, which is distant from Munroe by water 150 miles, and by land 75 miles. It is fortified, and offers what was considered a weak obstruction to the passage of the gunboats up the river to Munroe.

The steamer was one of the curious American river boats, which rise to a tremendous height out of the water, like great wooden castles. She was steered from a box at the very top of all, and this particular one was propelled by one wheel at her stern.

The river is quite beautiful; it is from 200 to 300 yards broad, very deep and tortuous, and the large trees grow right down to the very edge of the water.

Our captain at starting expressed in very plain

---

* General Hebert is the only man of education I met in the whole of my travels who spoke disagreeably about England in this respect. Most people say they think we are quite right to keep out of it as long as we can; but others think our government is foolish to miss such a splendid chance of "smashing the Yankees," with whom we must have a row sooner or later.

terms his extreme disgust at the expedition, and said he fully expected to run against a gunboat at any turn of the river.

Soon after leaving Munroe, we passed a large plantation. The negro quarters were larger than a great many Texan towns, and they held three hundred hands.

After we had proceeded about half an hour, we were stopped by a mounted orderly (called a courier), who from the bank roared out the pleasing information, "They're a-fighting at Harrisonburg." The captain on hearing this turned quite green in the face, and remarked that he'd be "dogged" if he liked running into the jaws of a lion, and he proposed to turn back; but he was jeered at by my fellow-travellers, who were all either officers or soldiers, wishing to cross the Mississippi to rejoin their regiments in the different Confederate armies.

One pleasant fellow, more warlike than the rest, suggested that as we had some Enfields on board, we should make "a little bit of a fight," or at least "make one butt at a gunboat." I was relieved to find that these insane proposals were not received with any enthusiasm by the majority.

The plantations, as we went further down the river, looked very prosperous; but signs of preparations for immediate skedaddling were visible in most of them, and I fear they are all destined to be soon desolate and destroyed.

We came to a courier picket every sixteen miles. At one of them we got the information, "Gunboats drove back," at which there was great rejoicing, and the captain, recovering his spirits, became quite jocose, and volunteered to give me letters of introduction to a "particular friend of his about here, called Mr. Farragut;" but the next news, "Still a-fightin'," caused us to tie ourselves to a tree at 8 P. M., off a little village called Columbia, which is half-way between Munroe and Harrisonburg.

We then lit a large fire, round which all the passengers squatted on their heels in Texan fashion, each man whittling a piece of wood, and discussing the merits of the different Yankee prisons at New Orleans or Chicago. One of them, seeing me, called out, "I reckon, Kernel, if the Yankees catch you with us, they'll say you're in d—d bad company;" which sally caused universal hilarity.

12th May (Tuesday).—Shortly after daylight three negroes arrived from Harrisonburg, and they described the fight as still going on. They said they were "dreadful skeered;" and one of them told me he would "rather be a slave to his master all his life, than a white man and a soldier."

During the morning some of the officers and soldiers left the boat, and determined to cut across country to Harrisonburg, but I would not abandon the scanty remains of my baggage until I was forced to do so.

During the morning twelve more negroes arrived from Harrisonburg. It appears that three hundred of them, the property of neighboring planters, had been engaged working on the fortifications, but they all with one accord bolted when the first shell was fired. Their only idea and hope at present seemed to be to get back to their masters. All spoke of the Yankees with great detestation, and expressed wishes to have nothing to do with such " bad people."

Our captain coolly employed them in tearing down the fences, and carrying the wood away on board the steamer for firewood.

We did nothing but this all day long, the captain being afraid to go on, and unwilling to return. In the evening a new alarm seized him—viz., that the Federal cavalry had cut off the Confederate line of couriers. During the night we remained in the same position as last night, head up stream, and ready to be off at a moment's notice.*

13th May (Wednesday).—There was a row on board last night; one of the officers having been too atten-

---

* One of the passengers on board this steamer was Captain Barney, of the Confederate States Navy, who has since, I believe, succeeded Captain Maffit in the command of the Florida.

tive to a lady, had to skedaddle suddenly into the
woods, in order to escape the fury of her protector,
and he has not thought it advisable to reappear. My
trusty companion for several days, the poor young
Missourian, was taken ill to-day, and told me he had
a "*right smart little fever*" on him." I doctored him
with some of the physic which Mr. Maloney had
given me, and he got better in the evening.

We had pickets out in the woods last night. Two
of my fellow-travellers on that duty fell in with a
negro, and pretending they were Yankees, asked him
to join them. He consented, and even volunteered
to steal his master's horses ; and he then received a
tremendous thrashing, administered by the two soldiers with their ramrods.

At 9 P. M., to the surprise of all, the captain suddenly made up his mind to descend the river at all
hazards, thinking, I suppose, that any thing was better
than the uncertainty of the last twenty-four hours.

The further we went, the more beautiful was the
scenery.

At 4 P. M. we were assured by a citizen on the bank
that the gunboats really had retreated ; and at 5.30
our doubts were set at rest, to our great satisfaction,
by descrying the Confederate flag flying from Fort
Beauregard, high above the little town of Harrisonburg. After we had landed, I presented my letter of
introduction from General Hebert to Colonel Logan,

who commands the fort. He introduced me to a German officer, the engineer.

They gave me an account of the attack and repulse of the four Federal gunboats under Commodore Woodford, and supposed to have been the Pittsburg ironclad), the General Price, the Arizona, and another.

Fort Beauregard is a much more formidable looking work than I expected to see, and its strength had evidently been much underrated at Munroe.

A hill 190 feet high, which rises just in rear of Harrisonburg, has been scarped and fortified. It is situated at an angle of the river, and faces a long "reach" of two miles.

The gunboats, after demanding an unconditional surrender, which was treated with great contempt by Colonel Logan, opened fire at 2 P. M. on Sunday, and kept it up till 6.30, throwing about one hundred and fifty 9 and 11 inch shell. The gunboats reopened again for about an hour on Monday afternoon, when they finally withdrew, the Arizona being crippled.

The fort fired altogether about forty-five 32-pound shot (smooth bore). The range was about a mile.

The garrison thought that they had loosened several of the Pittsburg's iron-plates. They felt confident they could have sunk the wooden vessels if they had attempted to force the passage; and they were naturally much elated with their success, which certainly had not been anticipated on board my steamer or at Munroe.

I had not time to visit the interior of the fort, but I saw the effect of the shell upon the outside. Those which fell in the sand did not burst. Only three men were wounded in the garrison. They told me the deck of the Pittsburg was furnished with a parapet of cotton-bales for riflemen.

The river at Harrisonburg is about 160 yards broad, and very deep, with a moderate current. The town, being between the vessels and the fort, had, of course, suffered considerably during the bombardment.

When the works are complete they will be much more formidable.

To our great joy Colonel Logan decided that our vessel should proceed at once to Trinity, which is fifteen miles nearer Natchez (on the Mississippi) than Harrisonburg. We arrived there at 8 P. M., and found that the gunboats had only just left, after having destroyed all the molasses and rum they could find, and carried away a few negroes.

Six of us pigged in one very small room, paying a dollar each for this luxury to an old woman, who was most inhospitable, and told us "she didn't want to see no soldiers, as the Yanks would come back and burn her house for harboring rebels." I am always taken for a Confederate officer, partly from being in their company, and partly on account of my clothes, which happen to be a gray shooting-suit, almost the same color as most of the soldiers' coats.

14*th May* (Thursday).—The officers and soldiers, about thirty in number, who came down the Wachita in my company, determined to proceed to Natchez to-day, and a very hard day's work we had of it.

As the Louisianian bank of the Mississippi is completely overflowed at this time of year, and the river itself is infested with the enemy's gunboats, which have run past Vicksburg and Port Hudson, the passage can only be made by a tedious journey in small boats through the swamps and bayous.

Our party left Trinity at 6 A. M. in one big yawl and three skiffs. In my skiff were eight persons, besides a negro oarsman named "Tucker." We had to take it in turns to row with this worthy, and I soon discovered to my cost the inconvenience of sitting in close proximity with a perspiring darkie. This negro was a very powerful man, very vain and susceptible of flattery. I won his heart by asking him if he wasn't worth 6,000 dollars. We kept him up to the mark throughout the journey by plying him with compliments upon his strength and skill. One officer declared to him that he should try to marry his mistress (a widow) on purpose to own him.

After beating up for about eight miles against one of three streams which unite at, and give its name to

5

Trinity, we turned off to the right, and got into a large dense swamp. The thicket was so tangled and impenetrable that we experienced the greatest difficulty in forcing our way through it; we were often obliged to get into the water up to our middles and shove, whilst most of the party walked along an embankment.

After two hours and a half of this sort of work we had to carry our boats bodily over the embankment into a bayou called Log Bayou, on account of the numerous floating logs which had to be encountered. We then crossed a large and beautiful lake, which led us into another dismal swamp, quite as tangled as the former one. Here we lost our way, and got aground several times; but at length, after great exertions, we forced ourselves through it, and reached Lake Concordia, a fine piece of water, several miles in extent, and we were landed at dusk on the plantation of a Mr. Davis. These bayous and swamps abound with alligators and snakes of the most venomous description. I saw many of the latter swimming about exposed to a heavy fire of six-shooters; but the alligators were frightened away by the leading boat.

The yawl and one of the skiffs beat us, and their passengers reached Natchez about 9 P. M., but the other skiff, which could not boast of a Tucker, was lost in the swamp, and passed the night there in a wretched plight.

The weather was most disagreeable, either a burning sun or a downpour of rain.

The distance we did in the skiff was about twenty-eight miles, which took us eleven hours to perform.

On landing we hired at Mr. Davis's a small cart for Mr. Douglas (the wounded Missourian) and our baggage, and we had to finish the day by a trudge of three miles through deep mud, until, at length, we reached a place called Vidalia, which is on the Louisianian bank of the Mississippi, just opposite Natchez.

At Vidalia I got the immense luxury of a pretty good bed, *all to myself*, which enabled me to take off my clothes and boots for the first time in ten days.

The landlord told us that three of the enemy's gunboats had passed during the day; and as he said their crews were often in the habit of landing at Vidalia, he cautioned the military to be ready to bolt into the woods at any time during the night.

There were two conscripts on board my skiff today, one an Irishman and the other a Pole. They confessed to me privately their extreme dislike of the military profession; but at the same time they acknowledged the enthusiasm of the masses for the war.

15th May (Friday).—I nearly slept round the clock after yesterday's exertions. Mr. Douglas and I crossed the father of rivers and landed on the Mississippi bank at 9 A.M.

Natchez is a pretty little town, and ought to contain about 6,000 inhabitants. It is built on the top of a high bluff overlooking the Mississippi river, which is about three quarters of a mile broad at this point.

When I reached Natchez I hired a carriage, and, with a letter of introduction which I had brought from San Antonio, I drove to the house of Mr. Haller Nutt, distant from the town about two miles.

The scenery about Natchez is extremely pretty, and the ground is hilly, with plenty of fine trees. Mr. Nutt's place reminded me very much of an English gentleman's country seat, except that the house itself is rather like a pagoda, but it is beautifully furnished.

Mr. Nutt was extremely civil, and was most anxious that I should remain at Natchez for a few days; but now that I was thoroughly wound up for travelling, I determined to push on to Vicksburg, as all the late news seemed to show that some great operations must take place there before long.

I had fondly imagined that after reaching Natchez my difficulties would have been over; but I very soon discovered that this was a delusive hope. I found that Natchez was full of the most gloomy rumors. Another Yankee raid seemed to have been made into the interior of Mississippi, more railroad is reported to be destroyed, and great doubts were expressed whether I should be able to get into Vicksburg at all.

However, as I found some other people as determined to proceed as myself, we hired a carriage for $100 to drive to Brookhaven, which is the nearest point on the railroad, and is distant from Natchez 66 miles.

My companions were a fat Government contractor from Texas, the wounded Missourian Mr. Douglas, and an ugly woman, wife to a soldier in Vicksburg.

We left Natchez at 12 noon, and were driven by a negro named Nelson; the carriage and the three horses belong to him, and he drives it for his own profit; but he is, nevertheless a slave, and pays his owner $4½ a-week to be allowed to work on his own account. He was quite as vain as and even more amusing than Tucker. He said he "didn't want to see no Yanks, nor to be no freer than he is;" and he thought the war had already lasted four or five years.

Every traveller we met on the road was eagerly asked the questions, "Are the Yanks in Brookhaven? Is the railroad open?" At first we received satisfactory replies; but at 6 P. M. we met an officer driving towards Natchez at a great pace; he gave us the alarming intelligence that *Jackson* was going to be evacuated. Now, as Jackson is the capital city of this State, a great railroad junction, and on the highroad to every civilized place from this, our feelings may be imagined, but we did not believe it possible. On the other hand we were told that General Joseph

Johnston had arrived and assumed the command in Mississippi. He appears to be an officer in whom every one places unbounded confidence.

We slept at a farm-house. All the males were absent at the war, and it is impossible to exaggerate the unfortunate condition of the women left behind in these farm-houses; they have scarcely any clothes, and nothing but the coarsest bacon to eat, and are in miserable uncertainty as to the fate of their relations, whom they can hardly ever communicate with. Their slaves, however, generally remain true to them.

Our hostess, though she was reduced to the greatest distress, was well-mannered, and exceedingly well educated; very far superior to a woman of her station in England.

16th May (Saturday).—We started a little before daylight, our team looking so very mean that we expressed doubts as to their lasting—to Mr. Nelson's great indignation.

We breakfasted at another little farm-house on some unusually tough bacon, and coffee made of sweet potatoes. The natives, under all their misery, were red-hot in favor of fighting for their independence to the last, and I constantly hear the words, " This is the most unjust war ever waged upon a people by mortal man."

At 11 A. M. we met a great crowd of negroes, who

had been run into the swamps to be out of the way
of the Yankees, and they were now returning to
Louisiana.

At 2 P. M. a wounded soldier gave us the deplorable information that the enemy really was on the
railroad between Jackson and Brookhaven, and that
Jackson itself was in his hands. This news stag-
gered us all, and Nelson became alarmed for the
safety of his wretched animals; but we all determined to go on at all hazards, and see what turned
up. We halted for dinner at a farm-house, in which
were seven virgins, seated all of a row. They were
all good-looking, but shy and bashful to a degree I
never before witnessed. All the young women in this
country seem to be either uncommonly free-spoken, or
else extremely shy. The further we went, the more
certain became the news of the fall of Jackson.

We passed the night in the veranda of an old
farmer. He told us that Grierson's Yankee raid had
captured him about three weeks ago. He thought
the Yankees were about 1,500 strong; they took all
good horses, leaving their worn-out ones behind.
They destroyed railroad, government property, and
arms, and paroled all men, both old and young, but
they committed no barbarities. In this manner they
traversed all the State of Mississippi without meeting any resistance. They were fine-looking men
from the Northwestern States.

17*th May* (Sunday).—We started again at 4.30
A. M., and met five wounded men, who had been captured and paroled by Banks, in Louisiana; they confirmed every thing about the fall of Jackson, which
made me consider myself particularly unfortunate,
and destined apparently to be always intercepted by
the Northern troops, which had happened to be at
Alexandria, at Harrisonburg, and now again at
Jackson. At 8 A. M. we reached the little town of
Brookhaven, which was full of travellers, principally
Confederate soldiers, anxious to rejoin their regiments.

Maxey's brigade left this place by road last night
to join General Johnston, who is supposed to be concentrating his forces at a place called Canton, not far
from Jackson.

I called on Captain Matthews, the officer who commanded at Brookhaven, and after introducing myself
to him, he promised to assist me, by every means in
his power, to join General Johnston.

I then went to a Methodist chapel; a good many
soldiers were there, and a great number of women.

At noon, just as I had begun to get in very low
spirits about the prospects of getting on, a locomotive
arrived from a station called Haslehurst, and brought
us the astonishing report that the Yankees had suddenly abandoned Jackson, after destroying all the
government, and a good deal of private, property.

This news caused our prospects to look brighter.

18*th May* (Monday).—On getting up this morning, every thing appeared very uncertain, and a
thousand contradictory reports and rumors were flying about.

At 8 o'clock I called on Captain Matthews, and
told him my earnest desire to get on towards Johnston's army at all risks.   He kindly introduced me
to the conductor of a locomotive, who offered to take
me to within a few miles of Jackson, if he was not
cut off by the enemy, which seemed extremely probable.   At 9 A. M. I seated myself, in company with
about twenty soldiers, on the engine, and we started
towards Jackson.

On reaching Crystal Springs, half-way to Jackson,
we found General Loring's division crossing the railroad and marching east.   It had been defeated, with
the loss of most of its artillery, three days before, and
was now cut off from General Pemberton.

At 5 P. M. the conductor stopped the engine, and
put us out at a spot distant nine miles from Jackson;
and as I could procure no shelter, food, or conveyance there, I found myself in a terrible fix.

At this juncture a French boy rode up on horseback, and volunteered to carry my saddle-bags as far
as Jackson, if I could walk and carry the remainder.

Gladly accepting this unexpected offer, I started
with him to walk up the railroad, as he assured me
the Yankees really had gone; and during the journey,

5*

he gave me a description of their conduct during the short time they had occupied the city.

On arriving within three miles of Jackson, I found the railroad destroyed by the enemy, who after pulling up the track, had made piles of the sleepers, and then put the rails in layers on the top of these heaps; they had then set fire to the sleepers, which had caused the rails to bend when red-hot; the wooden bridges had also been set on fire, and were still smoking.

When within a mile and a half of Jackson, I met four men, who stopped and questioned me very suspiciously, but they at length allowed me to proceed, saying that these "were curious times."

After another mile I reached a mild trench, which was dignified by the name of the fortifications of Jackson. A small fight had taken place there four days previous, when General Johnston had evacuated the city.

When I got inside this trench I came to the spot on which a large body of the Yankees had recently been encamped; they had set fire to a great quantity of stores and arms, which they had been unable to carry away with them, and which were still burning, and were partially destroyed. I observed also great numbers of pikes and pikeheads amongst the debris.

At the entrance to the town the French boy took me to the house of his relatives, and handed me my saddlebags. These French people told me they had been much ill-treated, notwithstanding their French nationality. They showed me their broken furniture, and they assured me that they had been robbed of every thing of any value. I then shouldered my saddlebags, and walked through the smoking and desolate streets towards the Bowmont House hotel.

I had not proceeded far before a man with long gray hair and an enormous revolver rode up to me, and offered to carry my saddlebags. He then asked me who I was; and after I told him, he thought a few moments, and then said, "Well, sir, you must excuse me, but if you are a British officer, I can't make out what on earth you are doing at Jackson just now." I could not but confess that this was rather a natural idea, and that my presence in this burning town must have seemed rather odd, more especially as I was obliged to acknowledge that I was there entirely of my own free will, and for my own amusement.

Mr. Smythe, for so this individual was named, then told me, that if I was really the person I represented myself, I should be well treated by all; but that if I could not prove myself to be an English officer, an event would happen which it was not difficult to foresee, and the idea caused a disagreeable sensation about the throat.

Mr. Smythe then gave me to understand that I must remain a prisoner for the present. He conducted me to a room in the Bowmont House hotel, and I found myself speedily surrounded by a group of eager and excited citizens, who had been summoned by Smythe to *conduct my examination.*

At first they were inclined to be disagreeable. They examined my clothes, and argued as to whether they were of English manufacture. Some, who had been in London, asked me questions about the streets of the metropolis, and about my regiment. One remarked that I was "*mighty young for a lootenant-colonel.*"

When I suggested that they should treat me with proper respect until I was proved to be a spy, they replied that their city had been brutally pillaged by the Yankees, and that there were many suspicious characters about.

Every thing now looked very threatening, and it became evident to me that nothing would relieve the minds of these men so much as a hanging match. I looked in vain for some one to take my part, and I could not even get any person to examine my papers.

At this critical juncture a new character appeared on the scene in the shape of a big heavy man who said to me, " My name is Dr. Russell; I'm an Irishman, and I hate the British Government and the English nation; but if you are really an officer in the Coldstream Guards there is nothing I won't do for you; you shall come to my house and I will protect you."

I immediately showed Dr. Russell my passport and letters of introduction to General Johnston and other Confederate officers; he pronounced them genuine, promised to stand by me, and wanted to take me away with him at once.

But observing that the countenances of Smythe and his colleagues did not by any means express satisfaction at this arrangement, I announced my determination to stay where I was until I was released by the military authorities, with whom I demanded an immediate audience.

A very handsome cavalry officer called Captain Yerger, shortly afterwards arrived, who released me at once—asked me to his mother's house, and promised that I should join a brigade which was to march for General Johnston's camp on the following morning.

All the citizens seemed to be satisfied by the result of my interview with Captain Yerger, and most of them insisted on shaking hands and "liquoring up," in horrible whiskey. Smythe, however, was an exception to this rule. He evidently thought he had effected a grand capture, and was not at all satisfied at the turn of affairs. I believe to his dying day he will think I am a spy; but it was explained to me that his house had been burnt down by the Yankees two days before, which had made him unusually venomous.

They told me that Dr. Russell had saved his prop-

erty from pillage in the following manner :—He had
seated himself in his veranda, with a loaded double-
barrelled gun on his knees, and when the pillagers
approached, he addressed them in the following manner : " No man can die more than once, and I shall
never be more ready to die than I am now : there is
nothing to prevent your going into this house, except that I shall kill the first two of you who move
with this gun. Now then, gentlemen, walk in."
This speech is said to have saved Dr. Russell from
further annoyance, and his property from the ruin
which overtook his neighbors.

Jackson, the capital of the State of Mississippi, is a
place of great importance. Four railroads meet here,
and have been destroyed in each direction for a distance of from three to five miles. All the numerous
factories have been burnt down by the enemy, who
were of course justified in doing so ; but during the
short space of thirty-six hours, in which General Grant
occupied the city, his troops had wantonly pillaged
nearly all the private houses. They had gutted all
the stores, and destroyed what they could not carry
away. All this must have been done under the very
eyes of General Grant, whose name was in the book
of the Bowmont House hotel.

I saw the ruins of the Roman Catholic church, the
priest's house, and the principal hotel, which were
still smoking, together with many other buildings

which could in no way be identified with the Confederate Government. The whole town was a miserable wreck, and presented a deplorable aspect.

Nothing could exceed the intense hatred and fury with which its excited citizens speak of the outrages they have undergone—of their desire for a bloody revenge, and of their hope that the Black Flag might be raised.*

I had previously heard the Jacksonians spoken of as not being particularly zealous in the war. Heaven knows General Grant had now converted them into good and earnest rebels.

At 8 P. M. I called at Captain Yerger's house, and found him with General Gist and another officer lying flat on their stomachs poring over a map. Captain Yerger then introduced me to the ladies of his family, who were extremely pretty, very amiable, and highly patriotic. The house is charming, and, being outside the town, it had by good luck escaped destruction and pillage. After supper, the ladies played and sang, and I ended an eventful day in a very agreeable manner. General Gist promised that I should accompany his brigade to-morrow on its march towards General Johnston, and Mrs. Yerger insisted that I should pass the night at her house.

---

* Since this date, the unfortunate city of Jackson has been again subjected to pillage by the Federals after the capture of Vicksburg.

In this part of the country the prospects of the Confederacy appeared to be very gloomy. General Joseph Johnston, who commands the whole Western Department, only arrived from Tennessee last Wednesday, and on the following day he found himself obliged to abandon Jackson to an overwhelming Northern army, after making a short fight to enable his baggage to escape.

General Pemberton, who had hitherto held the chief command, is abused by all. He was beaten on Saturday at Baker's Creek, where he lost the greater part of his artillery. He had retired into Vicksburg, and was now completely shut up there by the victorious Grant.

General Maxey's brigade, about 5,000 strong, was near Brookhaven, and was marching east when I was there. General Loring's force, cut off from Pemberton, was near Crystal Springs. General Johnston, with about 6,000 men, was supposed to be near Canton. General Gist's troops, about 5,500 strong, were close by, having arrived from South Carolina and Georgia, just too late to defend Jackson.

The enemy, under General Grant, in vastly superior force, was pressing Vicksburg very hard, and had now completely invested that fortress.

The great object of the Confederates must, of course, be to unite their scattered forces under so able a general as Johnston, and then relieve Vicksburg.

19*th May* (Tuesday).—The landlord of the Bowmont House gave a breakfast at 7 A. M. to General
Gist and his Staff, to which I also was invited.

Shortly afterwards I was given a seat in a curious
little vehicle belonging to Lieutenant Martino, a
Spaniard, in the Confederate army. This vehicle
caused considerable merriment amongst the soldiers,
who called it a chicken-wagon.

We left Jackson with the leading troops about 8
A. M., amidst a great waving of handkerchiefs and
showers of flowers, thrown by the few remaining
ladies who were still left in that dilapidated place.

The corps under General Gist consisted of three
weak brigades, the leading one composed of Georgians
and South Carolinians; the next were Texans, under
General Ector; and the last were Arkansians, under
General M'Nair. General Gist had twelve good-
looking Napoleon guns with him (twelve-pounders).
The horses were fine animals, and were in wonderful
good condition, considering that they had been ten
days on the railroad coming from South Carolina.

The troops were roughly but efficiently clothed;
their boots were in good order, and all were armed
with Enfield rifles.

The weather was very hot, and we were halted to
bivouac for the night, at a spot about seventeen miles
from Jackson, on the road towards Vicksburg.

The straggling of the Georgians was on the grandest scale conceivable; the men fell out by dozens, and seemed to suit their own convenience in that respect, without interference on the part of the officers. But I was told that these regiments had never done any marching before, having hitherto been quartered in forts and transported by railroad.

The country is much covered with woods, and is sandy, with very little water.

I did not consider that the troops were marched judiciously; they were halted too long at a time, and not often enough. The baggage was carried on country carts pressed into the service.

We bivouacked in the woods near a very pretty house, belonging to a planter called Colonel Robinson. These immense woods make admirable bivouacs.

General State Rights Gist is a South Carolinian, only thirty-two years of age, and although not educated as a soldier, he seems easily to have adapted himself to the military profession. He looks a determined man, and he takes responsibility very coolly. In the early part of the day he was very doubtful as to the exact whereabouts of General Johnston; but about noon a courier arrived, from whom he received important and satisfactory information, otherwise General Gist had made up his mind for some "nasty work" before the junction could be effected. He told me that the present expedition was rather inconvenient to him, as he had only been married three days before he left Charleston. He lent me a magnificent rug, and I slept very comfortably in the open air for the first time since I was in Texas.

20th May (Wednesday).—At 3 A. M. we were awoke by a great bombardment going on at Vicksburg, which lasted about three hours.*

The assembly was beaten at 7 A. M. by an old nigger, performing on a cracked drum, and its sound was hailed by the soldiers with loud yells.

General Gist, his Staff, and I, breakfasted with Mr. Robinson, whose house is charming, and beautifully furnished, and had not been visited by the Yankees.

We had a crazy old planter, named ——, with us, who insisted upon accompanying the column, mounted on a miserable animal which had been left him by the enemy as not being worth carrying away. The small remains of this poor old man's sense had been shattered by the Yankees a few days ago; they cleaned him completely out, taking his horses, mules, cows, and pigs, and stealing his clothes and any thing they wanted, destroying what they could not carry away. But what "riled" him most was that he had been visited by a Federal officer, disguised in the Confederate uniform. Poor old ——, full of rebel zeal, had, on being invited to do so, mounted *en croupe* behind

* I afterwards learnt that this bombardment preceded one of the unsuccessful assaults

this officer, and unbosomed himself to him; his fury
and rage may be imagined at finding himself shortly
afterwards in the very midst of the Federal camp;
but the Yankee General M'Pherson ordered him to
be released; and it appears that the reason of his being kidnapped, was to extract from him a large quantity of gold, which he was supposed to have hidden
somewhere.

This Mr. (or Major*) ——took a great fancy to me,
and insisted on picking some of the silk of Indian
corn, which he requested I would present to Queen
Victoria to show her how far advanced the crops were
in Mississippi. It was almost painful to hear the
manner in which this poor old man gloated over the
bodies of the dead Yankees at Jackson, and of his
intense desire to see more of them put to death.

The column reached the village or town of Living-
ston at 11 A. M., where I was introduced to a militia
general and his pretty daughter; the latter had been
married two days before to a wounded Confederate
officer, but the happy couple were just on the point
of starting for the Yazoo river, as they were afraid of
being disturbed in their felicity by the Yankees.

I now heard every one speaking of the fall of Vicksburg as very possible, and its jeopardy was laid at the
door of General Pemberton, for whom no language

* Nearly every man in this part of the country has a military
title.

could be too strong. He was freely called a coward and a traitor. He has the misfortune to be a Northerner by birth, which was against him in the opinion of all here.

General Gist and I cantered on in front of the column, and reached General Johnston's bivouac at 6 P. M.

General Johnston received me with much kindness, when I presented my letters of introduction, and stated my object in visiting the Confederate armies.

In appearance, General Joseph E. Johnston (commonly called Joe Johnston) is rather below the middle height, spare, soldierlike, and well set up; his features are good, and he has lately taken to wear a grayish beard. He is a Virginian by birth, and appears to be about fifty-seven years old. He talks in a calm, deliberate, and confident manner; to me he was extremely affable, but he certainly possesses the power of keeping people at a distance when he chooses, and his officers evidently stand in great awe of him. He lives very plainly, and at present his only cooking-utensils consisted of an old coffee-pot and frying-pan—both very inferior articles. There was only one fork (one prong deficient) between himself and Staff, and this was handed to me ceremoniously as the "guest."

He has undoubtedly acquired the entire confidence of all the officers and soldiers under him. Many of the officers told me they did not consider him inferior as a general to Lee or any one else.

He told me that Vicksburg was certainly in a critical situation, and was now closely invested by Grant. He said that he (Johnston) had 11,000 men with him (which includes Gist's), hardly any cavalry, and only sixteen pieces of cannon; but if he could get adequate reinforcements, he stated his intention of endeavoring to relieve Vicksburg.

I also made the acquaintance of the Georgian General Walker, a fierce and very warlike fire-eater, who was furious at having been obliged to evacuate Jackson after having only destroyed four hundred Yankees. He told me, "I know I couldn't hold the place, but I did want to kill a few more of the rascals."

At. 9 P. M I returned with General Gist to his camp, as my baggage was there. On the road we were met by several natives, who complained that soldiers were quartering themselves upon them and eating every thing.

The bivouacs are extremely pretty at night, the dense woods being lit up by innumerable camp-fires.

21st *May* (Thursday).—I rejoined General Johnston at 9 A. M., and was received into his mess. Major Eustis and Lieutenant Washington, officers of his Staff, are thorough gentlemen, and did all in their power to make me comfortable.   The first is a Louisianian of wealth (formerly) ; his negro always speaks French.   He is brother to the secretary of Mr. Slidell in Paris, and has learnt to become an excellent Staff officer.

I was presented to Captain Henderson, who commanded a corps of about fifty "scouts."   These are employed on the hazardous duty of hanging about the enemy's camps, collecting information, and communicating with Pemberton in Vicksburg.   They are a fine-looking lot of men, wild, and very picturesque in appearance.

At 12 noon a Yankee military surgeon came to camp.   He had been left behind by Grant to look after the Yankees wounded at Jackson, and he was now anxious to rejoin his general by flag of truce, but General Johnston very prudently refused to allow this, and desired that he should be sent to the North *via* Richmond.   By a very sensible arrangement, both sides have agreed to treat doctors as non-combatants, and not to make prisoners of war of them.

The chief surgeon in Johnston's army is a very clever and amusing Kentuckian, named Dr. Yandell. He told me he had been educated in England, and might have had a large practice there.

My friend "Major" —— very kindly took me to dine with a neighboring planter, named Harrold, at whose house I met General Gregg, a Texan, who, with his brigade, fought the Yankees at Raymond a few days ago.

After dinner, I asked Mr. Harrold to take me over the quarters of his slaves, which he did immediately. The huts were comfortable and very clean; the negroes seemed fond of their master, but he told me they were suffering dreadfully from the effects of the war—he had so much difficulty in providing them with clothes and shoes. I saw an old woman in one of the huts, who had been suffering from an incurable disease for thirteen years, and was utterly useless. She was evidently well cared for, and was treated with affection and care. At all events, she must have benefited largely by the "peculiar institution."

I have often told these planters that I thought the word "slave" was the most repulsive part of the institution, and I have always observed they invariably shirk using it themselves. They speak of their servant, their boy, or their negroes, but never of their slaves. They address a negro as boy or girl, or uncle or aunty.

In the evening I asked General Johnston what prospect he thought there was of early operations, and he told me that at present he was too weak to do any good, and he was unable to give me any definite idea as to when he might be strong enough to attack Grant. I therefore made up my mind to be off in a day or two, unless something turned up, as I could not afford to wait for events, I have still so much to see. General Johnston is a very well-read man, and agreeable to converse with. He told me that he considered Marlborough a greater general than Wellington. All Americans have an intense admiration for Napoleon; they seldom scruple to express their regret that he was beaten at Waterloo.

Remarking upon the extreme prevalence of military titles, General Johnston said, " You must be astonished to find how fond all Americans are of titles, though they are republicans; and as they can't get any other sort, they all take military ones."

Whilst seated round the camp fire in the evening, one of the officers remarked to me, " I can assure you, colonel, that nine men out of ten in the South would sooner become subjects of Queen Victoria than return to the Union." " Nine men out ten !" said General Johnston—" ninety-nine out of a hundred; I consider that few people in the world can be more fortunate in their government than the British colonies of North America." But the effect of these compliments was rather spoilt when some one else said they would prefer to serve under the Emperor of the French or the Emperor of Japan to returning to the dominion of Uncle Abe; and it was still more damaged when another officer alluded in an undertone to the infernal regions as a more agreeable alternative than reunion with the Yankees.

6

22d May (Friday).—The bombardment at Vicksburg was very heavy and continuous this morning.

I had a long conversation with General Johnston, who told me that the principal evils which a Confederate general had to contend against consisted in the difficulty of making combinations, owing to uncertainty about the time which the troops would take to march a certain distance, on account of their straggling propensities.

But from what I have seen and heard *as yet*, it appears to me that the Confederates possess certain great qualities as soldiers, such as individual bravery and natural aptitude in the use of firearms, strong, determined patriotism, and boundless confidence in their favorite generals, and in themselves. They are sober of necessity, as there is literally no liquor to be got. They have sufficient good sense to know that a certain amount of discipline is absolutely necessary; and I believe that instances of insubordination are extremely rare. They possess the great advantage of being led by men of talent and education as soldiers who thoroughly understand the people they have to lead, as well as those they have to beat. These generals, such as Lee, Johnston, Beauregard, or Longstreet, they would follow anywhere, and obey implicitly. But, on the other hand, many of their officers, looking forward to future political advancement, owing to their present military rank, will not punish

their men, or are afraid of making themselves obnoxious by enforcing rigid discipline.   The men are constantly in the habit of throwing away their knapsacks and blankets on a long march, if not carried
for them, and though actuated by the strongest and
purest patriotism, can often not be got to consider
their obligations as soldiers.   In the early part of the
war they were often, when victorious, nearly as disorganized as the beaten, and many would coolly walk
off home, under the impression that they had performed their share.   But they are becoming better
in these respects as the war goes on.*   All this
would account for the trifling benefits derived by the
Confederates from their numerous victories.

General Johnston told me that Grant had displayed more vigor than he had expected, by crossing
the river below Vicksburg, seizing Jackson by vastly
superior force, and, after cutting off communications,
investing the fortress thoroughly, so as to take it if
possible before a sufficient force could be got to relieve it.   His army is estimated at 75,000 men, and
General Johnston has very little opinion of the de-

* After having lived with the veterans of Bragg and Lee, I was
able to form a still higher estimate of Confederate soldiers.   Their
obedience and forbearance in success, their discipline under disaster, their patience under suffering, under hardships, or when
wounded, and their boundless devotion to their country under all
circumstances, are beyond all praise.

fences of Vicksburg on the land side. He said the garrison consisted of about 20,000 men.

News has been received that the Yankees were getting up the Yazoo river; and this morning General Walker's division left at 6 A. M. for Yazoo city.

The General with his staff and myself rode into Canton, six miles, and lodged in the house of a planter who owned 700 slaves.

Dr. Yandell is a wonderful mimic, and amused us much by taking off the marriage ceremony, as performed by General Polk in Tennessee—General Morgan of Kentucky notoriety being the bridegroom.*

One of Henderson's scouts caused much hilarity amongst the General's Staff this afternoon. He had brought in a Yankee prisoner, and *apologized* to General Johnston for doing so, saying, "I found him in a negro quarter, and *he surrendered so quick, I couldn't kill him.*" There can be no doubt that the conduct of the Federals in captured cities tends to create a strong indisposition on the part of the Confederates to take prisoners, particularly amongst these wild Mississippians.

General Johnston told me this evening that altogether he had been wounded ten times. He was the senior officer of the old army who joined the Confeder-

---

* When I was introduced to General Polk in Tennessee I recognized him at once by Dr. Yandell's imitation, which was most wonderfully accurate.

ates, and he commanded the Virginian army until he was severely wounded at the battle of "Seven Pines."*

23*d May* (Saturday).—General Johnston, Major Eustis, and myself, left Canton at 6 A. M. on a locomotive for Jackson.

On the way we talked a good deal about "Stonewall" Jackson. General Johnston said that although this extraordinary man did not possess any great qualifications as a strategist, and was perhaps unfit for the independent command of a large army; yet he was gifted with wonderful courage and determination, and a perfect faith in Providence that he was destined to destroy his enemy. He was much indebted to General Ewell in the Valley campaigns. Stonewall Jackson was also most fortunate in commanding the flower of the Virginian troops, and in being opposed to the most incapable Federal commanders, such as Fremont and Banks.

Before we had proceeded twelve miles we were forced to stop and collect wood from the roadside to feed our engine, and the General worked with so much energy as to cause his "Seven Pines" wound to give him pain.

We were put out at a spot where the railroad was destroyed, at about four miles from Jackson. A car-

---

* Called "Fair Oaks" by the Yankees.

riage ought to have been in waiting for us, but by
some mistake it had not arrived, so we had to foot it.
I was obliged to carry my heavy saddlebags. Major
Eustis very kindly took my knapsack, and the Gen-
eral carried the cloaks. In this order we reached
Jackson, much exhausted, at 9.30 A. M.

General Loring came and reported himself soon
after. He is a stout man with one arm. His division had arrived at Jackson from Crystal Springs
about 6,000 strong; Evans's brigade, about 3,000,
had also arrived from Charleston; and Maxey's brigade was in the act of marching into Jackson. I cal-
culate, therefore, that General Johnston must now have
nearly 25,000 men between Jackson and the Yazoo.

I took an affectionate farewell of him and his officers, and he returned to Canton at 3 P. M. I shall be
much surprised if he is not heard of before long.
That portion of his troops which I saw, though they
had been beaten and forced to retreat, were in excellent spirits, full of confidence, and clamoring to be
led against *only* double their numbers.

I renewed my acquaintance with Dr. Russell, for
whose timely protection I shall always feel myself
much indebted. I also sent my love to Smythe by
several different people.

At 3.30 P. M. I left Jackson in a Government ambulance, in company with Captain Brown of General
Johnston's Staff, who was extremely useful to me. I

had taken the precaution of furnishing myself with a pass from Colonel Ewell, the adjutant-general, which I afterwards discovered was absolutely necessary, as I was asked for it continually, and on the railroad every person's passport was rigidly examined.

We drove to the nearest point at which the railroad was in working order, a distance of nearly five miles.

We then got into the cars at 6 P. M. for Meridian. This piece of railroad was in a most dangerous state, and enjoys the reputation of being the very worst of all the bad railroads in the South. It was completely worn out, and could not be repaired. Accidents are of almost daily occurrence, and a nasty one had happened the day before.

After we had proceeded five miles, our engine ran off the track, which caused a stoppage of three hours. All male passengers had to get out to push along the cars.

24th May (Sunday).—We reached Meridian at 7.30 A. M., with sound limbs, and only five hours late.

We left for Mobile at 9 A. M., and arrived there at 7.15 P. M. This part of the line was in very good order.

We were delayed a short time, owing to a "*difficulty*" which had occurred in the up-train. The difficulty was this. The engineer had shot a passenger, and then unhitched his engine, cut the telegraph, and bolted up the line, leaving his train planted on a single track. He had allowed our train to pass by shunting himself, until we had done so without any suspicion. The news of this occurrence caused really hardly any excitement amongst my fellow-travellers; but I heard one man remark, that "it was mighty mean to leave a train to be run into like that." We avoided this catastrophe by singular good fortune.*

* I cut this out of a Mobile paper two days after :—

"ATTEMPT TO COMMIT MURDER.—We learn that while the up-train on the Mobile and Ohio Railroad was near Beaver Meadow, one of the employees, named Thomas Fitzgerald, went into one of the passenger cars and shot Lieutenant H. A. Knowles with a pistol, the ball entering his left shoulder, going out at the back of his neck, making a very dangerous wound. Fitzgerald then uncoupled the locomotive from the train and started off. When a few miles above Beaver Meadows he stopped and cut the telegraph wires, and then proceeded up the road. When near Lauderdale station he came in collision with the down-train, smashing the engine, and doing considerable damage to several of the cars.† It is thought he there took to the woods; at any rate he has made good his escape so far, as nothing of him has yet been heard. The shooting, as we are informed, was that of revenge. It will be remembered that a few months ago Knowles and a brother of Thomas Fitzgerald, named Jack, had a rencounter at Enterprise about a lady, and during which Knowles killed Jack Fitzgerald; afterwards it is stated that Thomas threatened to revenge the death of his brother; so on Sunday morning Knowles was on the train, as stated, going up to Enterprise to stand his trial. Thomas learning that he was on the train, hunted him up and shot him. Knowles, we learn, is now lying in a very critical condition."

---

† This is a mistake.

The universal practice of carrying arms in the South is undoubtedly the cause of occasional loss of life, and is much to be regretted; but, on the other hand, this custom renders altercations and quarrels of very rare occurrence, for people are naturally careful what they say when a bullet may be the probable reply.

By the intercession of Captain Brown, I was allowed to travel in the ladies' car. It was cleaner and more convenient, barring the squalling of the numerous children, who were terrified into good behavior by threats from their negro nurses of being given to the Yankees.

I put up at the principal hotel at Mobile—viz., the "Battlehouse." The living appeared to be very good by comparison, and cost $8 a-day. In consequence of the fabulous value of boots, they must not be left outside the door of one's room, from danger of annexation by a needy and unscrupulous warrior.

25th May (Monday).—I was disappointed in the aspect of Mobile. It is a regular rectangular American city, built on a sandy flat, and covering a deal of ground for its population, which is about 25,000.

I called on General Maury, for whom I brought a letter of introduction from General Johnston. He is a very gentlemanlike and intelligent but diminutive Virginian, and had only just assumed the command at Mobile.

6*

He was very civil, and took me in a steamer to see the sea defences. We were accompanied by General Ledbetter the engineer, and we were six hours visiting the forts.

Mobile is situated at the head of a bay thirty miles long. The blockading squadron, eight to ten in number, is stationed outside the bay, the entrance to which is defended by Forts Morgan and Gaines; but as the channel between these two forts is a mile wide, they might probably be passed.

Within two miles of the city, however, the bay becomes very shallow, and the ship channel is both dangerous and tortuous. It is, moreover, obstructed by double rows of pine piles, and all sorts of ingenious torpedoes, besides being commanded by carefully constructed forts, armed with heavy guns, and built either on islands or on piles.

Their names are Fort Pinto, Fort Spanish River, Apalache, and Blakeley.*

The garrisons of these forts complained of their being unhealthy, and I did not doubt the assertion. Before landing, we boarded two iron-clad floating-batteries. The Confederate fleet at Mobile is considerable, and reflects great credit upon the energy of the Mobilians, as it has been constructed since the commencement of the war. During the trip, I overheard

* A description of either its sea or land defences is necessarily omitted.

General Maury soliloquizing over a Yankee flag, and saying, "Well, I never should have believed that I could have lived to see the day in which I should detest that old flag." He is cousin to Lieutenant Maury, who has distinguished himself so much by his writings, on physical geography especially. The family seems to be a very military one. His brother is captain of the Confederate steamer Georgia.

After landing, I partook of a hasty dinner with General Maury and Major Cummins. I was then mounted on the General's horse, and was sent to gallop round the land defences with Brigadier-general Slaughter and his Staff. By great good fortune this was the evening of General Slaughter's weekly inspection, and all the redoubts were manned by their respective garrisons, consisting half of soldiers and half of armed citizens who had been exempted from the conscription either by their age or nationality, or had purchased substitutes. One of the forts was defended by a burly British guard, commanded by a venerable Captain Wheeler.*

After visiting the fortifications, I had supper at General Slaughter's house, and met there some of the refugees from New Orleans—these are now being huddled neck and crop out of that city for refusing to take the oath of allegiance to the United States. Great

* Its members were British subjects exempted from the conscription, but they had volunteered to fight in defence of the city.

numbers of women and children are arriving at Mobile every day; they are in a destitute condition, and they add to the universal feeling of exasperation. The propriety of raising the black flag, and giving no quarter, was again freely discussed at General Slaughter's, and was evidently the popular idea. I heard many anecdotes of the late "Stonewall Jackson," who was General Slaughter's comrade in the artillery of the old army. It appears that previous to the war he was almost a monomaniac about his health. When he left the U. S. service he was under the impression that one of his legs was getting shorter than the other; and afterwards his idea was that he only perspired on one side, and that it was necessary to keep the arm and leg of the other side in constant motion in order to preserve the circulation; but it seems that immediately the war broke out he never made any further allusion to his health. General Slaughter declared that on the night after the terrific repulse of Burnside's army at Fredericksburg, Stonewall Jackson had made the following suggestion:—"I am of opinion that we ought to attack the enemy at once; and in order to avoid the confusion and mistakes so common in a night attack, I recommend that we should all strip ourselves perfectly naked."* Blockade-running goes on very regularly at Mobile; the steamers nearly

* I always forgot to ask General Lee whether this story was a true one.

always succeed, but the schooners are generally captured.   To-morrow I shall start for the Tennessean army, commanded by General Braxton Bragg.

26th May (Tuesday).—When I took Colonel Ewell's pass to the provost-marshal's office this morning to be countersigned, that official hesitated about stamping it, but luckily a man in his office came to my rescue, and volunteered to say that, although he didn't know me himself, he had heard me spoken of by others as "a very respectable gentleman."   I was only just in time to catch the twelve o'clock steamer for the Montgomery railroad.   I overheard two negroes on board discussing affairs in general; they were deploring the war, and expressing their hatred of the Yankees for bringing "sufferment on us as well as our masters."   Both of them had evidently a great aversion to being "run off," as they called it.   One of them wore his master's sword, of which he was very proud, and he strutted about in a most amusing and consequential manner.

I got into the railroad cars at 2.30 P. M. ; the pace was not at all bad, had we not stopped so often and for such a long time for wood and water.   I sat opposite to a wounded soldier, who told me he was an Englishman from Chelsea.   He said he was returning to his regiment, although his wound in the neck often gave him great pain.   The spirit with which wounded men return to the front, even although their wounds are imperfectly healed, is worthy of all praise, and shows the indomitable determination of the Southern people. In the same car there were several quite young boys of fifteen or sixteen who were badly wounded, and one or two were minus arms and legs, of which deficiencies they were evidently very vain.

The country through which we passed was a dense pine forest, sandy soil, and quite desolate, very uninviting to an invading army. We travelled all night.

27th May (Wednesday).—Arrived at Montgomery, the capital of Alabama, at daylight, and left it by another railroad at 5.30 A. M.

All State capitals appear to resemble one another, and look like bits cut off from great cities. One or two streets have a good deal of pretension about them; and the inevitable " Capitol," with its dome, forms the principal feature. A sentry stands at the door of each railway car, who examines the papers of every passenger with great strictness, and even after that inspection the same ceremony is performed by an officer of the provost-marshal's department, who accompanies every train.* The officers and soldiers on this duty are very civil and courteous, and after

---

* This rigid inspection is necessary to arrest spies, and prevent straggling and absence without leave.

getting over their astonishment at finding that I am a British officer, they do all they can to make me comfortable. They ask all sorts of curious questions about the British army, and often express a strong wish to see *one of our regiments fight.* They can hardly believe that the Coldstream is really dressed in scarlet. To-day they entered gravely into discussion amongst themselves, as to whether British troops would have taken the position at Fredericksburg. The arguments on both sides were very amusing, and opinion was pretty evenly divided. We met three trains crammed full of soldiers for Johnston's army. They belonged to Breckenridge's division of Bragg's army, and all seemed in the highest spirits, cheering and yelling like demons. In the cars to-day I fell in with the Federal doctor who was refused leave to pass through General Johnston's lines; he was now *en route* for Richmond. He was in full Yankee uniform, but was treated with civility by all the Confederate soldiers. I had a long talk with him; he seemed a sensible man, and did not attempt to deny the universal enthusiasm and determination of the Southerners. He told me that General Grant had been very nearly killed at the taking of Jackson. He thought the war would probably terminate by a blow-up in the North.*

* Notwithstanding the exasperation with which every South-

I had to change cars at West Point and at Atlanta. At the latter place I was crammed into a desperately crowded train for Chattanooga. This country, Georgia, is much more inhabited and cultivated than Alabama. I travelled again all night.

28th May (Thursday).—I arrived at Chattanooga (Tennessee) at 4.30 A. M., and fell in with Captain Brown again ; his negro recognized me, and immediately rushed up to shake hands.

After breakfasting at Chattanooga, I started again at 7.30, by train, for Shelbyville, General Bragg's headquarters. This train was crammed to repletion with soldiers rejoining their regiments, so I was constrained to sit in the aisle on the floor of one of the cars. I thought myself lucky even then, for so great was the number of military, that all " *citizens*" were ordered out to make way for the soldiers; but my gray shooting-jacket and youthful appearance saved me from the imputation of being a " citizen." Two hours later, the passport officer, seeing who I was, procured me a similar situation in the ladies' car, where I was a little better off. After leaving Chattanooga the railroad winds alongside of the Tennessee

erner speaks of a Yankee, and all the talk about black flag and no quarter, yet I never saw a Federal prisoner ill treated or insulted in any way, although I have travelled hundreds of miles in their company.

river, the banks of which are high, and beautifully covered with trees—the river itself is wide, and very pretty; but from my position in the tobacco-juice I was unable to do justice to the scenery. I saw stockades at intervals all along the railroad, which were constructed by the Federals, who occupied all this country last year.

On arriving at Wartrace at 4 P. M., I determined to remain there, and ask for hospitality from General Hardee, as I saw no prospect of reaching Shelbyville in decent time. Leaving my baggage with the provost-marshal at Wartrace, I walked on to General Hardee's headquarters, which were distant about two miles from the railroad. They were situated in a beautiful country, green, undulating, full of magnificent trees, principally beeches, and the scenery was by far the finest I had seen in America as yet.

When I arrived, I found that General Hardee was in company with General Polk and Bishop Elliott of Georgia, and also with Mr. Vallandigham. The latter (called the Apostle of Liberty) is a good-looking man, apparently not much over forty, and had been turned out of the North three days before. Rosecrans had wished to hand him over to Bragg by flag of truce; but as the latter declined to receive him in that manner, he was, as General Hardee expressed it, "*dumped down*" in the neutral ground between the lines, and left there. He then received hospitality from the Confederates in the capacity of a destitute stranger. They do not in any way receive him officially, and it does not suit the policy of either party to be identified with one another. He is now living at a private house in Shelbyville, and had come over for the day, with General Polk, on a visit to Hardee. He told the generals, that if Grant was severely beaten in Mississippi by Johnston, he did not think the war could be continued on its present great scale.

When I presented my letters of introduction, General Hardee received me with the unvarying kindness and hospitality which I had experienced from all other Confederate officers. He is a fine, soldierlike man, broad-shouldered and tall. He looks rather like a French officer, and is a Georgian by birth. He bears the reputation of being a thoroughly good soldier, and he is the author of the drill-book still in use by both armies. Until quite lately, he was commanding officer of the military college at West Point. He distinguished himself at the battles of Corinth and Murfreesborough, and now commands the 2d *corps d'armée* of Bragg's army. He is a widower, and has the character of being a great admirer of the fair sex. During the Kentucky campaign last year, he was in the habit of availing himself of the privilege of his rank and years, and insisted upon kissing the wives and daughters of all the Kentuckian farmers. And although he is supposed to have converted many of the ladies to the Southern cause, yet in many instances their male relatives remained either neutral or undecided. On one occasion General Hardee had conferred the " accolade" upon a very pretty Kentuckian, to their mutual satisfaction, when, to his intense disgust, the proprietor produced two very ugly old females, saying, "Now, then, general, if you kiss any you must kiss them all round," which the discomfited general was forced to do, to the great amusement of his officers, who often allude to this *contretemps.*

Another rebuff which he received, and about which he is often chaffed by General Polk, was when an old lady told him he ought really to "leave off fighting *at his age.*" "Indeed, madam," replied Hardee, "and how old do you take me for?" "Why, about the same age as myself—seventy-five." The chagrin of the stalwart and gallant general, at having twenty years added to his age, may be imagined.

Lieutenant-general Leonidas Polk, Bishop of Louisiana, who commands the other *corps d'armée,* is a good-looking, gentlemanlike man, with all the manners and affability of a "grand seigneur." He is fifty-seven years of age—tall, upright, and looks much more the soldier than the clergyman. He is very rich; and I am told he owns seven hundred negroes. He is much beloved by the soldiers on account of his great personal courage and agreeable manners. I had already heard no end of anecdotes of him told me by my travelling companions, who always alluded to him with affection and admiration. In his clerical capacity I had always heard him spoken of with the greatest respect. When I was introduced to him he immediately invited me to come and stay at his headquarters at Shelbyville. He told me that he was educated at West Point, and was at that institution with the President, the two Johnstons, Lee, Magruder, &c., and that, after serving a short time in the artillery, he had entered the church.

Bishop Elliott, of Georgia, is a nice old man of venerable appearance and very courteous manners. He is here at the request of General Polk, for the purpose of confirming some officers and soldiers. He speaks English exactly like an English gentleman, and so, in fact, does General Polk, and all the well-bred Southerners, much more so than the ladies, whose American accent can always be detected. General Polk and Mr. Vallandigham returned to Shelbyville in an ambulance at 6.30 P. M.

General Hardee's headquarters were on the estate of Mrs. ——, a very hospitable lady. The two daughters of the General were staying with her, and also a Mrs. ——, who is a very pretty woman. These ladies are more violent against the Yankees than it is possible for a European to conceive; they beat their male relations hollow in their denunciations and hopes of vengeance. It was quite depressing to hear their innumerable stories of Yankee brutality, and I was much relieved when, at a later period of the evening, they subsided into music. After Bishop Elliott had read prayers, I slept in the same room with General Hardee.

29th May (Friday).—I took a walk before breakfast with Dr. Quintard, a zealous Episcopal chaplain, who began life as a surgeon, which enables him to attend to the bodily as well as the spiritual wants of the Tennessean regiment to which he is chaplain. The enemy is about fifteen miles distant, and all the tops of the intervening hills are occupied as signal stations, which communicate his movements by flags in the daytime, and by beacons at night. A signal corps has been organized for this service. The system is most ingenious, and answers admirably. We all breakfasted at Mrs. ——'s. The ladies were more excited even than yesterday in their diatribes against the Yankees. They insisted on cutting the accompanying paragraph out of to-day's newspaper, which they declared was a very fair exposition of the average treatment they received from the enemy.* They re-

* "LOSSES OF WILLIAM F. RICKS.—The Yankees did not treat us very badly as they returned from pursuing our men beyond Leighton (at least no more than we expected); they broke down our smokehouse door and took seven hams, went into the kitchen

proved Mrs. —— for having given assistance to the
wounded Yankees at Wartrace last year; and a sister of Mrs. ——'s, who is a very strong-minded lady,
gave me a most amusing description of an interview

and helped themselves to cooking utensils, tin ware, &c.; searched
the house, but took nothing. As they passed up the second time
we were very much annoyed by them, but not seriously injured;
they took the only two mules we had, a cart, our milch cows, and
more meat. It was on their return from this trip that our losses
were so grievous. They drove their wagons up in our yard and
loaded them with the last of our meat, all of our sugar, coffee,
molasses, flour, meal, and potatoes. I went to a lieut.-colonel
who seemed very busy giving orders, and asked him what he expected me to do; they had left me no provisions at all, and I had
a large family, and my husband was away from home. His reply
was short and pointed—'Starve, and be d—d, madam.' They
then proceeded to the carriage-house, took a fine new buggy that
we had never used, the cushions and harness of our carriage, then
cut the carriage up and left it. They then sent about sixty of the
slyest, smoothest-fingered rogues I have ever seen in the Federal
army (all the rogues I ever did see were in that army), into the
house to search for whiskey and money, while the officers remained
in the back-yard trying to hire the servants to tell them where we
had money hid. Their search proving fruitless, they loaded themselves with our clothing, bed-clothing, &c.; broke my dishes; stole
my knives and forks; refused the keys and broke open my trunks,
closets, and other doors. Then came the worst of all—the burn-
ers, or, as they call themselves, the 'Destroying Angels.' They
burned our gin-house and press. with 125 bales of cotton, seven
cribs containing 600 bolls of corn, our logs, stables, and six stacks
of fodder, a wagon, and four negro cabins, our lumber-room, fine
spinning-machine and 500 dollars' worth of thread, axes, hoes,

she had had at Huntsville with the astronomer
Mitchell, in his capacity of a Yankee general.   It has
often been remarked to me that, when this war is
over, the independence of the country will be due, in
a great measure, to the women ; for they declare that

scythe-blades, and all other plantation implements.   Then they
came with their torches to burn our house, the last remaining
building they had left besides the negro quarter.   That was too
much ; all my pride, and the resolutions that I had made (and until now kept up) to treat them with cool contempt, and never, let
the worst come, humble myself to the thievish cutthroats, forsook
me at the awful thought of my home in ruins ; I must do something, and that quickly ;—hardened, thieving villains, as I knew
them to be, I would make one effort for the sake of my home.
I looked over the crowd, as they huddled together to give orders
about the burning, for one face that showed a trace of feeling, or
an eye that beamed with a spark of humanity, but, finding none,
I approached the nearest group, and pointing to the children (my
sister's), I said, 'You will not burn the house, will you ? you drove
those little ones from one home and took possession of it, and this
is the only sheltering place they have.'   'You may thank your
God, madam,' said one of the ruffians, 'that we have left you and
your d—d brats with heads to be sheltered.'   Just then an officer
galloped up—pretended to be very much astonished and terribly
beset about the conduct of his men—cursed a good deal, and told
a batch of falsehoods about not having given orders to burn any
thing but corn—made divers threats that were forgotten in utter-
ance, and ordered his 'Angels' to fall into line,—thereby winding
up the troubles of the darkest day I have ever seen.

MRS. RICKS.

"Losses before this last raid : six mules, five horses, one wagon
(four-horse), fifty-two negroes."

had the women been desponding they could never
have gone through with it; but, on the contrary, the
women have invariably set an example to the men of
patience, devotion, and determination. Naturally
proud, and with an innate contempt for the Yankees,
the Southern women have been rendered furious and
desperate by the proceedings of Butler, Milroy,
Turchin, &c.   They are all prepared to undergo any
hardships and misfortunes rather than submit to the
rule of such people; and they use every argument
which woman can employ to infuse the same spirit
into their male relations.

At noon I took leave for the present of General
Hardee, and drove over in his ambulance to Shelbyville, eight miles, in company with Bishop Elliott and
Dr. Quintard.   The road was abominable, and it was
pouring with rain.   On arriving at General Polk's,
he invited me to take up my quarters with him during my stay with Bragg's army, which offer I accepted with gratitude.   After dinner General Polk
told me that he hoped his brethren in England did
not very much condemn his present line of conduct.
He explained to me the reasons which had induced
him temporarily to forsake the cassock and return to
his old profession.   He stated the extreme reluctance
he had felt in taking this step; and he said that so
soon as the war was over, he should return to his
episcopal avocations, in the same way as a man, find-

ing his house on fire, would use every means in his power to extinguish the flames, and would then resume his ordinary pursuits. He commanded the Confederate forces at the battle of Perryville and Belmont, as well as his present *corps d'armée* at the battles of Shiloh (Corinth) and Murfreesborough.

At 6.30 P. M., I called on General Bragg, the Commander-in-chief. This officer is in appearance the least prepossessing of the Confederate generals. He is very thin; he stoops, and has a sickly, cadaverous, haggard appearance, rather plain features, bushy black eyebrows which unite in a tuft on the top of his nose, and a stubby iron-gray beard : but his eyes are bright and piercing. He has the reputation of being a rigid disciplinarian, and of shooting freely for insubordination. I understand he is rather unpopular on this account, and also by reason of his occasional acerbity of manner. He was extremely civil to me, and gave me permission to visit the outposts, or any part of his army. He also promised to help me towards joining Morgan in Kentucky, and he expressed his regret that a boil on his hand would prevent him from accompanying me to the outposts. He told me that Rosecrans' position extended about forty miles, Murfreesborough (twenty-five miles distant) being his headquarters. The Confederate cavalry inclosed him in a semicircle extending over a hundred miles of country. He told me that West

7

Tennessee, occupied by the Federals, was devoted to the Confederate cause, whilst East Tennessee, now in possession of the Confederates, contained numbers of people of Unionist proclivities. This very place, Shelbyville, had been described to me by others as a "Union hole."

After my interview with General Bragg, I took a ride along the Murfreesborough road with Colonel Richmond, A. D. C. to General Polk. About two miles from Shelbyville, we passed some lines made to defend the position. The trench itself was a very mild affair, but the higher ground could be occupied by artillery in such a manner as to make the road impassable. The thick woods were being cut down in front of the lines for a distance of eight hundred yards to give range.

During our ride I met Major-general Cheetham, a stout, rather rough-looking man, but with the reputation of "a great fighter." It is said that he does all the necessary swearing in the 1st *corps d'armée*, which General Polk's clerical character incapacitates him from performing. Colonel Richmond gave me the particulars of General Van Dorn's death, which occurred about forty miles from this. His loss does not seem to be much regretted, as it appears he was always ready to neglect his military duties for an assignation. In the South it is not considered necessary to put yourself on an equality with a man in such a case as Van Dorn's by calling him out. His life belongs to the aggrieved husband, and "shooting down" is universally esteemed the correct thing, even if it takes place after a lapse of time, as in the affair between General Van Dorn and Dr. Peters.

News arrived this evening of the capture of Helena by the Confederates, and of the hanging of a negro regiment with forty Yankee officers. Every one expressed sorrow for the blacks, but applauded the destruction of their officers.*

I slept in General Polk's tent, he occupying a room in the house adjoining. Before going to bed, General Polk told me an affecting story of a poor widow in humble circumstances, whose three sons had fallen in battle one after the other, until she had only one left, a boy of sixteen. So distressing was her case that General Polk went himself to comfort her. She looked steadily at him, and replied to his condolences by the sentence, "As soon as I can get a few things together, General, you shall have Harry too." The tears came into General Polk's eyes as he related this episode, which he ended by saying, "*How can you subdue such a nation as this!*"

30*th May* (Saturday).—It rained hard all last night, but General Polk's tent proved itself a good one. We

---

* This afterwards turned out to be untrue.

have prayers both morning and evening, by Dr. Quintard, together with singing, in which General Polk joins with much zeal. Colonel Gale, who is son-in-law and volunteer aid-de-camp to General Polk, has placed his negro Aaron and a mare at my disposal during my stay.

General Polk explained to me, from a plan, the battle of Murfreesborough. He claimed that the Confederates had only 30,000 troops, including Breckenridge's division, which was not engaged on the first day. He put the Confederate loss at 10,000 men, and that of the Yankees at 19,000. With regard to the battle of Shiloh,* he said that Beauregard's order to retire was most unfortunate, as the gunboats were doing no real harm, and if they (the Confederates) had held on, nothing could have saved the Federals from capture or destruction. The misfortune of Albert Johnston's death, together with the fact of Beauregard's illness and his not being present at that particular spot, were the causes of this battle not being a more complete victory.

Ever since I landed in America, I had heard of the exploits of an Englishman called Colonel St. Leger Grenfell, who is now Inspector-general of Cavalry to Bragg's army. This afternoon I made his acquaintance, and I consider him one of the most extraordinary

* Called Pittsburg Landing and Corinth.

characters I ever met.   Although he is a member of a
well-known English family, he seems to have devoted
his whole life to the exciting career of a soldier of
fortune.   He told me that in early life he had served
three years in a French lancer regiment, and had risen
from a private to be a sous-lieutenant.   He after
wards became a sort of consular agent at Tangier,
under old Mr. Drummond Hay.   Having acquired a
perfect knowledge of Arabic, he entered the service of
Abd-el-Kader, and under that renowned chief he
fought the French for four years and a half.   At another time of his life he fitted out a yacht, and carried
on a private war with the Riff pirates.   He was bri-
gade-major in the Turkish contingent during the
Crimean war, and had some employment in the Indian mutiny.   He has also been engaged in war in
Buenos Ayres and the South American republics.
At an early period of the present troubles he ran the
blockade and joined the Confederates.   He was adjutant-general and right-hand man to the celebrated
John Morgan for eight months.   Even in this army,
which abounds with foolhardy and desperate characters, he has acquired the admiration of all ranks by
his reckless daring and gallantry in the field.   Both
Generals Polk and Bragg spoke to me of him as a
most excellent and useful officer, besides being a man
who never lost an opportunity of trying to throw his
life away.   He is just the sort of a man to succeed in

this army, and among the soldiers his fame for bravery has outweighed his unpopularity as a rigid disciplinarian. He is the terror of all absentees, stragglers, and deserters, and of all commanding officers who are unable to produce for his inspection the number of horses they have been drawing forage for. He looks about forty-five, but in reality he is fifty-six. He is rather tall, thin, very wiry and active, with a jovial English expression of countenance; but his eyes have a wild, roving look, which is common amongst the Arabs. When he came to me he was dressed in an English staff blue coat, and he had a red cavalry forage-cap, which latter, General Polk told me, he always wore in action, so making himself more conspicuous. He talked to me much about John Morgan, whose marriage he had tried to avert, and of which he spoke with much sorrow. He declared that Morgan was enervated by matrimony, and would never be the same man as he was. He said that in one of the celebrated telegraph tappings in Kentucky, Morgan, the operator, and himself, were seated for twelve hours on a clay-bank during a violent storm, but the interest was so intense, that the time passed like three hours.*

* This was the occasion when they telegraphed such a quantity of nonsense to the Yankee general, receiving valuable information in return, and such necessary stores by train as Morgan was in need of.

General Polk's son, a young artillery lieutenant, told me this evening that "Stonewall Jackson" was a professor at the military school at Lexington, in which he was a cadet. "Old Jack" was considered a persevering but rather dull master, and was often made a butt of by cheeky cadets, whose great ambition it was to irritate him, but, however insolent they were, he never took the slightest notice of their impertinence at the time, although he always had them punished for it afterwards. At the outbreak of the war, he was called upon by the cadets to make a speech, and these were his words: "Soldiers make short speeches: *be slow to draw the sword in civil strife, but when you draw it, throw away the scabbard.*" Young Polk says that the enthusiasm created by this speech of old Jack's was beyond description.

31*st May* (Sunday).—The Bishop of Georgia preached to-day to a very large congregation in the Presbyterian church. He is a most eloquent preacher; and he afterwards confirmed about twenty people,—amongst others, Colonel Gale (over forty years old), and young Polk. After church, I called again on General Bragg, who talked to me a long time about the battle of Murfreesborough (in which he commanded). He said that he retained possession of the ground he had won for three days and a half, and only retired on account of the exhaustion of his troops, and after carrying off over 6,000 prisoners, much cannon, and other trophies.   He allowed that Rosecrans had displayed much firmness, and was " *the only man in the Yankee army who was not badly beaten.*"   He showed me, on a plan, the exact position of the two armies, and also the field of operations of the renowned guerillas, Morgan and Forrest.

Colonel Grenfell called again, and I arranged to visit the outposts with him on Tuesday.   He spoke to me in high terms of Bragg, Polk, Hardee, and Cleburne ; but he described some of the others as " political" generals, and others as good fighters, but illiterate and somewhat addicted to liquor.   He deplored the effects of politics upon military affairs as very injurious in the Confederate army, though not so bad as it is in the Northern.

At 2 P. M. I travelled in the cars to Wartrace, in company with General Bragg and the Bishop of Georgia.   We were put into a baggage-car, and the General and the Bishop were the only persons provided with seats.   Although the distance from Shelbyville to Wartrace is only eight miles, we were one hour and ten minutes in effecting the *trajet*, in such a miserable and dangerous state were the rails.   On arriving at Wartrace we were entertained by Major-general Cleburne.   This officer gave me his history.   He is the son of a doctor at or near Ballincolig.   At

the age of seventeen he ran away from home, and
enlisted in her Majesty's 41st regiment of foot, in
which he served three years as private and corporal.
He then bought his discharge, and emigrated to Arkansas, where he studied law, and, eschewing politics, he got a good practice as a lawyer. At the outbreak of the war he was elected captain of his company, then colonel of his regiment, and has since, by
his distinguished services in all the Western campaigns, been appointed to the command of a division
(10,000 men)—the highest military rank which has
been attained by a foreigner in the Confederate service.   He told me that he ascribed his advancement
mainly to the useful lessons which he had learnt in
the ranks of the British army, and he pointed with a
a laugh to his general's white facings, which he said
his 41st experience enabled him to keep cleaner than
any other Confederate general.*   He is now thirty-
five years of age ; but, his hair having turned gray,
he looks older.   Generals Bragg and Hardee both
spoke to me of him in terms of the highest praise, and
said that he had risen entirely by his own personal
merit.

   At 5 P. M. I was present at a great open-air preach-

   * The 41st regiment wears white facings ; so do the Generals
in the Confederate army. M. de Polignac has recently been appointed a brigadier: he and Cleburne are the only two generals
amongst the Confederates who are foreigners.

ing at General Wood's camp. Bishop Elliott preached
most admirably to a congregation composed of nearly
3,000 soldiers, who listened to him with the most
profound attention. Generals Bragg, Polk, Hardee,
Withers, Cleburne, and endless brigadiers, were also
present. It is impossible to exaggerate the respect
paid by all ranks of this army to Bishop Elliott; and
although most of the officers are Episcopalians, the
majority of the soldiers are Methodists, Baptists, &c.
Bishop Elliott afterwards explained to me that the
reason most of the people had become dissenters was
because there had been no bishops in America during
the " British dominion;" and all the clergy having
been appointed from England, had almost without
exception stuck by the King in the Revolution, and
had had their livings forfeited.

I dined and slept at General Hardee's, but spent
the evening at Mrs. ——'s, where I heard renewed
philippics directed by the ladies against the Yankees.

I find that it is a great mistake to suppose that the
Press is gagged in the South, as I constantly see the
most violent attacks upon the President—upon the
different generals and their measures. To-day I heard
the officers complaining bitterly of the " Chattanooga
Rebel," for publishing an account of Breckenridge's
departure from this army to reinforce Johnston in
Mississippi, and thus giving early intelligence to the
enemy.

1st *June* (Monday).—We all went to a review of General Liddell's brigade at Bellbuckle, a distance of six miles. There were three carriages full of ladies, and I rode an excellent horse, the gift of General John Morgan to General Hardee. The weather and the scenery were delightful. General Hardee asked me particularly whether Mr. Mason had been kindly received in England. I replied that I thought he had, by private individuals. I have often found the Southerners rather touchy on this point.

General Liddell's brigade was composed of Arkansas troops—five very weak regiments which had suffered severely in the different battles, and they cannot be easily recruited on account of the blockade of the Mississippi. The men were good-sized, healthy, and well clothed, but without any attempt at uniformity in color or cut; but nearly all were dressed either in gray or brown coats and felt hats. I was told that even if a regiment was clothed in proper uniform by the Government, it would become particolored again in a week, as the soldiers preferred wearing the coarse home-spun jackets and trousers made by their mothers and sisters at home. The Generals very wisely allow them to please themselves in this respect, and insist only upon their arms and accoutrements being kept in proper order. Most of the officers were dressed in uniform which is neat and serviceable—viz., a bluish-gray frock-coat of a color similar to Austrian yagers. The infantry wear blue facings, the artillery red, the doctors black, the staff white, and the cavalry yellow; so it is impossible to mistake the branch of the service to which an officer belongs—nor is it possible to mistake his rank. A second lieutenant, first lieutenant, and captain, wear respectively one, two, and three bars on the collar. A major, lieutenant-colonel, and colonel, wear one, two, and three stars on the collar.

Before the marching past of the brigade, many of the soldiers had taken off their coats and marched past the general in their shirt-sleeves, on account of the warmth. Most of them were armed with Enfield rifles captured from the enemy. Many, however, had lost or thrown away their bayonets, which they don't appear to value properly, as they assert that they have never met any Yankees who would wait for that weapon. I expressed a desire to see them form square, but it appeared they were "not drilled to such a manœuvre" (except square two deep). They said the country did not admit of cavalry charges, even if the Yankee cavalry had stomach to attempt it.

Each regiment carried a "battle-flag," blue, with a white border, on which were inscribed the names "Belmont," "Shiloh," "Perryville," "Richmond, Ky.," and "Murfreesborough." They drilled tolerably well, and an advance in line was remarkably good; but General Liddell had invented several dodges of his own, for which he was reproved by General Hardee. The review being over, the troops were harangued by Bishop Elliott in an excellent address, partly religious, partly patriotic. He was followed by a Congress man of vulgar appearance, named Hanley, from Arkansas, who delivered himself of a long and uninteresting political oration, and ended by announcing himself as a candidate for re-election. This speech seemed to me (and to others) particularly ill-timed, out of place, and ridiculous, addressed as it was to soldiers in front of the enemy. But this was one of the results of universal suffrage. The soldiers afterwards wanted General Hardee to say something, but he declined. I imagine that the discipline in this army is the strictest in the Confederacy, and that the men are much better marchers than those I saw in Mississippi.

A soldier was shot in Wartrace this afternoon. We heard the volley just as we left in the cars for Shelbyville. His crime was desertion to the enemy; and as the prisoner's brigade was at Tullahoma (twenty miles off), he was executed without ceremony by the provost-guard. Spies are hung every now and then; but General Bragg told me it was almost impossible for either side to stop the practice.

Bishop Elliott, Dr. Quintard, and myself got back to General Polk's quarters at 5 P. M., where I was introduced to a Colonel Styles, who was formerly

United States minister at Vienna. In the evening I made the acquaintance of General Wheeler, Van Dorn's successor in the command of the cavalry of this army, which is over 24,000 strong. He is a very little man, only twenty-six years of age, and was dressed in a coat much too big for him. He made his reputation by protecting the retreat of the army through Kentucky last year. He was a graduate of West Point, and seems a remarkably zealous officer, besides being very modest and unassuming in his manners. General Polk told me that, notwithstanding the departure of Breckenridge, this army is now much stronger than it was at the time of the battle of Murfreesborough. I think that probably 45,000 infantry and artillery could be brought together immediately for a battle.

2d June (Tuesday).—Colonel Grenfell and I rode to the outposts, starting on the rode to Murfreesborough at 6 A. M. It rained hard nearly all day. He explained to me the method of fighting adopted by the Western cavalry, which he said was admirably adapted for this country; but he denied that they could, under any circumstances, stand a fair charge of regular cavalry in the open. Their system is to dismount and leave their horses in some secure place. One man is placed in charge of his own and three other horses, whilst the remainder act as infantry skirmishers in the dense woods and broken country, making a tremendous row, and deceiving the enemy as to their numbers, and as to their character as infantry or cavalry. In this manner Morgan, assisted by two small guns, called bull-dogs, attacked the Yankees with success in towns, forts, stockades, and steamboats; and by the same system, Wheeler and Wharton kept a large pursuing army in check for twenty-seven days, retreating and fighting every day, and deluding the enemy with the idea that they were being resisted by a strong force composed of all three branches of the service.

Colonel Grenfell told me that the only way in which an officer could acquire influence over the Confederate soldiers was by his personal conduct under fire. They hold a man in great esteem who in action sets them an example of contempt for danger; but they think nothing of an officer who is not in the habit of *leading* them; in fact such a man could not possibly retain his position. Colonel Grenfell's expression was, "every atom of authority has to be purchased by a drop of your blood." He told me he was in desperate hot water with the civil authorities of the State, who accuse him of illegally impressing and appropriating horses, and also of conniving at the escape of a negro from his lawful owner, and he said that the military authorities were afraid or unable to give him proper protection.

For the first nine miles our road was quite straight and hilly, with a thick wood on either side. We then reached a pass in the hills called Guy's Gap, which, from the position of the hills, is very strong, and could be held by a small force. The range of hills extends as far as Wartrace, but I understand the position could be turned on the left. About two miles beyond Guy's Gap were the headquarters of General Martin, the officer who commands the brigade of cavalry stationed in the neighborhood. General Martin showed me the letter sent by the Yankees a few days ago by flag of truce with Mr. Vallandigham. This letter was curiously worded, and ended, as far as I can remember, with this expression: "Mr. Vallandigham is therefore handed over to the respectful attention of the Confederate authorities." General Martin told me that skirmishing and bushwhacking went on nearly every day, and that ten days ago the enemy's cavalry, by a bold dash, had captured a field-piece close to his own quarters. It was, however, retaken, and its captors were killed.

One of General Martin's Staff officers conducted us to the bivouac of Colonel Webb (three miles further along the road), who commanded the regiment on outpost duty there—51st Alabama Cavalry. This Colonel Webb was a lawyer by profession, and seemed a capital fellow; and he insisted on riding with us to the videttes in spite of the rain, and he also desired his regiment to turn out for us by the time we returned. The extreme outposts were about two miles beyond Colonel Webb's post, and about sixteen miles from Shelbyville. The neutral ground extended for about three miles. We rode along it as far as it was safe to do so, and just came within sight of the Yankee videttes. The Confederate videttes were at an interval of from 300 to 400 yards of each other. Colonel Webb's regiment was in charge of two miles of the front; and, in a similar manner, the chain of videttes was extended by other corps right and left for more than eighty miles. Scouts are continually sent forward by both sides to collect information. Rival scouts and pickets invariably fire on one another whenever they meet; and Colonel Webb good-naturedly offered, if I was particularly anxious to see their customs and habits, to send forward a few men and have a little fight. I thanked him much for his kind offer, but begged he wouldn't trouble himself so far on my account. He showed me the house where Vallandigham had been "dumped down" between the outposts when they refused to receive him by flag of truce.

The woods on both sides of the road showed many signs of the conflicts which are of daily occurrence. Most of the houses by the roadside had been destroyed; but one plucky old lady had steadfastly refused to turn out, although her house was constantly an object of contention, and showed many marks of bullets and shell. Ninety-seven men were employed every day in Colonel Webb's regiment to patrol the front. The remainder of the 51st Alabama were mounted and drawn up to receive Colonel Grenfell on our return from the outposts. They were uniformly armed with long rifles and revolvers, but without sabres, and they were a fine body of young men. Their horses were in much better condition than might have been expected, considering the scanty food and hard duty they had had to put up with for the last five months, without shelter of any kind, except the trees. Colonel Grenfell told me they were a very fair specimen of the immense number of cavalry with Bragg's army. I got back to Shelbyville at 4.30 P. M., just in time to be present at an interesting ceremony peculiar to America. This was a baptism at the Episcopal Church. The ceremony was performed in an impressive manner by Bishop Elliott, and the person baptized was no less than the commander-in-chief of the army. The bishop took the general's hand in his own (the latter kneeling in front of the font), and said, "Braxton, if thou hast not already been baptized, I baptize thee," &c. Immediately afterwards he confirmed General Bragg, who then shook hands with General Polk, the officers of their respective Staffs, and myself, who were the only spectators.

The soldiers on sentry at General Polk's quarters

this afternoon were deficient both of shoes and stockings. These were the first barefooted soldiers I had as yet seen in the Confederacy.

I had intended to have left Shelbyville to-morrow with Bishop Elliott; but as I was informed that a reconnoissance in force was arranged for to-morrow, I accepted General Polk's kind offer of further hospitality for a couple of days more. Four of Polk's brigades with artillery move to the front to-morrow, and General Hardee is also to push forward from Wartrace. The object of this movement is to ascertain the enemy's strength at Murfreesborough, as rumor asserts that Rosecrans is strengthening Grant in Mississippi, which General Bragg is not disposed to allow with impunity. The weather is now almost chilly.

3d June (Wednesday).—Bishop Elliott left for Savannah at 6 A. M., in a downpour of rain, which continued nearly all day. Grenfell came to see me this morning in a towering rage. He had been arrested in his bed by the civil power on a charge of horse-stealing, and conniving at the escape of a negro from his master. General Bragg himself had stood bail for him, but Grenfell was naturally furious at the indignity. But, even according to his own account, he seems to have acted indiscreetly in the affair of the negro, and he will have to appear before the civil court next October. General Polk and his officers were all much vexed at the occurrence, which, however, is an extraordinary and convincing proof that the military had not superseded the civil power in the Southern States; for here was an important officer arrested, in spite of the commander-in-chief, when in the execution of his office before the enemy. By standing bail, General Bragg gave a most positive proof that he exonerated Grenfell from any malpractices.*

---

* I cut this out of a Charleston paper some days after I had parted from Colonel Grenfell: Colonel Grenfell was only obeying General Bragg's orders in depriving the soldier of his horse, and temporarily of his money :—

"COLONEL ST. LEGER GRENFELL.—The Western army correspondent of the 'Mobile Register' writes as follows :—The famous Colonel St. Leger Grenfell, who served with Morgan last summer, and since that time has been Assistant Inspector-general of General Bragg, was arrested a few days since by the civil authorities. The sheriff and his officers called upon the bold Englishman before he had arisen in the morning, and after the latter had performed his toilet duties he buckled on his belt and trusty pistols. The officer of the law remonstrated, and the Englisher damned, and a struggle of half an hour ensued, in which the stout Britisher made a powerful resistance, but, by overpowering force, was at last placed *hors de combat* and disarmed.† The charges were, that he retained in his possession the slave of a Confederate citizen, and refused to deliver him or her up; that meeting a soldier coming

---

† This is all nonsense—the myrmidons of the law took very good care to pounce upon Colonel Grenfell when he was in bed and asleep.

In the evening, after dark, General Polk drew my attention to the manner in which the signal beacons were worked. One light was stationary on the ground, whilst another was moved backwards and forwards over it. They gave us intelligence that General Hardee had pushed the enemy to within five miles of Murfreesborough, after heavy skirmishing all day.

I got out of General Polk the story of his celebrated adventure with the —— Indiana (Northern) regiment, which resulted in the almost total destruction of that corps. I had often during my travels heard officers and soldiers talking of this extraordinary feat of the "Bishop's." The modest yet graphic manner in which General Polk related this wonderful instance of coolness and bravery was ex-

to the army leading a horse, he accused him of being a deserter, dismounted him, took his horses and equipments and *money*, stating that deserters were not worthy to have either horses or money, and sent the owner thereof off where he would not be heard of again. The result of the affair was, that Colonel Grenfell, whether guilty or not guilty, delivered up the negro, horses, and money to the civil authorities. If the charges against him are proven true, then there is no doubt that the course of General Bragg will be to dismiss him from his Staff; but if, on the contrary, malicious slanders are defaming this ally, he is Hercules enough and brave enough to punish them. His bravery and gallantry were conspicuous throughout the Kentucky campaign, and it is hoped that this late tarnish on his fame will be removed; or if it be not, that he will."

tremely interesting, and I now repeat it, as nearly as
I can, in his own words.

"Well, sir, it was at the battle of Perryville, late in
the evening—in fact, it was almost dark when Liddell's brigade came into action. Shortly after its arrival I observed a body of men, whom I believed to
be Confederates, standing at an angle to this brigade,
and firing obliquely at the newly arrived troops. I
said, 'Dear me, this is very sad, and must be stopped;'
so I turned round, but could find none of my young
men, who were absent on different messages; so I
determined to ride myself and settle the matter.
Having cantered up to the colonel of the regiment
which was firing, I asked him in angry tones what he
meant by shooting his own friends, and I desired him
to cease doing so at once. He answered with surprise, 'I don't think there can be any mistake about
it; I am sure they are the enemy." 'Enemy!' I
said; 'why, I have only just left them myself. Cease
firing, sir; what is your name, sir?' '*My name is
Colonel ——, of the —— Indiana; and pray, sir,
who are you?*'

"Then for the first time I saw, to my astonishment,
that he was a Yankee, and that I was in rear of a regiment of Yankees. Well, I saw that there was no
hope but to brazen it out; my dark blouse and the
increasing obscurity befriended me, so I approached
quite close to him and shook my fist in his face, say-

ing, 'I'll soon show you who I am, sir; cease firing, sir, at once.' I then turned my horse and cantered slowly down the line, shouting in an authoritative manner to the Yankees to cease firing; at the same time I experienced a disagreeable sensation, like screwing up my back, and calculating how many bullets would be between my shoulders every moment. I was afraid to increase my pace until I got to a small copse, when I put the spurs in and galloped back to my men. I immediately went up to the nearest colonel, and said to him, 'Colonel, I have reconnoitred those fellows pretty closely—and I find there is no mistake who they are; you may get up and go at them.' And I assure you, sir, that the slaughter of that Indiana regiment was the greatest I have ever seen in the war."*

It is evident to me that a certain degree of jealous feeling exists between the Tennesseean and Virginian armies. This one claims to have had harder fighting than the Virginian army, and to have been opposed to the best troops and best generals of the North.

The Southerners generally appear to estimate highest the northwestern Federal troops, which compose in a great degree the armies of Grant and Rosecrans; they come from the States of Ohio, Iowa, Indiana, &c. The Irish Federals are also respected for

* If these lines should ever meet the eyes of General Polk, I hope he will forgive me if I have made any error in recording his adventure.

their fighting qualities; whilst the genuine Yankees and Germans (Dutch) are not much esteemed.

I have been agreeably disappointed in the climate of Tennessee, which appears quite temperate to what I had expected.

4th June (Thursday).—Colonel Richmond rode with me to the outposts, in order to be present at the reconnoissance which was being conducted under the command of General Cheetham. We reached the field of operations at 2 P. M., and found that Martin's cavalry (dismounted) had advanced upon the enemy about three miles, and, after some brisk skirmishing, had driven in his outposts. The enemy showed about 2,000 infantry, strongly posted, his guns commanding the turnpike-road. The Confederate infantry was concealed in the woods, about a mile in rear of the dismounted cavalry.

This being the position of affairs, Colonel Richmond and I rode along the road so far as it was safe to do so. We then dismounted, and sneaked on in the wood alongside the road until we got to within 800 yards of the Yankees, whom we then reconnoitred leisurely with our glasses. We could only count about seventy infantry soldiers, with one field-piece in the wood at an angle of the road, and we saw several staff officers galloping about with orders. Whilst we were thus engaged, some heavy firing and loud cheering suddenly commenced in the woods on our left; so, fearing to be outflanked, we remounted and rode back to an open space, about 600 yards to the rear, where we found General Martin giving orders for the withdrawal of the cavalry horses in the front, and the retreat of the skirmishers.

It was very curious to see three hundred horses suddenly emerge from the wood just in front of us, where they had been hidden—one man to every four horses, riding one and leading the other three, which were tied together by the heads. In this order I saw them cross a cotton-field at a smart trot, and take up a more secure position; two or three men cantered about in the rear, flanking up the led horses. They were shortly afterwards followed by the men of the regiment, retreating in skirmishing order under Colonel Webb, and they lined a fence parallel to us. The same thing went on on our right.

As the firing on our left still continued, my friends were in great hopes that the Yankees might be inveigled on to follow the retreating skirmishers until they fell in with the two infantry brigades, which were lying in ambush for them; and it was arranged, in that case, that some mounted Confederates should then get in their rear, and so capture a good number; but this simple and ingenious device was frustrated by the sulkiness of the enemy, who now stubbornly refused to advance any further.

The way in which the horses were managed was very pretty, and seemed to answer admirably for this sort of skirmishing. They were never far from the men, who could mount and be off to another part of the field with rapidity, or retire to take up another position, or act as cavalry as the case might require. Both the superior officers and the men behaved with the most complete coolness; and, whilst we were waiting in hopes of a Yankee advance, I heard the soldiers remarking that they "didn't like being done out of their good boots"—one of the principal objects in killing a Yankee being apparently to get hold of his valuable boots.

A tremendous row went on in the woods during this bushwhacking, and the trees got knocked about in all directions by shell; but I imagine that the actual slaughter in these skirmishes is very small, unless they get fairly at one another in the open cultivated spaces between the woods. I did not see or hear of anybody being killed to-day, although there were a few wounded and some horses killed. Colonel Richmond and Colonel Webb were much disappointed that the inactivity of the enemy prevented my seeing the skirmish assume larger proportions, and General Cheetham said to me, "We should be very happy to see you, Colonel, when we are in our regular way of doing business."

After waiting in vain until 5 P. M., and seeing no

signs of any thing more taking place, Colonel Richmond and I cantered back to Shelbyville. We were
accompanied by a detachment of General Polk's
body-guard, which was composed of young men of
good position in New Orleans. Most of them spoke
in the French language, and nearly all had slaves in
the field with them, although they ranked only as
private soldiers, and had to perform the onerous duties of orderlies (or couriers, as they are called). On
our way back we heard heavy firing on our left, from
the direction in which General Withers was conducting his share of the reconnoissance with two other
infantry brigades.

After dark, General Polk got a message from
Cheetham, to say that the enemy had after all advanced in heavy force about 6.15 P. M., and obliged
him to retire to Guy's Gap. We also heard that
General Cleburne, who had advanced from Wartrace,
had had his horse shot under him. The object of the
reconnoissance seemed, therefore, to have been attained, for apparently the enemy was still in strong
force at Murfreesborough, and manifested no intention of yielding it without a struggle.

I took leave of General Polk before I turned in.
His kindness and hospitality have exceeded any thing
I could have expected. I shall always feel grateful
to him on this account, and I shall never think of
him without admiration for his character as a sincere

patriot, a gallant soldier, and a perfect gentleman.
His aids-de-camp, Colonels Richmond and Yeatman,
are also excellent types of the higher class of Southerner. Highly educated, wealthy, and prosperous
before the war, they have abandoned all for their
country. They, and all other Southern gentlemen
of the same rank, are proud of their descent from
Englishmen. They glory in speaking English as we
do, and that their manners and feelings resemble
those of the upper classes in the old country. No
Staff officers could perform their duties with more
zeal and efficiency than these gentlemen, although
they were not educated as soldiers.

5th June (Friday).—I left Shelbyville at 6 A. M.,
after having been shaken hands with affectionately
by "Aaron," and arrived at Chattanooga at 4 P. M.
As I was thus far under the protection of Lieutenant
Donnelson, of General Polk's Staff, I made this journey under more agreeable auspices than the last time.
The scenery was really quite beautiful.

East Tennessee is said to contain many people who
are more favorable to the North than to the South,
and its inhabitants are now being conscripted by the
Confederates; but they sometimes object to this operation, and, taking to the hills and woods, commence
bushwhacking there.

I left Chattanooga for Atlanta at 4.30 P. M.   The

train was much crowded with wounded and sick soldiers returning on leave to their homes. A goodish-
looking woman was pointed out to me in the cars as
having served as a private soldier in the battles of
Perryville and Murfreesborough. Several men in
my car had served with her in a Louisianian regiment, and they said she had been turned out a short
time since for her bad and immoral conduct. They
told me that her sex was notorious to all the regiment, but no notice had been taken of it so long as
she conducted herself properly. They also said that
she was not the only representative of the female sex
in the ranks. When I saw her she wore a soldier's
hat and coat, but had resumed her petticoats.

6th June (Saturday).—Arrived at Atlanta at 3 A. M.,
and took three hours' sleep at the Trouthouse hotel.
After breakfasting, I started again for Augusta at 7
A. M. (174 miles); but the train had not proceeded
ten miles before it was brought up by an obstruction,
in the shape of a broken-down freight train, one of
whose cars was completely smashed. This delayed
us for about an hour, but we made up for it afterwards, and arrived at Augusta at 5.15 P. M.

The country through Georgia is undulating, well
cultivated, and moderately covered with trees; and
this part of the Confederacy has as yet suffered but
little from the war. At some of the stations provi-

sions for the soldiers were brought into the cars by ladies, and distributed gratis. When I refused on the ground of not being a soldier, these ladies looked at me with great suspicion, mingled with contempt, and as their looks evidently expressed the words, " Then why are you not a soldier ?" I was obliged to explain to them who I was, and show them General Bragg's pass, which astonished them not a little. I was told that Georgia was the only State in which soldiers were still so liberally treated—they have become so very common everywhere else. On reaching Augusta, I put up at the Planters'-house hotel, which seemed very luxurious to me after so many hours of the cars. But the Augusta climate is evidently much hotter than Tennessee.

7th June (Sunday).—Augusta is a city of 20,000 inhabitants; but its streets being extremely wide, and its houses low, it covers a vast space. No place that I have seen in the Southern States shows so little traces of the war, and it formed a delightful contrast to the war-worn, poverty-stricken, dried-up towns I had lately visited. I went to the Episcopal church, and might almost have fancied myself in England: the ceremonies were exactly the same, and the church was full of well-dressed people.

At 2 P. M. I dined at the house of Mr. Carmichael, son-in-law to Bishop Elliott, who told me there were

2,000 volunteers in Augusta, regularly drilled and prepared to resist raids. These men were exempted from the conscription, either on account of their age, nationality, or other cause—or had purchased substitutes. At 3 P. M. Mr. Carmichael sent me in his buggy to call on Colonel Rains, the superintendent of the Government works here. My principal object in stopping at Augusta was to visit the powder manufactory and arsenal; but, to my disappointment, I discovered that the present wants of the State did not render it necessary to keep these establishments open on Sundays.

I had a long and most interesting conversation with Colonel Rains, who is a very clever, highly-educated, and agreeable officer. He was brought up at West Point, and after a short service in the United States army, he became Professor of Chemistry at the Military College. He was afterwards much engaged in the manufacture of machinery in the Northern States. At the commencement of this war, with his usual perspicacity, President Davis selected Colonel Rains as the most competent person to build and to work the Government factories at Augusta, giving him *carte blanche* to act as he thought best; and the result has proved the wisdom of the President's choice. Colonel Rains told me that at the beginning of the troubles, scarcely a grain of gunpowder was manufactured in the whole of the Southern States. The Augusta powder-mills and arsenal were then commenced, and *no less than 7,000 lbs. of powder are now made every day* in the powder manufactory. The cost to the Government of making the powder is only four cents a pound. The saltpetre (nine-tenths of which runs the blockade from England) cost formerly seventy-five cents, but has latterly been more expensive. In the construction of the powder-mills, Colonel Rains told me he had been much indebted to a pamphlet by Major Bradley of Waltham Abbey.

At the cannon foundry, one Napoleon 12-pounder is turned out every two days; but it is hoped very soon that one of these guns may be finished daily. The guns are made of a metal recently invented by the Austrians, and recommended to the Confederate Government by Mr. Mason. They are tested by a charge of ten pounds of powder, and by loading them to the muzzle with bolts. Two hundred excellent mechanics are exempted from the conscription, to be employed at the mills. The wonderful speed with which these works have been constructed, their great success, and their immense national value, are convincing proofs of the determined energy of the Southern character, now that it has been roused; and also of the zeal and skill of Colonel Rains. He told me that Augusta had been selected as a site for these works on account of its remoteness from the probable seats of war, of its central position, and of its great facilities of transport; for this city can boast of a navigable river and a canal, besides being situated on a central railroad. Colonel Rains said, that although the Southerners had certainly been hard up for gunpowder at the early part of the war, they were still harder up for percussion caps. An immense number (I forget how many) of these are now made daily in the Government factory at Atlanta.

I left Augusta at 7 P. M. by train for Charleston. My car was much crowded with Yankee prisoners.

8th June (Monday).—I arrived at Charleston at 5 A. M., and drove at once in an omnibus to the Charleston hotel. At nine o'clock I called at General Beauregard's office, but, to my disappointment, I found that he was absent on a tour of inspection in Florida. He is, however, expected to return in two or three days.

I then called on General Ripley, who commands the garrison and forts of Charleston. He is a jovial character, very fond of the good things of this life; but it is said that he never allows this propensity to interfere with his military duties, in the performance of which he displays both zeal and talent. He has the reputation of being an excellent artillery officer, and although by birth a Northerner, he is a red-hot and indefatigable rebel. I believe he wrote a book about the Mexican war, and after leaving the old

8*

army, he was a good deal in England, connected with the small-arms factory at Enfield, and other enterprises of the same sort. Nearly all the credit of the efficiency of the Charleston fortifications is due to him. And notwithstanding his Northern birth and occasional rollicking habits, he is generally popular.

I then called on Mr. Robertson, a merchant, for whom I had brought a letter of introduction from England. This old gentleman took me a drive in his buggy at 6 P. M. It appears that at this time of year the country outside the city is quite pestilential, for when we reached the open, Mr. Robertson pointed to a detached house and said, "Now, I am as fond of money as any Jew, yet I wouldn't sleep in that house for one night if you gave it to me for doing so."

I had intended to have visited Mr. Blake, an Eng lish gentleman for whom I had a letter, on his Combahee plantation, but Mr. Robertson implored me to abandon this idea. Mr. Robertson was full of the disasters which had resulted from a recent Yankee raid of the Combahee river. It appears that a vast amount of property had been destroyed and slaves carried off. This morning I saw a poor old planter in Mr. Robertson's office, who had been suddenly and totally ruined by this raid. The raiders consisted principally of Northern armed negroes, and as they met with no Southern whites to resist them, they were able to effect their depredations with total impunity.

It seems that a good deal of the land about Charleston belongs either to Blakes or Heywards. Mr. Blake lost thirty negroes in the last raid, but he has lost since the beginning of the war about 150.

Mr. Robertson afterwards took me to see Mrs. ——, who is Mr. Walter Blake's daughter. To me, who had roughed it for ten weeks to such an extent, Charleston appeared most comfortable and luxurious. But its inhabitants must, to say the least, be suffering great inconvenience. The lighting and paving of the city had gone to the bad completely. Most of the shops were shut up. Those that were open contained but very few goods, and those were at famine prices. I tried to buy a black scarf, but I couldn't find such an article in all Charleston.

An immense amount of speculation in blockade-running was going on, and a great deal of business is evidently done in buying and selling negroes, for the papers are full of advertisements of slave auctions. That portion of the city destroyed by the great fire presents the appearance of a vast wilderness in the very centre of the town, no attempt having been made towards rebuilding it; this desert space looks like the Pompeian ruins, and extends, Mr. Robertson says, for a mile in length by half a mile in width. Nearly all the distance between the Mills House hotel and Charleston hotel is in this desolate state. The fire began quite by accident, but the violent wind which suddenly arose rendered all attempts to stop the flames abortive. The deserted state of the wharves is melancholy—the huge placards announcing lines of steamers to New York, New Orleans, and to different parts of the world, still remain, and give one an idea of what a busy scene they used to be. The people, however, all seem happy, contented, and determined. Both the great hotels are crowded; and well dressed, handsome ladies are plentiful; the fare is good, and the charge at the Charleston hotel is eight dollars a day.

9th June (Tuesday).—A Captain Feilden came to call upon me at 9 A. M. He is an Englishman, and formerly served in the 42d Highlanders. He is now in the Confederate army, and is on the staff of General Beauregard's army. I remember his brother quite well at Sandhurst. Captain Feilden accompanied me to General Ripley's office, and at 12 o'clock the latter officer took us in his boat to inspect Fort Sumter. Our party consisted of an invalid General Davis, a Congressman named Nutt, Captain Feilden, the general, and myself. We reached Fort Sumter after a pull of about three-quarters of an hour.* This now celebrated fort is a pentagonal work built of red brick. It has two tiers of casemates, besides a heavy

* As Fort Sumter must be in a very different state now to what it was when I saw it, I think there can be no harm in describing the fort as it then stood.—Nov., 1863.

barbette battery. Its walls are twelve feet thick at the piers, and six feet thick at the embrasures. It rises sheer out of the water, and is apparently situated in the centre of the bay, but on its side towards James Island the water is extremely shallow. It mounts sixty-eight guns, of a motley but efficient description. Ten-inch columbiads predominate, and are perhaps the most useful. They weigh 14,000 lb. (125 cwt.), throw a solid shot weighing 128 lb., and are made to traverse with the greatest ease by means of Yates's system of cogwheels. There are also eight-inch columbiads, rifled forty-two pounders, and Brook guns to throw flat-headed projectiles (General Ripley told me that these Brook guns, about which so much is said, differ but little from the Blakely cannon); also there are Parrot guns and Dahlgrens; in fact, a general assortment of every species of ordnance except Whitworths and Armstrongs. But the best gun in the fort is a fine new eleven-inch gun, which had just been fished up from the wreck of the Keokuk; the sister gun from the same wreck is at ——. The garrison consists of 350 enlisted soldiers under Colonel Rhett. They are called Confederate States regulars, and certainly they saluted in a more soldier-like way than the ordinary volunteers. A great proportion of them are foreigners.

Fort Sumter now shows but little signs of the battering it underwent from the ironclads eight weeks

ago.   The two faces exposed to fire have been patched
up so that large pieces of masonry have a newer appearance than the mass of the building.   The guns
have been removed from the casemates on the eastern
face, and the lower tier of casemates has been filled
up with earth to give extra strength, and prevent the
balls from coming right through into the interior of
the work, which happened at the last attack.   There
is consequently a deep hole in the parade inside Fort
Sumter, from which the earth had been taken to fill
up these casemates.   The angles of Sumter are being
strengthened outside by stone buttresses.   Some of
the cheeks of the upper embrasures have been faced
with blocks of iron three feet long, eight inches thick,
and twelve inches wide.   I saw the effect of a heavy
shot on one of these blocks which had been knocked
right away, and had fallen in two pieces on the rocks
below, but it had certainly saved the embrasure from
further injury that time.   I saw some solid fifteen-inch
shot which had been fired by the enemy : they weigh
425 lb.   I was told that several fifteen-inch shell had
stuck in the walls and burst there, tearing away great
flakes of masonry, and making holes two feet deep at
the extreme.   None of the ironclads would approach
nearer than nine hundred yards, and the Keokuk,
which was the only one that came thus close, got out
of order in five minutes, and was completely disabled
in a quarter of an hour.   She sank on the following

morning. Solid ten-inch shot and seven-inch flat-heads were used upon her. Ripley said he would give a great deal for some more eleven-inch guns, but he can't get them except by such chances as the Keokuk.

The fight only lasted two hours and twenty-five minutes. Fort Sumter bore nearly the whole weight of the attack, assisted in a slight degree by Moultrie. Only one man was killed, which was caused by the fall of the flagstaff. The Confederates were unable to believe until some time afterwards the real amount of the damage they had inflicted; nor did they discover until next day that the affair was a serious attack, and not a reconnoissance. General Ripley spoke with the greatest confidence of being able to repulse any other attack of the same sort. Colonel Rhett, the commandant, entertained us with luncheon in one of the casemates. He is a handsome and agreeable man, besides being a zealous officer. He told me that one of the most efficient of his subordinates was Captain Mitchell, son to the so-called Irish patriot, who is editor of one of the Richmond newspapers.

From the summit of Fort Sumter a good general view is obtained of the harbor, and of the fortifications commanding the approach to Charleston. Castle Pinckney and Fort Sumter are two old masonry works built on islands—Pinckney being much closer to the city than Sumter. Between them is Fort Ripley, which mounts —— heavy guns. Moultrieville,

with its numerous forts, called Battery Bee, Fort
Moultrie, Fort Beauregard, &c., is on Sullivan's
Island, one mile distant from Fort Sumter. There
are excellent arrangements of ——, and other con-
trivances, to foul the screw of a vessel between Sumter and Moultrie. On the other side of Fort Sumter
is Fort Johnson, on James Island, Fort Cummins
Point, and Fort Wagner, on Morris Island. In fact,
both sides of the harbor for several miles appear to
bristle with forts mounting heavy guns.

The bar, beyond which we counted thirteen blockaders, is nine miles from the city. Sumter is three
and a half miles from the city. Two or three thou-·
sand Yankees are now supposed to be on Folly Island,
which is next beyond Morris Island, and in a day or
two they are to be shelled from the Confederate batteries on Morris Island. The new Confederate flag,
which bears a strong resemblance to the British white
ensign, was flying from most of the forts.

In returning we passed several blockade-runners,
amongst others the steamer Kate, with the new double
screw. These vessels are painted the same color as
the water; as many as three or four often go in and
out with impunity during one night; but they never
attempt it except in cloudy weather. They are very
seldom captured, and charge an enormous price for
passengers and freight. It is doubtful whether the
traffic of the private blockade-runners doesn't do m re

harm than good to the country by depreciating its currency, and they are generally looked upon as regular gambling speculations. I have met many persons who are of opinion that the trade ought to be stopped, except for government stores and articles necessary for the public welfare.

After we had landed, Captain Fielden took me on board one of the new ironclads which are being built, and which are supposed to be a great improvement upon the Chicora and Palmetto State; these are already afloat, and did good service last February by issuing suddenly forth, and driving away the whole blockading squadron for one day. Last night these two active little vessels were out to look after some blockaders which were supposed to have ventured inside the bar.

At 5 P. M. I dined with General and Mrs. Ripley. The dinner was a very sumptuous one, for a " blockade" dinner, as General Ripley called it. The other guests were Gen. Jordan, Chief of the Staff to Beauregard; Gen. Davis, Mr. Nutt, and Col. Rhett, of Fort Sumter. The latter told me that if the ironclads had come any closer than they did, he should have dosed them with flat-headed bolts out of the smoothbore guns, which, he thinks, could travel accurately enough for 500 or 600 yards. Mrs. H—— asked me to an evening party, but the extreme badness of my clothes compelled me to decline the invitation.

10th June (Wednesday).—I dined with Mr. and Mrs. H—— this afternoon, and after dinner they drove me to the Battery, which is the popular promenade. A great many well-dressed people and a few carriages were there, but the H——s say it is nothing to what it was. Most of the horses and carriages have been sent out of Charleston since the last attack. Mrs. H—— told me all the ladies began to move out of Charleston on the morning after the repulse of the Monitors, the impression being that the serious attack was about to begin. I talked to her about the smart costumes of the negro women on Sundays; she said the only difference between them and their mistresses is, that a mulatto woman is not allowed to wear a veil.

11th June (Thursday).—General Ripley took me in his boat to Morris Island. We passed Fort Sumter on our left, and got aground for five minutes in its immediate neighborhood; then bearing off towards the right, we passed Fort Cummins Point, and (after entering a narrow creek) Fort Wagner on our left. The latter is a powerful, well-constructed field-work, mounting nine heavy guns, and it completely cuts across Morris Island at the end nearest to Fort Sumter. General Ripley pointed at Fort Wagner with some pride.

We landed near the house of the colonel who commanded the troops in Morris Island,* and borrowed his horses to ride to the further extremity of the island. We passed the wreck of the Keokuk, whose turret was just visible above the water, at a distance from the shore of about 1500 yards. On this beach I also inspected the remains of the so-called "Yankee Devil," a curious construction, which on the day o. the attack had been pushed into the harbor by one of the Monitors. This vessel, with her appendage, happened to be the first to receive the fire of Fort Sumter, and after a quarter of an hour Monitor and Devil got foul of one another, when both came to grief, and the latter floated harmlessly ashore. It seems to have been composed of double twenty-inch beams, forming a sort of platform or stage fifty feet long by twenty broad, from which depended chains with grappling irons to rake up hostile torpedoes. The machine was also provided with a gigantic torpedo of its own, which was to blow up piles or other obstacles.

Morris Island is a miserable, low, sandy desert, and at its further extremity there is a range of low sand-

---

* This must have been about the spot from whence Fort Sumter was afterwards bombarded. I cannot help thinking that the Confederates made a great mistake in not fortifying the further end of Morris Island and keeping a larger garrison there, for when the Federals landed, they met with no fortification until they reached Fort Wagner.

hills, which form admirable natural parapets. About
ten guns and mortars were placed behind them, and
two companies of regular artillery were stationed at
this point under the command of Captain Mitchell
(the " patriot's" son), to whom I was introduced. He
seemed a quiet, unassuming man, and was spoken or
by General Ripley as an excellent officer. He told
me he expected to be able to open fire in a day or
two upon the Yankees in Folly Island and Little
Folly; and he expressed a hope that a few shell
might drive them out from Little Folly, which is only
distant 600 yards from his guns. The enemy's large
batteries are on Folly Island, 3400 yards off, but
within range of Captain Mitchell's rifled artillery, one
of which was a twelve-pounder Whitworth.

A blockade-runner, named the Ruby, deceived by
some lights on Folly Island, ran ashore at one o'clock
this morning in the narrow inlet between Morris
Island and Little Folly. The Yankees immediately
opened fire on her, and her crew, despairing of getting her off, set her on fire—a foolish measure, as she
was right under Captain Mitchell's guns—and whenever a group of Yankees approached the wreck, a
shell was placed in their midst, which effectually
checked their curiosity. The Ruby was therefore
burning in peace. Her crew had escaped, all except
one man, who was drowned in trying to save a valuable trunk.

After having conversed some time with Captain Mitchell and his brother officers, we took leave of them; and General Ripley, pursuing his tour of inspection, took me up some of the numerous creeks which intersect the low marshy land of James Island. In one of these I saw the shattered remains of the sham Keokuk, which was a wooden imitation of its equally short-lived original, and had been used as a floating target by the different forts.

In passing Fort Sumter, I observed that the eastern face, from which the guns (except those *en barbette*) had been removed, was being further strengthened by a facing of twelve feet of sand, supported by logs of wood. There can be no doubt that Sumter could be destroyed, if a vessel could be found impervious enough to lie pretty close in and batter it for five hours; but with its heavy armament and plunging fire, this catastrophe was not deemed probable. General Ripley told me that, in his opinion, the proper manner to attack Charleston, was to land on Morris Island, take Forts Wagner and Cummings Point, and then turn their guns on Fort Sumter. He does not think much of the 15-inch guns. The enemy does not dare use more than 35 lb. of powder to propel 425 lb. of iron; the velocity consequently is very trifling. He knows and admires the British 68-pounder, weighing 95 cwt., but he does not think it heavy enough effectually to destroy iron-clads. He considers the 11-inch gun, throwing a shot of 170 lb., as the most efficient for that purpose.

In returning from Morris Island, we passed two steamers, which had successfully run the blockade last night, besides the luckless Ruby, which had also passed the blockading squadron before she came to grief. The names of the other two are the Anaconda and Racoon, both fine-looking vessels.

I dined at Mr. Robertson's, at the corner of Rutledge-street, and met Captain Tucker of the navy there. He is a very good fellow, and a perfect gentleman. He commands the Chicora gunboat, and it was he who, with his own and another gunboat (Palmetto State), crossed the bar last February, and raised the blockade for a few hours. He told me that several Yankee blockaders surrendered, but could not be taken possession of, and the others bolted at such a pace as to render pursuit hopeless, for these little gunboats are very slow. They made the attack at daylight, and though much fired at were never struck. They seem to have taken the Yankees by surprise, and to have created great alarm; but at that time the blockading squadron consisted entirely of improvised men-of-war. Since this exploit, the frigate Ironsides, and the sloop of war Powhatan, have been added to its strength.

It poured with rain during the evening, and we

had a violent thunderstorm. General Beauregard returned to Charleston this afternoon.

12th June (Friday).—I called at an exchange office this morning, and asked the value of gold; they offered me six to one for it. I went to a slave auction at 11; but they had been so quick about it that the whole affair was over before I arrived, although I was only ten minutes late. The negroes—about fifteen men, three women, and three children—were seated on benches, looking perfectly contented and indifferent. I saw the buyers opening the mouths and showing the teeth of their new purchases to their friends in a very business-like manner. This was certainly not a very agreeable spectacle to an Englishman, and I know that many Southerners participate in the same feeling; for I have often been told by people that they had never seen a negro sold by auction, and never wished to do so. It is impossible to mention names in connection with such a subject, but I am perfectly aware that many influential men in the South feel humiliated and annoyed with several of the incidents connected with slavery; and I think that if the Confederate States were *left alone,* the system would be much modified and amended, although complete emancipation cannot be expected; for the Southerners believe it to be as impracticable to cultivate cotton on a large scale in the South, without forced black labor, as the British have found it to produce sugar in Jamaica; and they declare that the example the English have set them of sudden emancipation in that island is by no means encouraging. They say that that magnificent colony, formerly so wealthy and prosperous, is now nearly valueless—the land going out of cultivation—the Whites ruined—the Blacks idle, slothful, and supposed to be in a great measure relapsing into their primitive barbarism.

At twelve o'clock I called by appointment on Captain Tucker, on board the Chicora.* The accommodation below is good, considering the nature and peculiar shape of the vessel; but in hot weather the quarters are very close and unhealthy, for which reason she is moored alongside a wharf, on which her crew live. Captain Tucker expressed great confidence in his vessel during calm weather, and when not exposed to a plunging fire. He said he should not hesitate to attack even the present blockading squadron, if it were not for certain reasons which he explained to me.

Captain Tucker expects great results from certain newly-invented submarine inventions, which he thinks are sure to succeed. He told me that, in the April attack, these two gunboats were placed in the rear

* I have omitted a description of this little gunboat, as she is still doing good service in Charleston harbor.—November, 1863.

of Fort Sumter, and if, as was anticipated, the Monitors had managed to force their way past Sumter, they would have been received from different directions by the powerful battery Bee on Sullivan's Island, by this island, Forts Pinckney and Ripley, by the two gunboats, and by Fort Johnson on James Island—a nest of hornets from which perhaps they would never have returned.

At 1 p. m. I called on General Beauregard, who is a man of middle height, about forty-seven years of age. He would be very youthful in appearance were it not for the color of his hair, which is much grayer than his earlier photographs represent. Some persons account for the sudden manner in which his hair turned gray by allusions to his cares and anxieties during the last two years; but the real and less romantic reason is to be found in the rigidity of the Yankee blockade, which interrupts the arrival of articles of toilet. He has a long straight nose, handsome brown eyes, and a dark mustache without whiskers, and his manners are extremely polite. He is a New Orleans creole, and French is his native language.

He was extremely civil to me, and arranged that I should see some of the land fortifications to-morrow. He spoke to me of the inevitable necessity, sooner or later, of a war between the Northern States and Great Britain; and he remarked that, if England

9*

would join the South at once, the Southern armies, relieved of the present blockade and enormous Yankee pressure, would be able to march right into the Northern States, and, by occupying their principal cities, would give the Yankees so much employment that they would be unable to spare many men for Canada. He acknowledged that in Mississippi, General Grant had displayed uncommon vigor, and met with considerable success, considering that he was a man of no great military capacity. He said that Johnston was certainly acting slowly and with much caution; but then he had not the veteran troops of Bragg or Lee. He told me that he (Beauregard) had organized both the Virginian and Tennessean armies. Both are composed of the same materials, both have seen much service, though, on the whole, the first had been the most severely tried. He said that in the Confederate organization a brigade is composed of four regiments, a division ought to number 10,000 men, and a *corps d'armée* 40,000. But I know that neither Polk nor Hardee have got any thing like that number.*

At 5.30 P. M. the firing on Morris Island became distinctly audible. Captain Mitchell had evidently commenced his operations against Little Folly.

While I was walking on the battery this evening, a

* A division does nearly always number 10,000 men, but then there are generally only two or three divisions in a *corps d'armée.*

gentleman came up to me and recalled himself to my recollection as Mr. Meyers of the Sumter, whom I had known at Gibraltar a year ago. This was one of the two persons who were arrested at Tangier by the acting United States consul in such an outrageous manner. He told me that he had been kept in iron during his whole voyage, in the merchant vessel, to the United States; and, in spite of the total illegality of his capture on neutral ground, he was imprisoned for four months in Fort Warren, and not released until regularly exchanged as a prisoner of war. Mr. Meyers was now most anxious to rejoin Captain Semmes, or some other rover.

I understand that when the attack took place in April, the garrison of Fort Sumter received the Monitors with great courtesy as they steamed up. The three flagstaffs were dressed with flags, the band from the top of the fort played the national airs, and a salute of twenty-one guns was fired, after which the entertainment provided was of a more solid description.

13th June (Saturday).—Colonel Rice, aid-de-camp to General Beauregard, rode with me to "Secessionville" this morning. I was mounted on the horse which the General rode at Manassas and Shiloh. We reached James Island by crossing the long wooden bridge which spans the river Ashley. The land of James Island is low and marshy, and is both by re-

pute and in appearance most unhealthy. Three years
ago no white men would have dreamed of occupying
it at this time of year; but now that the necessity
has arisen, the troops, curiously enough, do not appear to suffer.

" Secessionville," the most advanced and most important of the James Island fortifications, is distant
by road eight miles from Charleston bridge, with
which it is connected by a chain of forts. It was surprised by the enemy just a year ago (June, 1862), and
was the scene of a desperate conflict, which resulted
in the repulse of the Federals with a loss of nearly 800
men. The Confederates lost 150 men on this occasion, which as yet has been the only serious loss of
life at Charleston during the war. Colonel Lamar,
who commanded the garrison with great gallantry,
was one of the few victims to yellow fever last year.
The Yankees attacked the fort three times with much
bravery and determination, and actually reached the
superior slope of the parapet before they were driven
back. They were within an ace of being successful;
and although they deserved great credit for their behavior on that occasion, yet it is understood that the
officer who organized the attack has either been dis-
missed the service or otherwise punished.

Lieutenant-colonel Brown, the commandant, who
showed me over the fort and bomb-proofs, is quite
young, full of zeal, and most anxious to be attacked;

he has —— artillerymen to man this and the neighboring works, and two regiments of infantry are also encamped within a short distance.

At the time of the attack on Charleston last April, there were 30,000 men to defend it; since that time 20,000 had been sent into Mississippi to reinforce Johnston. I imagine that, as the fortifications are so very extensive, the Charleston garrison ought to consist of at least 30,000 men.

14th June (Sunday).—I went to church at St. Michael's, which is one of the oldest churches in America, and is supposed to have been built a hundred and fifty years ago. The Charlestonians are very proud of it, and I saw several monuments of the time of the British dominion.

This morning I made the acquaintance of a Mr. Sennec, an officer in the Confederate States navy, who, with his wife and daughter, were about to face the terrors and dangers of running the blockade, Mr. Sennec having got an appointment in Europe. The ladies told me they had already made one start, but after reaching the bar, the night was not considered propitious, so they had returned. Mr. Sennec is thinking of going to Wilmington, and running from thence, as it is more secure than Charleston.

I dined at Mr. Robertson's this evening, and met a very agreeable party there—viz., two young ladies, who were extremely pretty, General Beauregard, Captain Tucker of the Chicora, and Major Norris, the chief of the secret intelligence bureau at Richmond.

I had a long conversation with General Beauregard, who said he considered the question of ironclads *versus* forts as settled, especially when the fire from the latter is plunging. If the other Monitors had approached as close as the Keokuk, they would probably have shared her fate. He thought that both flat-headed rifled 7-inch bolts and solid 10-inch balls penetrated the ironclads when within 1,200 yards. He agreed with General Ripley that the 15-inch gun is rather a failure; it is so unwieldy that it can only be fired very slowly, and the velocity of the ball is so small that it is very difficult to strike a moving object. He told me that Fort Sumter was to be covered by degrees with the long green moss which in this country hangs down from the trees: he thinks that when this is pressed it will deaden the effect of the shot without being inflammable; and he also said that, even if the walls of Fort Sumter were battered down, the barbette battery would still remain, supported on the piers.

The Federal frigate Ironsides took up her position, during the attack, over 3,000 lb. of powder, which was prevented from exploding owing to some misfortune connected with the communicating wire. General Beauregard and Captain Tucker both seemed to ex-

pect great things from a newly invented and extra-
diabolical torpedo-ram.

After dinner, Major Norris showed us a copy of a
New York illustrated Newspaper of the same character as our "Punch." In it the President Davis and
General Beauregard were depicted shoeless and in
rags, contemplating a pair of boots, which the latter
suggested had better be eaten. This caricature excited considerable amusement, especially when its
merits were discussed after Mr. Robertson's excellent
dinner. General Beauregard told me he had been
educated in the North, and used to have many friends
there, but that *now* he would sooner submit to the
Emperor of China than return to the Union.

Mr. Walter Blake arrived soon after dinner; he
had come up from his plantation on the Combahee
river on purpose to see me. He described the results
of the late Yankee raid up that river : forty armed
negroes and a few whites in a miserable steamer were
able to destroy and burn an incalculable amount of
property, and carry off hundreds of negroes. Mr.
Blake got off very cheap, having only lost twenty-
four this time, but he only saved the remainder by
his own personal exertions and determination. He
had now sent all his young males two hundred miles
into the interior for greater safety. He seemed to
have a very rough time of it, living all alone in that
pestilential climate. A neighboring planter, Mr.

Lowndes, had lost 290 negroes, and a Mr. Kirkland was totally ruined.

At 7 P. M. Mr. Blake and I called at the office of General Ripley, to whom Mr. Blake, notwithstanding that he is an Englishman of nearly sixty years of age, had served as aid-de-camp during some of the former operations against Charleston. General Ripley told us that shelling was still going on vigorously between Morris and Folly Islands, the Yankees being assisted every now and then by one or more of their gunboats. The General explained to us that these light-draft armed vessels—*river-gropers*, as he called them—were indefatigable at pushing up the numerous creeks, burning and devastating every thing. He said that when he became acquainted with the habits of one of these "critturs," he arranged an ambuscade for her, and with the assistance of "his fancy Irishman" (Captain Mitchell), he captured her. This was the case with the steamer Stono, a short time since, which, having been caught in this manner by the army, was lost by the navy shortly afterwards off Sullivan's Island.

News has just been received that Commodore Foote is to succeed Dupont in the command of the blockading squadron. Most of these officers appeared to rejoice in this change, as they say Foote is younger, and likely to show more sport than the venerable Dupont.

15th June (Monday).—I called on General Beauregard to say good-by. Before parting, he told me
that his official orders, both from the Government
and from the Town-Council, were, that he was to
allow Charleston to be laid in ashes sooner than surrender it; the Confederates being unanimous in their
determination that, whatever happened, the capital
of South Carolina should never have to submit to the
fate of New Orleans. But General Beauregard did
not at all anticipate that such an alternative was im
minent. In answer to my thanks for his kindness
and courtesy, he said that the more Europeans that
came to the South, the more the Southerners were
pleased, as *seeing* was the only way to remove many
prejudices. He declared every thing here was open
and above board, and I really believe this is the case.
Most certainly the civil law is not overruled by the
military, except in cases of the strongest emergency.
The press is allowed the most unlimited freedom, and
even license. Whenever excesses take place, and the
law is violated, this is caused by the violence of the
people themselves, who take the law into their own
hands. General Beauregard sent his love to Sir
James Fergusson, who had visited him during the
early part of the war; so also did General Jordan,
Chief of the Staff.

Before taking my departure from the hotel, I was
much gratified by meeting M'Carthy, who had just

9*

returned from Richmond. He had had the good
fortune to cross the Mississippi a little later than me,
and he had encountered comparatively few obstacles.

I left Charleston by rail at 2 P. M., in company with
Mr. Sennec, his wife, and daughter ; and Major Norris, who was extremely kind and useful to me. I declined travelling in the ladies' car, although offered
that privilege—the advantage of a small amount of
extra cleanliness being outweighed by the screaming
of the children, and the constant liability of being
turned out of one's place for a female.

Major Norris told me many amusing anecdotes
connected with the secret intelligence department,
and of the numerous ingenious methods for communicating with the Southern partisans on the other
side of the Potomac.

We reached Florence at 9 P. M., where we were de-
tained for some time owing to a break-down of another train. We then fought our way into some
desperately crowded cars, and continued our journey
throughout the night.

16th June (Tuesday).—Arrived at Wilmington at
5 A. M., and crossed the river there in a steamer. This
river was quite full of blockade runners. I counted
eight large steamers, all handsome leaden-colored
vessels, which ply their trade with the greatest regularity. Half these ships were engaged in carrying

goods on Government account; and I was told that
the quantity of boots, clothing, saltpetre, lead, and
tin, which they bring into the country, is very great.
I cannot suppose that in ordinary times there would
be any thing like such a trade as this, at a little place
like Wilmington, which shows the absurdity of calling the blockade an efficient one.

This blockade running is an extraordinary instance
of British energy and enterprise. When I was at
Charleston, I asked Mr. Robertson whether any
French vessels had run the blockade. In reply he
told me it was a very peculiar fact that " one of the
partners of Fraser & Co. being a Frenchman, was
extremely anxious to engage a French vessel in the
trade. Expense was no object; the ship and the
cargo were forthcoming; nothing was wanted but a
French captain and a French crew (to make the ship
legally French); but although any amount of money
was offered as an inducement, they were not to be
found, and this obstacle was insurmountable." Not
the slightest difficulty is experienced at Liverpool in
officering and manning any number of ships for this
purpose.

Major Norris went to call upon Mr. Vallandigham,
whom he had escorted to Wilmington as a sort of
semi-prisoner some days ago. Mr. Vallandigham was
in bed. He told Major Norris that he intended to
run the blockade this evening for Bermuda, from

whence he should find his way to the Clifton Hotel, Canada, where he intended to publish a newspaper, and agitate Ohio across the frontier. Major Norris found him much elated by the news of his having been nominated for the governorship of Ohio; and he declared if he was duly elected, his State could dictate peace.

In travelling through the country to Wilmington, these two used to converse much on politics; and Major Norris once said to him, " Now, from what you have seen and heard in your journey through the South, you must know that a reconstruction of the old Union, under any circumstances, is utterly impossible." Vallandigham had replied, " Well, all I can say is, *I hope*, and at all events I know, that my scheme of a suspension of hostilities is the only one which has any prospect of ultimate success."*

At Wilmington I took leave with regret of Mr. Sennec and his family, who were also to run the blockade this evening. Miss Sennec is much too pretty to risk a collision with a fragment of a shell; but here no one seems to think any thing of the risk of passing through the Yankee fleet, as the "runners," though often fired at, are very seldom hit or captured,

---

* I have often heard Southerners speak of this proposal of Vallandigham's as *most insidious* and dangerous; but the opinion now is that things have gone too far to permit reunion under any circumstances.

and their captains are becoming more and more knowing every day. I was obliged to go to the provost-marshal's office to get Beauregard's pass renewed there, as North Carolina is out of his district: in doing so I very nearly missed the train.

I left Wilmington at 7 A. M. The weather was very hot and oppressive, and the cars dreadfully crowded all day. The luxuries of Charleston had also spoiled me for the "road," as I could no longer appreciate at their proper value the "hog and hominy" meals which I had been so thankful for in Texas; but I found Major Norris a very agreeable and instructive companion. We changed cars again at Weldon, where I had a terrific fight for a seat, but I succeeded; for experience had made me very quick at this sort of business. I always carry my saddlebags and knapsack with me into the car.

17th June (Wednesday).—We reached Petersburgh at 3 A. M., and had to get out and traverse this town in carts, after which we had to lie down in the road until some other cars were opened. We left Petersburgh at 5 A. M. and arrived at Richmond at 7 A. M., having taken forty-one hours coming from Charleston.

The railroad between Petersburgh and Richmond is protected by extensive field-works, and the woods have been cut down to give range. An irruption of the enemy in this direction has evidently been contemplated; and we met a brigade of infantry half-way between Petersburgh and Richmond on its way to garrison the latter place, as the Yankees are reported to be menacing in that neighborhood.

The scenery near Richmond is very pretty, and rather English-looking. The view of the James River from the railway bridge is quite beautiful, though the water is rather low at present. The weather was extremely hot and oppressive, and, for the first time since I left Havana, I really suffered from the heat.

At 10 A. M., I called on General Cooper, Adjutant-general to the Confederate forces, and senior general in the army. He is brother-in-law to Mr. Mason, the Southern Commissioner in London. I then called upon Mr. Benjamin, the Secretary of State, who made an appointment with me to meet him at his house at 7 P. M. The public offices are handsome stone buildings, and seem to be well arranged for business. I found at least as much difficulty in gaining access to the great men as there would be in European countries; but when once admitted, I was treated with the greatest courtesy. The anterooms were crowded with people patiently waiting for an audience. The streets of Richmond are named and numbered in a most puzzling manner, and the greater part of the houses are not numbered at all. It is the most hilly city I have ever seen in America, and its population is unnaturally swollen since the commencement of the war. The fact of there being abundance of ice appeared to me an immense luxury, as I had never seen any before in the South; but it seems that the winters are quite severe in Northern Virginia. I was sorry to hear in the highest quarters the gloomiest forebodings with regard to the fate of Vicksburg. This fortress is in fact *given up*, and all now despair of General Johnston's being able to effect any thing towards its relief.

I kept my appointment with Mr. Benjamin at 7 o'clock. He is a stout dapper little man, evidently of Hebrew extraction, and of undoubted talent. He is a Louisianian, and was senator for that State in the old United States Congress, and I believe he is accounted a very clever lawyer and a brilliant orator. He told me that he had filled the onerous post of Secretary of War during the first seven months of the Secession, and I can easily believe that he found it no sinecure. We conversed for a long time about the origin of Secession, which he indignantly denied was brought about, as the Yankees assert, by the interested machinations of individuals. He declared that, for the last ten years, the Southern statesmen had openly stated in Congress what would take place; but the Northerners never would believe they were in earnest, and had often replied by the taunt, " The South was

so bound to, and dependent on the North, that *she
couldn't be kicked out of the Union."*

He said that the Southern armies had always been
immensely outnumbered in all their battles, and that
until recently General Lee could never muster more
than 60,000 effective men. He confessed that the
Southern forces consisted altogether of about 350,000
to 400,000 men; and when I asked him where they
all were, he replied that, on account of the enormous
tract of country to be defended, and the immense advantages the enemy possessed by his facilities for sea
and river transportation, the South was obliged to
keep large bodies of men unemployed, and at great
distances from each other, awaiting the sudden inva-
sions or raids to which they were continually exposed.
Besides which, the Northern troops, which numbered
(he supposed) 600,000 men, having had as yet but
little defensive warfare, could all be employed for ag-
gressive purposes.

He asserted that England had still, and always had
had it in her power to terminate the war by recognition, and by making a commercial treaty with the
South; and he denied that the Yankees really would
dare to go to war with Great Britain for doing so,
however much they might swagger about it: he said
that recognition would not increase the Yankee hatred
of England, for this, whether just or unjust, was already as intense as it could possibly be. I then al-

luded to the supposed ease with which they could overrun Canada, and to the temptation which its unprotected towns must offer to the large numbers of Irish and German mercenaries in the Northern armies. He answered, " They probably could not do that so easily as some people suppose, and they know perfectly well that you could deprive them of California (a far more serious loss) with much greater ease." This consideration, together with the certainty of an entire blockade of their ports, the total destruction of their trade, and an invasion on a large scale by the Southern troops, in reality prevents the possibility of their declaring war upon England at the present time, any more than they did at the period of their great national humiliation in the Mason-Slidell affair.

Mr. Benjamin told me that his property had lately been confiscated in New Orleans, and that his two sisters had been turned, neck and crop, into the streets there, with only one trunk, which they had been forced to carry themselves. Every one was afraid to give them shelter, except an Englishwoman, who protected them until they could get out of the city.

Talking of the just admiration which the English newspapers accorded to Stonewall Jackson, he expressed, however, his astonishment that they should have praised so highly his strategic skill in out-manœuvring Pope at Manassas, and Hooker at Chan-llorsville, totally ignoring that in both cases the movements were planned and ordered by General Lee, for whom (Mr. Benjamin said) Jackson had the most "childlike reverence."

Mr. Benjamin complained of Mr. Russell of the "Times" for holding him up to fame as a "gambler" —a story which he understood Mr. Russell had learnt from Mr. Charles Sumner at Washington. But even supposing that this was really the case, Mr. Benjamin was of opinion that such a revelation of his private life was in extremely bad taste, after Mr. Russell had partaken of his (Mr. Benjamin's) hospitality at Montgomery.

He said the Confederates were more amused than annoyed at the term "rebel," which was so constantly applied to them; but he only wished mildly to remark, that in order to be a "rebel," a person must rebel against some one who has a right to govern him; and he thought it would be very difficult to discover such a right as existing in the Northern over the Southern States.

In order to prepare a treaty of peace, he said, "It would only be necessary to write on a blank sheet of paper the words '*self-government.*' Let the Yankees accord that, and they might fill up the paper in any manner they chose. We don't want any State that doesn't want us; but we only wish that each State should decide fairly upon its own destiny. All we are struggling for is to be let alone."

At 8 p. m. Mr. Benjamin walked with me to the President's dwelling, which is a private house at the other end of the town. I had tea there, and uncommonly good tea, too—the first I had tasted in the Confederacy. Mrs. Davis was unfortunately unwell and unable to see me.

Mr. Jefferson Davis struck me as looking older than I expected. He is only fifty-six, but his face is emaciated, and much wrinkled. He is nearly six feet high, but is extremely thin, and stoops a little. His features are good, especially his eye, which is very bright, and full of life and humor. I was afterwards told he had lost the sight of his left eye from a recent illness. He wore a linen coat and gray trousers, and he looked what he evidently is, a well-bred gentleman. Nothing can exceed the charm of his manner, which is simple, easy, and most fascinating. He conversed with me for a long time, and agreed with Benjamin that the Yankees did not really intend to go to war with England if she recognized the South; and he said that, when the inevitable smash came—and that separation was an accomplished fact—the State of Maine would probably try to join Canada, as most of the intelligent people in that State have a horror of being "*under the thumb of Massachusetts*." He added, that Maine was inhabited by a hardy, thrifty, seafaring population, with different ideas to the people in the other

New England States. When I spoke to him of the wretched scenes I had witnessed in his own State (Mississippi), and of the miserable, almost desperate, situation in which I had found so many unfortunate women, who had been left behind by their male relations; and when I alluded in admiration to the quiet, calm, uncomplaining manner in which they bore their sufferings and their grief, he said, with much feeling, that he always considered *silent despair* the most painful description of misery to witness, in the same way that he thought *mute insanity* was the most awful form of madness.

He spoke to me of Grenfell, who, he said, seemed to be serving the Confederacy in a disinterested and loyal manner. He had heard much of his gallantry and good services, and he was very sorry when I told him of Grenfell's quarrel with the civil power.

He confirmed the truth of my remark, that a Confederate general is either considered an Admirable Crichton by the soldiers, or else abused as every thing bad; and he added, the misfortune was, that it is absolutely necessary, in order to insure success, that a general must obtain and preserve this popularity and influence with his men, who were, however, generally very willing to accord their confidence to any officer deserving of it.

With regard to the black-flag-and-no-quarter agitation, he said people would talk a great deal, and even go into action determined to give no quarter; "but," he added, "I have yet to hear of Confederate soldiers putting men to death who have thrown down their arms and held up their hands."

He told me that Lord Russell confessed that the impartial carrying out of the neutrality laws had pressed hard upon the South; and Mr. Davis asserted that the pressure might have been equalized, and yet retained its impartiality, if Great Britain, instead of closing her ports, had opened them to the prizes of both parties; but I answered that perhaps this might be over-doing it a little on the other side.

When I took my leave about 9 o'clock, the President asked me to call upon him again. I don't think it is possible for any one to have an interview with him without going away most favorably impressed by his agreeable, unassuming manners, and by the charm of his conversation. While walking home, Mr. Benjamin told me that Mr. Davis's military instincts still predominate, and that his eager wish was to have joined the army instead of being elected President.

During my travels, many people have remarked to me that Jefferson Davis seems in a peculiar manner adapted for his office. His military education at West Point rendered him intimately acquainted with the higher officers of the army; and his post of Secretary of War under the old government brought officers of all ranks under his immediate personal knowledge

and supervision. No man could have formed a more
accurate estimate of their respective merits. This is
one of the reasons which gave the Confederates such
an immense start in the way of generals; for having
formed his opinion with regard to appointing an
officer, Mr. Davis is always most determined to carry
out his intention in spite of every obstacle. His
services in the Mexican war gave him the prestige
of a brave man and a good soldier. His services as
a statesman pointed him out as the only man who,
by his unflinching determination and administrative
talent, was able to control the popular will. People
speak of any misfortune happening to him as an ir-
reparable evil too dreadful to contemplate.

Before we reached the Spottswood Hotel, we met
——, to whom Mr. Benjamin introduced me. They
discussed the great topic of the day—viz., the recapture of Winchester by General Ewell, the news ot
which had just arrived, and they both expressed their
regret that General Milroy should have escaped. It
appears that this Yankee commander, for his alleged
crimes, had been put *hors de la loi* by the Confederates in the same manner as General Butler. ——
said to me, " We hope he may not be taken alive;
but if he is, we will not shrink from the responsibility
of putting him to death."

18*th June* (Thursday).—At 10 A. M., I called by

appointment on Mr. Sedden, the Secretary at War.
His anteroom was crowded with applicants for an
interview, and I had no slight difficulty in getting in.
Mr. Sedden is a cadaverous but clever-looking man;
he received me with great kindness, and immediately
furnished me with letters of introduction for Generals
Lee and Longstreet.

My friend Major Norris then took me to the President's office and introduced me to the aids-de-camp of
the President—viz., Colonels Wood, Lee, and Johnston. The two latter are sons to General Lee and
General Albert Sidney Johnston, who was killed at
Shiloh.

Major Norris then took me to the capitol, and introduced me to Mr. Thompson the librarian, and to
Mr. Meyers, who is now supposed to look after British interests since the abrupt departure of Mr. Moore,
the consul. I was told that Mr. Moore had always
been considered a good friend to the Southern cause,
and had got into the mess which caused his removal
entirely by his want of tact and discretion. There is
a fine view from the top of the capitol; the librarian
told me that last year the fighting before Richmond
could easily be seen from thence, and that many ladies
used to go up for that purpose. Every one said, that
notwithstanding the imminence of the danger, the
population of Richmond continued their daily avocations, and that no alarm was felt as to the result.

The interior of the capitol is decorated with numerous flags captured from the enemy. They are very gorgeous, all silk and gold, and form a great contrast to the little bunting battle-flags of the Confederates. Among them I saw two colors which had belonged to the same regiment, the 37th New York (I think). These were captured in different battles; and on the last that was taken there is actually inscribed as a victory the word *Fair-oaks*, which was the engagement in which the regiment had lost its first color.

Mr. Butler King, a member of Congress, whose acquaintance I had made in the Spottswood Hotel, took me to spend the evening at Mrs. S——'s, a charming widow, for whom I had brought a letter from her only son, aid-de-camp to General Magruder, in Texas.

Mrs. S—— is clever and agreeable. She is a highly patriotic Southerner; but she told me that she had stuck fast to the Union until Lincoln's proclamation calling out 75,000 men to coerce the South, which converted her and such a number of others into strong Secessionists. I spent a very pleasant evening with Mrs. S——, who had been much in England, and had made a large acquaintance there.

Mr. Butler King is a Georgian gentleman, also very agreeable and well informed. It is surprising to hear the extraordinary equanimity with which he and hundreds of fellow-sufferers talk of their entire ruin and the total destruction of their property. I know

many persons in England suppose that Great Britain
has now made enemies both of the North and South;
but I do not believe this is the case with respect to
the South, whatever certain Richmond papers may
say. The South looks to England for every thing
when this war is over;—she wants our merchants to
buy her cotton, she wants our ships to carry it;—she
is willing that England should supply her with all
the necessaries which she formerly received from the
North. It is common to hear people declare they
would rather pay twice the price for English goods
than trade any more with Yankeedom.

19th June (Friday).—I embarked at 10 A. M. on
board a small steamer to visit Drewry's Bluff on the
James River, the scene of the repulse of the ironclads Monitor and Galena. The stream exactly opposite Richmond is very shallow and rocky, but it
becomes navigable about a mile below the city.
Drewry's Bluff is about eight miles distant, and,
before reaching it, we had to pass through two
bridges—one of boats, and the other a wooden
bridge. I was shown over the fortifications by Captain Chatard, Confederate States navy, who was in
command during the absence of Captain Lee. A
flotilla of Confederate gunboats was lying just above
the obstructions, and nearly opposite to the bluff.
Amongst them was the Yorktown, *alias* Patrick
10

Henry, which, under the command of my friend Captain Tucker, figured in the memorable Merrimac attack. There was also an ironclad called the Richmond, and two or three smaller craft. Beyónd Drewry's Bluff, on the opposite side of the river, is Chaffin's Bluff, which mounts —— heavy guns, and forms the extreme right of the Richmond defences on that side of the river.

At the time of the attack by the two Federal ironclads, assisted by several wooden gunboats, there were only three guns mounted on Drewry's Bluff, which is from 80 to 90 feet high. These had been hastily removed from the Yorktown, and dragged up there by Captain Tucker on the previous day. They were either smooth-bore 32-pounders or 8-inch guns, I forget which. During the contest the Monitor, notwithstanding her recent exploits with the Merrimac, kept herself out of much danger, partly concealed behind the bend of the river; but her consort, the ironclad Galena, approached boldly to within 500 yards of the bluff. The wooden gunboats remained a considerable distance down the river. After the fight had lasted about four hours the Galena withdrew much crippled, and has never, I believe, been known to fame since. The result of the contest goes to confirm the opinion expressed to me by General Beauregard—viz., that ironclads cannot resist the plunging fire of forts, even though that latter can only boast of the old smooth-bore guns.

A Captain Maury took me on board the Richmond ironclad, in which vessel I saw a 7-inch treble-banded Brook gun, weighing, they told me, 21,000 lbs., and capable of standing a charge of 25 lbs. of powder. Amongst my fellow-passengers from Richmond I had observed a very Hibernian-looking prisoner in charge of one soldier. Captain Maury informed me that this individual was being taken to Chaffin's Bluff, where he is to be shot at 12 noon to-morrow for desertion.

Major Norris and I bathed in James River at 7 P. M. from a rocky and very pretty island in the centre of the stream.

I spent another very agreeable evening at Mrs. S——'s, and met General Randolph, Mr. Butler King, and Mr. Conrad there; also Colonel Johnston, aid-de-camp to the President, who told me that they had been forced, in order to stop Burnside's executions in Kentucky, to select two Federal captains, and put them under orders for death. General Randolph looks in weak health. He had for some time filled the post of Secretary of War; but it is supposed that he and the President did not quite hit it off together. Mr. Conrad as well as Mr. King is a member of Congress, and he explained to me that, at the beginning of the war, each State was most desirous of being put (without the slightest necessity) under military law, which they thought was quite the correct remedy for all evil; but so sick did they soon become of this *régime* that at the last session Congress had refused the President the power of putting any place under military law, which is just as absurd in the other direction.

I hear every one complaining dreadfully of General Johnston's inactivity in Mississippi, and all now despair of saving Vicksburg. They deplore its loss, more on account of the effects its conquest may have in prolonging the war, than for any other reason. No one seems to fear that its possession, together with Port Hudson, will really enable the Yankees to navigate the Mississippi; nor do they fear that the latter will be able to prevent communication with the trans-Mississippi country.

Many of the Richmond papers seem to me scarcely more respectable than the New York ones. Party spirit runs high. Liberty of the press is carried to its fullest extent.

20th June (Saturday).—Armed with letters of introduction from the Secretary at War for Generals Lee and Longstreet, I left Richmond at 6 A. M., to join the Virginian army. I was accompanied by a sergeant of the Signal Corps, sent by my kind friend Major Norris, for the purpose of assisting me in getting on. We took the train as far as Culpepper, and arrived there at 5.30 P. M., after having changed cars at Gordonsville, near which place I observed an enormous pile of excellent rifles rotting in the open air. These had been captured at Chancellorsville; but the Confederates have already such a superabundant stock of rifles that apparently they can afford to let them spoil. The weather was quite cool after the rain of last night. The country through which we passed had been in the enemy's hands last year, and was evacuated by them after the battles before Richmond; but at that time it was not their custom to burn, destroy, and devastate —every thing looked green and beautiful, and did not in the least give one the idea of a hot country.

In his late daring raid, the Federal General Stoneman crossed this railroad, and destroyed a small portion of it, burned a few buildings, and penetrated to within three miles of Richmond; but he and his men were in such a hurry that they had not time to do much serious harm.

Culpepper was, until five days ago, the headquarters of Generals Lee and Longstreet; but since Ewell's recapture of Winchester, the whole army had advanced with rapidity, and it was my object to catch it up as quickly as possible. On arriving at Culpepper, my sergeant handed me over to another myrmidon of Major Norris, with orders from that officer to supply me with a horse, and take me himself to join Mr. Lawley, who had passed through for the same purpose as myself three days before.

Sergeant Norris, my new chaperon, is cousin to Major Norris, and is a capital fellow.   Before the war he was a gentleman of good means in Maryland, and was accustomed to a life of luxury; he now lives the life of a private soldier with perfect contentment, and is utterly indifferent to civilization and comfort.   Although he was unwell when I arrived, and it was pouring with rain, he proposed that we should start at once—6 P. M.   I agreed, and we did so.   Our horses had both sore backs, were both unfed, except on grass, and mine was deficient of a shoe.   They nevertheless travelled well, and we reached a hamlet called Woodville, fifteen miles distant, at 9.30.   We had great difficulty in procuring shelter; but at length we overcame the inhospitality of a native, who gave us a feed of corn for our horses, and a blanket on the floor for ourselves.

21st June (Sunday).—We got the horse shod with some delay, and after refreshing the animals with corn and ourselves with bacon, we effected a start at 8.15 A. M.   We experienced considerable difficulty in carrying my small saddle-bags and knapsack, on account of the state of our horses' backs.   Mine was not very bad, but that of Norris was in a horrid state. We had not travelled more than a few miles when

the latter animal cast a shoe, which took us an hour
to replace at a village called Sperryville. The country is really magnificent, but as it has supported two
large armies for two years, it is now completely
cleaned out. It is almost uncultivated, and no animals are grazing where there used to be hundreds.
All fences have been destroyed, and numberless
farms burnt, the chimneys alone left standing. It is
difficult to depict and impossible to exaggerate the
sufferings which this part of Virginia has undergone.
But the ravages of war have not been able to destroy
the beauties of nature—the verdure is charming, the
trees magnificent, the country undulating, and the
Blue Ridge mountains form the background.

Being Sunday, we met about thirty negroes going
to church, wonderfully smartly dressed, some (both
male and female) riding on horseback, and others in
wagons; but Mr. Norris informs me that two years
ago we should have numbered them by hundreds.
We soon began to catch up the sick and broken-down
men of the army, but not in great numbers; most of
them were well shod, though I saw two without
shoes.

After crossing a gap in the Blue Ridge range, we
reached Front Royal at 5 P. M., and we were now in
the well-known Shenandoah Valley—the scene of
Jackson's celebrated campaigns. Front Royal is a
pretty little place, and was the theatre of one of the

earliest fights in the war, which was commenced by
a Maryland regiment of Confederates, who, as Mr.
Norris observed, "jumped on to" a Federal regiment
from the same State, and "whipped it badly." Since
that time the village has changed hands continually,
and was visited by the Federals only a few days previous to Ewell's rapid advance ten days ago.

After immense trouble we procured a feed of corn
for the horses, and, to Mr. Norris's astonishment, I
was impudent enough to get food for ourselves by
appealing to the kind feelings of two good-looking
female citizens of Front Royal, who, during our supper, entertained us by stories of the manner they
annoyed the Northern soldiers by disagreeable allusions to "Stonewall" Jackson.

We started again at 6.30, and crossed two branches
of the Shenandoah river, a broad and rapid stream.
Both the railway and carriage bridges having been
destroyed, we had to ford it; and as the water was
deep, we were only just able to accomplish the passage. The soldiers, of whom there were a number
with us, took off their trousers, and held their rifles
and ammunition above their heads. Soon afterwards
our horses became very leg-weary; for although the
weather had been cool, the roads were muddy and
hard upon them. At 8.30 we came up with Pender's division encamped on the sides of hills, illu-
minated with innumerable camp-fires, which looked

very picturesque. After passing through about two miles of bivouacs, we begged for shelter in the hay-loft of a Mr. Mason: we turned our horses into a field, and found our hayloft most luxurious after forty-six miles' ride at a foot's pace.

Stonewall Jackson is considered a regular demigod in this country.

22d *June* (Monday).—We started without food or corn at 6.30 A. M., and soon became entangled with Pender's division on its line of march, which delayed us a good deal. My poor brute of a horse also took this opportunity of throwing two more shoes, which we found it impossible to replace, all the blacksmiths' shops having been pressed by the troops.

The soldiers of this division are a remarkably fine body of men, and look quite seasoned and ready for any work. Their clothing is serviceable, so also are their boots; but there is the usual utter absence of uniformity as to color and shape of their garments and hats: gray of all shades, and brown clothing, with felt hats, predominate. The Confederate troops are now entirely armed with excellent rifles, mostly Enfields. When they first turned out they were in the habit of wearing numerous revolvers and bowie-knives. General Lee is said to have mildly remark-ed: "Gentlemen, I think you will find an Enfield rifle, a bayonet, and sixty rounds of ammunition, as

10*

much as you can conveniently carry in the way of arms." They laughed, and thought they knew better; but the six-shooters and bowie-knives gradually disappeared; and now none are to be seen among the infantry.

The artillery horses are in poor condition, and only get 3 lb. of corn* a-day. The artillery is of all kinds —Parrots, Napoleons, rifled and smooth bores, all shapes and sizes; most of them bear the letters U. S., showing that they have changed masters.

The colors of the regiments differ from the blue battle-flags I saw with Bragg's army. They are generally red, with a blue St. Andrew's Cross showing the stars. This pattern is said to have been invented by General Joseph Johnston, as not so liable to be mistaken for the Yankee flag. The new Confederate flag has evidently been adopted from this battle-flag, as it is called. Most of the colors in this division bear the names Manassas, Fredericksburg, Seven Pines, Harper's Ferry, Chancellorsville, &c.

I saw no stragglers during the time I was with Pender's division; but although the Virginian army certainly does get over a deal of ground, yet they move at a slow dragging pace, and are evidently not good marchers naturally. As Mr. Norris observed to me, " Before this war we were a lazy set of devils;

* Indian corn.

our niggers worked for us, and none of us ever dreamt of walking, though we all rode a great deal."

We reached Berryville (eleven miles) at 9 A. M. The headquarters of General Lee were a few hundred yards beyond this place. Just before getting there, I saw a general officer of handsome appearance, who must, I knew from description, be the Commander-in-chief; but as he was evidently engaged I did not join him, although I gave my letter of introduction to one of his Staff. Shortly afterwards, I presented myself to Mr. Lawley, with whom I became immediately great friends.* He introduced me to General Chilton, the Adjutant-general of the army, to Colonel Cole, the Quartermaster-general, to Major Taylor, Captain Venables, and other officers of General Lee's Staff; and he suggested, as the headquarters were so busy and crowded, that he and I should ride to Winchester at once, and afterwards ask for hospitality from the less busy Staff of General Longstreet. I was also introduced to Captain Schreibert, of the Prussian army, who is a guest sometimes of General Lee and sometimes of General Stuart of the cavalry. He had been present at one of the late severe cavalry skirmishes, which have been of constant occurrence since the sudden advance of this army. This advance has

* The Honorable F. Lawley, author of the admirable letters from the Southern States, which appeared in the "Times" newspaper.

been so admirably timed as to allow of the capture of
Winchester, with its Yankee garrison and stores, and
at the same time of the seizure of the gaps of the
Blue Ridge range. All the officers were speaking
with regret of the severe wound received in this skirmish by Major Von Borke, another Prussian, but
now in the Confederate States service, and aid-de-
camp to Jeb Stuart.

After eating some breakfast, Lawley and I rode
ten miles into Winchester. My horse, minus his fore-
shoes, showed signs of great fatigue, but we struggled
into Winchester at 5 P. M., where I was fortunate
enough to procure shoes for the horse, and, by Lawley's introduction, admirable quarters for both of us at
the house of the hospitable Mrs. ——, with whom he
had lodged seven months before, and who was charmed
to see him. Her two nieces, who are as agreeable as
they are good-looking, gave us a miserable picture of
the three captivities they have experienced under
the Federal commanders, Banks, Shields, and Milroy.

The unfortunate town of Winchester seems to have
been made a regular shuttlecock of by the contending
armies. Stonewall Jackson rescued it once, and last
Sunday week his successor, General Ewell, drove out
Milroy. The name of Milroy is always associated
with that of Butler, and his rule in Winchester seems
to have been somewhat similar to that of his illustrious
rival in New Orleans. Should either of these two in-

dividuals fall alive into the hands of the Confederates, I imagine that Jeff Davis himself would be unable to save their lives, even if he were disposed to do so.

Before leaving Richmond, I heard every one ex pressing regret that Milroy should have escaped, as the recapture of Winchester seemed to be incomplete without him. More than 4,000 of his men were taken in the two forts which overlook the town, and which were carried by assault by a Louisianian brigade with trifling loss. The joy of the unfortunate inhabitants may easily be conceived at this sudden and unexpect- ed relief from their last captivity, which had lasted six months. During the whole of this time they could not legally buy an article of provisions without taking the oath of allegiance, which they magnanimously refused to do. They were unable to hear a word of their male relations or friends, who were all in the Southern army; they were shut up in their houses after 8 P. M., and sometimes deprived of light; part of our kind entertainer's house was forcibly occupied by a vulgar, ignorant, and low-born Federal officer, *ci-devant* driver of a street car; and they were con- stantly subjected to the most humiliating insults, on pretence of searching the house for arms, documents, &c. To my surprise, however, these ladies spoke of the enemy with less violence and rancor than almost any other ladies I had met with during my travels through the whole Southern Confederacy. When I told them so, they replied that they who had seen many men shot down in the streets before their own eyes knew what they were talking about, which other and more excited Southern women did not.

Ewell's division is in front and across the Potomac; and before I left headquarters this morning, I saw Longstreet's corps beginning to follow in the same direction.

23*d June* (Tuesday).—Lawley and I went to inspect the site of Mr. Mason's (the Southern Commissioner in London) once pretty house—a melancholy scene. It had been charmingly situated near the outskirts of the town, and by all accounts must have been a delightful little place. When Lawley saw it seven months ago, it was then only a ruin; but since that time Northern vengeance (as directed by General Milroy) has satiated itself by destroying almost the very foundations of the house of this arch-traitor, as they call him. Literally not one stone remains standing upon another; and the *débris* seems to have been carted away, for there is now a big hole where the principal part of the house stood. Troops have evidently been encamped upon the ground, which was strewed with fragments of Yankee clothing, accoutrements, &c.

I understand that Winchester used to be a most agreeable little town, and its society extremely pleas-

ant. Many of its houses are now destroyed or converted into hospitals; the rest look miserable and
dilapidated. Its female inhabitants (for the able-
bodied males are all absent in the army) are familiar
with the bloody realities of war. As many as 5,000
wounded have been accommodated here at one time.
All the ladies are accustomed to the bursting of shells
and the sight of fighting, and all are turned into hospital nurses or cooks.

From the utter impossibility of procuring corn, I
was forced to take the horses out grazing a mile beyond the town for four hours in the morning and two
in the afternoon. As one mustn't lose sight of them
for a moment, this occupied me all day, while Lawley
wrote in the house. In the evening we went to visit
two wounded officers in Mrs. ——'s house, a major and
a captain in the Louisianian brigade which stormed
the forts last Sunday week. I am afraid the captain
will die. Both are shot through the body, but are
cheery. They served under Stonewall Jackson until
his death, and they venerate his name, though they
both agree that he has got an efficient successor in
Ewell, his former companion in arms; and they confirmed a great deal of what General Johnston had
told me as to Jackson having been so much indebted
to Ewell for several of his victories. They gave us an
animated account of the spirits and feeling of the
army. At no period of the war, they say, have the

men been so well equipped, so well clothed, so eager
for a fight, or so confident of success—a very different state of affairs from that which characterized the
Maryland invasion of last year, when half of the
army were barefooted stragglers, and many of the remainder unwilling and reluctant to cross the Potomac.

Miss —— told me to-day that dancing and horse-
racing are forbidden by the Episcopal Church in this
part of Virginia.

24th June (Wednesday).—Lawley being in weak
health, we determined to spend another day with our
kind friends in Winchester. I took the horses out
again for six hours to graze, and made acquaintance
with two Irishmen, who gave me some cut grass and
salt for the horses. One of these men had served and
had been wounded in the Southern army. I remarked to him that he must have killed lots of his own
countrymen; to which he replied, " Oh yes, but faix
they must all take it as it comes." I have always
observed that Southern Irishmen make excellent
" Rebs," and have no sort of scruple in killing as
many of their Northern brethren as they possibly can.

I saw to-day many new Yankee graves, which the
deaths among the captives are constantly increasing.
Wooden head-posts are put at each grave, on which
's written, " An Unknown Soldier, U. S. A. Died of

wounds received upon the field of battle, June 21, 22, or 23, 1863."

A sentry stopped me to-day as I was going out of town, and when I showed him my pass from General Chilton, he replied with great firmness, but with perfect courtesy, "I'm extremely sorry, sir; but if you were the Secretary of War, or Jeff Davis himself, you couldn't pass without a passport from the Provost-marshal."

25th June (Thursday).—We took leave of Mrs. —— and her hospitable family, and started at 10 A. M. to overtake Generals Lee and Longstreet, who were supposed to be crossing the Potomac at Williamsport. Before we had got more than a few miles on our way, we began to meet horses and oxen, the first fruits of Ewell's advance into Pennsylvania. The weather was cool and showery, and all went swimmingly for the first fourteen miles, when we caught up M'Laws's division, which belongs to Longstreet's corps. As my horse about this time began to show signs of fatigue, and as Lawley's pickaxed most alarmingly, we turned them into some clover to graze, whilst we watched two brigades pass along the road. They were commanded, I think, by Semmes and Barksdale,* and

* Barksdale was killed, and Semmes mortally wounded, at the battle of Gettysburg

were composed of Georgians, Mississippians, and South Carolinians. They marched very well, and there was no attempt at straggling; quite a different state of things from Johnston's men in Mississippi. All were well shod and efficiently clothed. In rear of each regiment were from twenty to thirty negro slaves, and a certain number of unarmed men carrying stretchers and wearing in their hats the red badges of the ambulance corps;—this is an excellent institution, for it prevents unwounded men falling out on pretence of taking wounded to the rear. The knapsacks of the men still bear the names of the Massachusetts, Vermont, New Jersey, or other regiments to which they originally belonged. There were about twenty wagons to each brigade, most of which were marked U. S., and each of these brigades was about 2,800 strong. There are four brigades in M'Laws's division. All the men seem in the highest spirits, and were cheering and yelling most vociferously.

We reached Martinsburg (twenty-two miles) at 6 P. M., by which time my horse nearly broke down, and I was forced to get off and walk. Martinsburg and this part of Virginia are supposed to be more Unionist than Southern; however, many of the women went through the form of cheering M'Laws's division as it passed. I dare say they would perform the same ceremony in honor of the Yankees to-morrow.

Three miles beyond Martinsburg we were forced
by the state of our horses to insist upon receiving the
unwilling hospitality of a very surly native, who was
evidently Unionist in his proclivities. We were obliged to turn our horses into a field to graze during
the night. This was most dangerous, for the Confederate soldier, in spite of his many virtues, is, as a
rule, the most incorrigible horse-stealer in the world.

26th June (Friday).—I got up a little before daylight, and, notwithstanding the drenching rain, I
secured our horses, which, to my intense relief, were
present. But my horse showed a back rapidly getting
worse, and both looked "mean" to a degree. Lawley being ill, he declined starting in the rain, and our
host became more and more surly when we stated
our intention of remaining with him. However, the
sight of *real gold* instead of Confederate paper, or
even greenbacks, soothed him wonderfully, and he
furnished us with some breakfast. All this time
M'Laws's division was passing the door; but so strict
was the discipline, that the only man who loafed in
was immediately pounced upon and carried away
captive. At 2 P. M., the weather having become a
little clearer, we made a start, but under very un-
promising circumstances. Lawley was so ill that he
could hardly ride; his horse was most unsafe, and
had cast a shoe;—my animal was in such a miserable

state that I had not the inhumanity to ride him ;— but, by the assistance of his tail, I managed to struggle through the deep mud and wet.

We soon became entangled with M'Laws's division, and reached the Potomac, a distance of nine miles and a half, at 5 P. M.; the river is both wide and deep, and in fording it (for which purpose I was obliged to mount) we couldn't keep our legs out of the water. The little town of Williamsport is on the opposite bank of the river, and we were now in Maryland. We had the mortification to learn that Generals Lee and Longstreet had quitted Williamsport this morning at 11 o'clock, and were therefore obliged to toil on to Hagerstown, six miles further. This latter place is evidently by no means rebel in its sentiments, for all the houses were shut up, and many apparently abandoned. The few natives that were about stared at the troops with sulky indifference.

After passing through Hagerstown, we could obtain no certain information of the whereabouts of the two generals, nor could we get any willing hospitality from any one; but at 9 P. M., our horses being quite exhausted, we forced ourselves into the house of a Dutchman, who became a little more civil at the sight of gold, although the assurance that we were English travellers, and not rebels, had produced no effect. I had walked to-day, in mud and rain, seven-

teen miles, and I dared not take off my solitary pair
of boots, because I knew I should never get them on
again.

27th *June* (Saturday).—Lawley was so ill this
morning that he couldn't possibly ride. I therefore
mounted his horse a little before daybreak, and
started in search of the generals. After riding eight
miles, I came up with General Longstreet, at 6.30
A. M., and was only just in time, as he was on the
point of moving. Both he and his Staff were most
kind, when I introduced myself and stated my difficulties. He arranged that an ambulance should
fetch Lawley, and he immediately invited me to join
his mess during the campaign. He told me (which
I did not know) that we were now in Pennsylvania,
the enemy's country—Maryland being only ten miles
broad at this point. He declared that bushwhackers
exist in the woods, who shoot unsuspecting stragglers,
and it would therefore be unsafe that Lawley and I
should travel alone. General Longstreet is an Alabamian—a thickset, determined-looking man, forty-
three years of age. He was an infantry Major in
the old army, and now commands the 1st *corps d'armée*. He is never far from General Lee, who relies
very much upon his judgment. By the soldiers he
is invariably spoken of as "the best fighter in the
whole army." Whilst speaking of entering upon

the enemy's soil, he said to me, that although it might be fair, in just retaliation, *to apply the torch*, yet that doing so would demoralize the army and ruin its now excellent discipline. Private property is to be therefore rigidly protected.

At 7 A. M. I returned with an orderly (or courier, as they are called) to the farm-house in which I had left Lawley; and after seeing all arranged satisfactorily about the ambulance, I rode slowly on to rejoin General Longstreet, near Chambersburg, which is a Pennsylvanian town, distant twenty-two miles from Hagerstown. I was with M'Laws's division, and observed that the moment they entered Pennsylvania, the troops opened the fences and enlarged the road about twenty yards on each side, which enabled the wagons and themselves to proceed together. This is the only damage I saw done by the Confederates. This part of Pennsylvania is very flourishing, highly cultivated, and, in comparison with the Southern States, thickly peopled.   But all the cattle and horses having been seized by Ewell, farm-labor had now come to a complete standstill.

In passing through Greencastle we found all the houses and windows shut up, the natives in their Sunday clothes standing at their doors regarding the troops in a very unfriendly manner.   I saw no straggling into the houses, nor were any of the inhabitants disturbed or annoyed by the soldiers.   Sentries were placed at the doors of many of the best houses, to prevent any officer or soldier from getting in on any pretence.

I entered Chambersburg at 6 P. M.   This is a town of some size and importance.   All its houses were shut up; but the natives were in the streets, or at the upper windows, looking in a scowling and bewildered manner at the Confederate troops, who were marching gayly past to the tune of Dixie's Land.   The women (many of whom were pretty and well dressed) were particularly sour and disagreeable in their remarks.   I heard one of them say, "Look at Pharaoh's army going to the Red Sea."   Others were pointing and laughing at Hood's ragged Jacks, who were passing at the time.   This division, well known for its fighting qualities, is composed of Texans, Alabamians, and Arkansians, and they certainly are a queer lot to look at.   They carry less than any other troops; many of them have only got an old piece of carpet or rug as baggage; many have discarded their shoes in the mud; all are ragged and dirty, but full of good-humor and confidence in themselves and in their general, Hood.   They answered the numerous taunts of the Chambersburg ladies with cheers and laughter.   One female had seen fit to adorn her ample bosom with a huge Yankee flag, and she stood at the door of her house, her countenance expressing the greatest contempt for the barefooted Rebs; several companies passed her without taking any notice; but at length a Texan gravely remarked, " Take care, madam, for Hood's boys are great at storming breast-works when the Yankee colors is on them." After this speech the patriotic lady beat a precipitate retreat.

Sentries were placed at the doors of all the princi-pal houses, and the town was cleared of all but the military passing through or on duty. Some of the troops marched straight through the town, and biv-ouacked on the Carlisle road. Others turned off to the right, and occupied the Gettysburg turnpike. I found Generals Lee and Longstreet encamped on the latter road, three-quarters of a mile from the town.

General Longstreet and his Staff at once received me into their mess, and I was introduced to Major Fairfax, Major Latrobe, and Captain Rogers of his personal Staff; also to Major Moses, the Chief Com-missary, whose tent I am to share. He is the most jovial, amusing, clever son of Israel I ever had the good fortune to meet. The other officers of Long-street's Headquarter Staff are Colonel Sorrell, Lieu-tenant-colonel Manning (ordnance officer), Major Walton, Captain Goree, and Major Clark, all excel-lent good fellows, and most hospitable.*

* Having lived at the headquarters of all the principal Confed-erate Generals, I am able to affirm that the relation between their Staffs and themselves, and the way the duty is carried on, is very

Lawley is to live with three doctors on the Head-quarter Staff: their names are Cullen, Barksdale, and Maury; they form a jolly trio, and live much more luxuriously than their generals.

Major Moses tells me that his orders are to open the stores in Chambersburg by force, and seize all that is wanted for the army in a regular and official manner, giving in return its value in Confederate money on a receipt. The storekeepers have doubt-less sent away their most valuable goods on the ap-proach of the Confederate army. Much also has been already seized by Ewell, who passed through nearly a week ago. But Moses was much elated at having already discovered a large supply of excellent felt hats, hidden away in a cellar, which he "an-nexed" at once.

I was told this evening the numbers which have crossed the Potomac, and also the number of pieces of artillery. There is a large train of ammunition; for if the army advances any deeper into the enemy's country, General Lee cannot expect to keep his com-munications open to the rear; and as the Staff offi-cers say, "In every battle we fight we must capture

similar to what it is in the British army. All the Generals—Johnston, Bragg, Polk, Hardee, Longstreet, and Lee—are thorough soldiers, and their Staffs are composed of gentlemen of position and education, who have now been trained into excellent and zealous Staff officers.

11

as much ammunition as we use." This necessity, however, does not seem to disturb them, as it has hitherto been their regular style of doing business.

Ewell, after the capture of Winchester, had advanced rapidly into Pennsylvania, and has already sent back great quantities of horses, mules, wagons, beeves, and other necessaries; he is now at or beyond Carlisle, laying the country under contribution, and making Pennsylvania support the war, instead of poor, used-up, and worn-out Virginia. The corps of Generals A. P. Hill and Longstreet are now near this place, all full of confidence and in high spirits.

28th June (Sunday).—No officer or soldier under the rank of a general is allowed into Chambersburg without a special order from General Lee, which he is very chary of giving; and I hear of officers of rank being refused this pass.

Moses proceeded into town at 11 A. M., with an official requisition for three days' rations for the whole army in this neighborhood. These rations he is to seize by force, if not voluntarily supplied.

I was introduced to General Hood this morning; he is a tall, thin, wiry-looking man, with a grave face and a light-colored beard, thirty-three years old, and is accounted one of the best and most promising officers in the army. By his Texan and Alabamian troops he is adored; he formerly commanded the

Texan brigade, but has now been promoted to the command of a division. His troops are accused of being a wild set, and difficult to manage; and it is the great object of the chiefs to check their innate plundering propensities by every means in their power.

I went into Chambersburg at noon, and found Lawley ensconced in the Franklin Hotel. Both he and I had much difficulty in getting into that establishment—the doors being locked, and only opened with the greatest caution. Lawley had had a most painful journey in the ambulance yesterday, and was much exhausted. No one in the hotel would take the slightest notice of him, and all scowled at me in a most disagreeable manner. Half-a-dozen Pennsylvanian viragos surrounded and assailed me with their united tongues to a deafening degree. Nor would they believe me when I told them I was an English spectator and a non-combatant: they said I must be either a Rebel or a Yankee—by which expression I learned for the first time that the term Yankee is as much used as a reproach in Pennsylvania as in the South. The sight of gold, which I exchanged for their greenbacks, brought about a change, and by degrees they became quite affable. They seemed very ignorant, and confused Texans with Mexicans.

After leaving Lawley pretty comfortable, I walked about the town and witnessed the pressing operations

of Moses and his myrmidons. Neither the Mayor
nor the corporation were to be found anywhere, nor
were the keys of the principal stores forthcoming
until Moses began to apply the axe. The citizens
were lolling about the streets in a listless manner,
and showing no great signs of discontent. They had
left to their women the task of resisting the commis-
saries—a duty which they were fully competent to
perform. No soldiers but those on duty were visible
in the streets.

In the evening I called again to see Lawley, and
found in his room an Austrian officer, in the full uniform of the Hungarian hussars. He had got a year's
leave of absence, and has just succeeded in crossing
the Potomac, though not without much trouble and
difficulty. When he stated his intention of wearing
his uniform, I explained to him the invariable custom
of the Confederate soldiers, of never allowing the
smallest peculiarity of dress or appearance to pass
without a torrent of jokes, which, however good-
humored, ended in becoming rather monotonous.

I returned to camp at 6 P. M. Major Moses did
not get back till very late, much depressed at the ill-
success of his mission. He had searched all day
most indefatigably, and had endured much contumely
from the Union ladies, who called him " a thievish
little rebel scoundrel," and other opprobrious epithets.
But this did not annoy him so much as the manner

in which every thing he wanted had been sent away or hidden in private houses, which he was not allowed by General Lee's order to search. He had only managed to secure a quantity of molasses, sugar, and whiskey. Poor Moses was thoroughly exhausted ; but he endured the chaff of his brother officers with much good-humor, and they made him continually repeat the different names he had been called. He said that at first the women refused his Confederate " trash" with great scorn, but they ended in being very particular about the odd cents.

29th June (Monday).—We are still at Chambersburg. Lee has issued a remarkably good order on non-retaliation, which is generally well received ; but I have heard of complaints from fire-eaters, who want vengeance for their wrongs ; and when one considers the numbers of officers and soldiers with this army who have been totally ruined by the devastations of Northern troops, one cannot be much surprised at this feeling.

I went into Chambersburg again, and witnessed the singular good behavior of the troops towards the citizens. I heard soldiers saying to one another, that they did not like being in a town in which they were very naturally detested. To any one who has seen *as I have* the ravages of the Northern troops in Southern towns, this forbearance seems most commendable and surprising. Yet these Pennsylvanian Dutch* don't seem the least thankful, and really appear to be unaware that their own troops have been for two years treating Southern towns with ten times more harshness. They are the most unpatrioti people I ever saw, and openly state that they don't care which side wins, provided they are left alone. They abuse Lincoln tremendously.

Of course, in such a large army as this there must be many instances of bad characters, who are always ready to plunder and pillage whenever they can do so without being caught: the stragglers, also, who remain behind when the army has left, will doubtless do much harm. It is impossible to prevent this; but every thing that can be done is done to protect private property and non-combatants, and I can say, from my own observation, with wonderful success. I hear instances, however, in which soldiers, meeting well-dressed citizens, have made a "long arm" and changed hats, much to the disgust of the latter, who are still more annoyed when an exchange of boots is also proposed: their superfine broadcloth is never in any danger.

General Longstreet is generally a particularly taciturn man; but this evening he and I had a long talk about Texas, where he had been quartered a long time.

---

* This part of Pennsylvania is much peopled with the descendants of Germans, who speak an unintelligible language.

He remembered many people whom I had met quite well, and was much amused by the description of my travels through that country. I complimented him upon the manner in which the Confederate sentries do their duty, and said that they were quite as strict as, and ten times more polite than, regular soldiers. He replied, laughing, that a sentry, after refusing you leave to enter a camp, might very likely, if properly asked, show you another way in, by which you might avoid meeting a sentry at all.

I saw General Pendleton and General Pickett to-day. Pendleton is Chief of Artillery to the army, and was a West-Pointer; but in more peaceable times he fills the post of Episcopal clergyman in Lexington, Virginia. Unlike General Polk, he unites the military and clerical professions together, and continues to preach whenever he gets a chance. On these occasions he wears a surplice over his uniform.

G⹂⹂⹂al Pickett commands one of the divisions in Longstreet's corps.* He wears his hair in long ringlets, and is altogether rather a desperate looking character. He is the officer who, as Captain Pickett of the U. S. army, figured in the difficulty between the British and United States in the San Juan Island affair, under General Harney, four or five years ago.

* M'Laws, Hood, and Pickett, are the three divisional commanders or major-generals in Longstreet's *corps d'armée*.

30th June (Tuesday).—This morning, before marching from Chambersburg, General Longstreet introduced me to the Commander-in-chief. General Lee is, almost without exception, the handsomest man of his age I ever saw. He is fifty-six years old, tall, broad-shouldered, very well made, well set up—a thorough soldier in appearance; and his manners are most courteous and full of dignity. He is a perfect gentleman in every respect. I imagine no man has so few enemies, or is so universally esteemed. Throughout the South, all agree in pronouncing him to be as near perfection as a man can be. He has none of the small vices, such as smoking, drinking, chewing, or swearing, and his bitterest enemy never accused him of any of the greater ones. He generally wears a well-worn long gray jacket, a high black felt hat, and blue trousers tucked into his Wellington boots. I never saw him carry arms;* and the only mark of his military rank are the three stars on his collar. He rides a handsome horse, which is extremely well groomed. He himself is very neat in his dress and person, and in the most arduous marches he always looks smart and clean.†

---

* I never saw either Lee or Longstreet carry arms. A. P. Hill generally wears a sword.

† I observed this during the three days' fighting at Gettysburg, and in the retreat afterwards, when every one else looked, and was, extremely dirty.

In the old army he was always considered one of its best officers; and at the outbreak of these troubles, he was Lieutenant-colonel of the 2d cavalry. He was a rich man, but his fine estate was one of the first to fall into the enemy's hands. I believe he has never slept in a house since he has commanded the Virginian army, and he invariably declines all offers of hospitality, for fear the person offering it may afterwards get into trouble for having sheltered the Rebel General. The relations between him and Longstreet are quite touching—they are almost always together. Longstreet's corps complain of this sometimes, as they say that they seldom get a chance of detached service, which falls to the lot of Ewell. It is impossible to please Longstreet more than by praising Lee. I believe these two Generals to be as little ambitious and as thoroughly unselfish as any men in the world. Both long for a successful termination of the war, in order that they may retire into obscurity. Stonewall Jackson (until his death the third in command of their army) was just such another simple-minded servant of his country. It is understood that General Lee is a religious man, though not so demonstrative in that respect as Jackson; and, unlike his late brother in arms, he is a member of the Church of England. His only faults, so far as I can learn, arise from his excessive amiability.

Some Texan soldiers were sent this morning into
11*

Chambersburg to destroy a number of barrels of excellent whiskey, which could not be carried away.
This was a pretty good trial for their discipline, and
they did think it rather hard lines that the only time
they had been allowed into the enemy's town was for
the purpose of destroying their beloved whiskey.
However, they did their duty like good soldiers.

We marched six miles on the road towards Gettysburg, and encamped at a village called (I think)
Greenwood. I rode Lawley's old horse, he and the
Austrian using the doctor's ambulance. In the evening General Longstreet told me that he had just received intelligence that Hooker had been disrated,
and that Meade was appointed in his place. Of
course he knew both of them in the old army, and
he says that Meade is an honorable and respectable
man, though not, perhaps, so bold as Hooker.

I had a long talk with many officers about the approaching battle, which evidently cannot now be delayed long, and will take place on this road instead of
in the direction of Harrisburg, as we had supposed.
Ewell, who has laid York as well as Carlisle under
contribution, has been ordered to reunite. Every one,
of course, speaks with confidence. I remarked that
it would be a good thing for them if on this occasion they had cavalry to follow up the broken infantry in the event of their succeeding in beating
them. But to my surprise they all spoke of their

cavalry as not efficient for that purpose. In fact, Stuart's men, though excellent at making raids, capturing wagons and stores, and cutting off communications, seem to have no idea of charging infantry under any circumstances. Unlike the cavalry with Bragg's army, they wear swords, but seem to have little idea of using them—they hanker after their carbines and revolvers. They constantly ride with their swords between their left leg and the saddle, which has a very funny appearance; but their horses are generally good, and they ride well. The infantry and artillery of this army don't seem to respect the cavalry very much, and often jeer at them. I was forced to abandon my horse here, as he was now lame in three legs, besides having a very sore back.

1st July (Wednesday).—We did not leave our camp till noon, as nearly all General Hill's corps had to pass our quarters on its march towards Gettysburg. One division of Ewell's also had to join in a little beyond Greenwood, and Longstreet's corps had to bring up the rear. During the morning I made the acquaintance of Colonel Walton, who used to command the well-known Washington Artillery, but he is now chief of artillery to Longstreet's *corps d'armée.* He is a big man, *ci-devant* auctioneer in New Orleans, and I understand he pines to return to his hammer.

Soon after starting we got into a pass in the South Mountain, a continuation, I believe, of the Blue Ridge range, which is broken by the Potomac at Harper's Ferry. The scenery through the pass is very fine. The first troops, alòngside of whom we rode, belonged to Johnson's division of Ewell's corps. Among them I saw, for the first time, the celebrated "Stonewall" Brigade, formerly commanded by Jackson. In appearance the men differ little from other Confederate soldiers, except, perhaps, that the brigade contains more elderly men and fewer boys. All (except, I think, one regiment) are Virginians. As they have nearly always been on detached duty, few of them knew General Longstreet, except by reputation. Numbers of them asked me whether the General in front was Longstreet; and when I answered in the affirmative, many would run on a hundred yards in order to take a good look at him. This I take to be an immense compliment from any soldier on a long march.

At 2 P. M. firing became distinctly audible in our front, but although it increased as we progressed, it did not seem to be very heavy.

A spy who was with us insisted upon there being " a pretty tidy bunch of *blue-bellies* in or near Gettysburg," and he declared that he was in their society three days ago.

After passing Johnson's division, we came up to a

Florida brigade, which is now in Hill's corps; but as it had formerly served under Longstreet, the men knew him well. Some of them (after the General had passed) called out to their comrades, "Look out for work now, boys, for here's the old bull-dog again."

At 3 P. M. we began to meet wounded men coming to the rear, and the number of these soon increased most rapidly, some hobbling alone, others on stretchers carried by the ambulance corps, and others in the ambulance wagons. Many of the latter were stripped nearly naked, and displayed very bad wounds. This spectacle, so revolting to a person unaccustomed to such sights, produced no impression whatever upon the advancing troops, who certainly go under fire with the most perfect nonchalance. They show no enthusiasm or excitement, but the most complete indifference. This is the effect of two years' almost uninterrupted fighting.

We now began to meet Yankee prisoners coming to the rear in considerable numbers. Many of them were wounded, but they seemed already to be on excellent terms with their captors, with whom they had commenced swapping canteens, tobacco, &c. Among them was a Pennsylvanian Colonel, a miserable object from a wound in his face. In answer to a question, I heard one of them remark, with a laugh, "We're pretty nigh whipped already." We next came to a Confederate soldier carrying a Yankee color, belonging, I think, to a Pennsylvania regiment, which he told us he had just captured.

At 4.30 P. M. we came in sight of Gettysburg, and joined General Lee and General Hill, who were on the top of one of the ridges which form the peculiar feature of the country round Gettysburg. We could see the enemy retreating up one of the opposite ridges, pursued by the Confederates with loud yells. The position into which the enemy had been driven was evidently a strong one. His right appeared to rest on a cemetery, on the top of a high ridge to the right of Gettysburg, as we looked at it.

General Hill now came up and told me he had been very unwell all day, and in fact he looks very delicate. He said he had had two of his divisions engaged, and had driven the enemy four miles into his present position, capturing a great many prisoners, some cannon, and some colors. He said, however, that the Yankees had fought with a determination unusual to them. He pointed out a railway cutting, in which they had made a good stand ; also, a field in the centre of which he had seen a man plant the regimental color, round which the regiment had fought for some time with much obstinacy, and when at last it was obliged to retreat, the color-bearer retired last of all, turning round every now and then to shake his fist at the advancing rebels.

General Hill said he felt quite sorry when he saw this gallant Yankee meet his doom.

General Ewell had come up at 3.30, on the enemy's right (with part of his corps), and completed his discomfiture. General Reynolds, one of the best Yankee generals, was reported killed. Whilst we were talking, a message arrived from General Ewell, requesting Hill to press the enemy in the front, whilst he performed the same operation on his right. The pressure was accordingly applied in a mild degree, but the enemy were too strongly posted, and it was too late in the evening for a regular attack. The town of Gettysburg was now occupied by Ewell, and was full of Yankee dead and wounded. I climbed up a tree in the most commanding place I could find, and could form a pretty good general idea of the enemy's position, although the tops of the ridges being covered with pine-woods, it was very difficult to see any thing of the troops concealed in them. The firing ceased about dark, at which time I rode back with General Longstreet and his Staff to his headquarters at Cashtown, a little village eight miles from Gettysburg. At that time troops were pouring along the road, and were being marched towards the position they are to occupy to-morrow.

In the fight to-day nearly 6,000 prisoners had been taken, and 10 guns. About 20,000 men must have been on the field on the Confederate side. The

enemy had two *corps d'armée* engaged. All the
prisoners belong, I think, to the 1st and 11th corps.
This day's work is called a "brisk little scurry," and
all anticipate a "big battle" to-morrow.

I observed that the artillerymen in charge of the
horses dig themselves little holes like graves, throwing up the earth at the upper end. They ensconce
themselves in these holes when under fire.

At supper this evening, General Longstreet spoke
of the enemy's position as being "very formidable."
He also said that they would doubtless intrench
themselves strongly during the night.* The Staff
officers spoke of the battle as a certainty, and the
universal feeling in the army was one of profound
contempt for an enemy whom they have beaten so
constantly, and under so many disadvantages.

2d July (Thursday).—We all got up at 3.30 A. M.,
and breakfasted a little before daylight. Lawley in
sisted on riding, notwithstanding his illness. Captain
—— and I were in a dilemma for horses; but I was
accommodated by Major Clark (of this Staff), whilst
the stout Austrian was mounted by Major Walton.
The Austrian, in spite of the early hour, had shaved

* I have the best reason for supposing that the fight came off
prematurely, and that neither Lee nor Longstreet intended that
it should have begun that day. I also think that their plans were
deranged by the events of the first.

his cheeks and *ciréd* his mustaches as beautifully as if he was on parade at Vienna.

Colonel Sorrell, the Austrian, and I arrived at 5 A. M. at the same commanding position we were on yesterday, and I climbed up a tree in company with Captain Schreibert of the Prussian army. Just below us were seated Generals Lee, Hill, Longstreet, and Hood, in consultation—the two latter assisting their deliberations by the truly American custom of *whittling* sticks. General Heth was also present; he was wounded in the head yesterday, and although not allowed to command his brigade, he insists upon coming to the field.

At 7 A. M. I rode over part of the ground with General Longstreet, and saw him disposing of M'Laws's division for to-day's fight. The enemy occupied a series of high ridges, the tops of which were covered with trees, but the intervening valleys between their ridges and ours were mostly open, and partly under cultivation. The cemetery was on their right, and their left appeared to rest upon a high rocky hill. The enemy's forces, which were now supposed to comprise nearly the whole Potomac army, were concentrated into a space apparently not more than a couple of miles in length. The Confederates inclosed them in a sort of semicircle, and the extreme extent of our position must have been from five to six miles at least. Ewell was on our left; his headquarters in a church (with a high cupola) at Gettysburg; Hill in the centre; and Longstreet on the right, Our ridges were also covered with pine-woods at the tops, and generally on the rear slopes. The artillery of both sides confronted each other at the edges of these belts of trees, the troops being completely hidden. The enemy was evidently intrenched, but the Southerners had not broken ground at all. A dead silence reigned till 4.45 P. M., and no one would have imagined that such masses of men and such a powerful artillery were about to commence the work of destruction at that hour.

Only two divisions of Longstreet were present to-day—viz., M'Laws's and Hood's—Pickett being still in the rear. As the whole morning was evidently to be occupied in disposing the troops for the attack, I rode to the extreme right with Colonel Manning and Major Walton, where we ate quantities of cherries, and got a feed of corn for our horses. We also bathed in a small stream, but not without some trepidation on my part, for we were almost beyond the lines, and were exposed to the enemy's cavalry.

At 1 P. M. I met a quantity of Yankee prisoners who had been picked up straggling. They told me they belonged to Sickles's corps (3d, I think), and had arrived from Emmetsburg during the night. About this time skirmishing began along part of the line, but not heavily.

At 2 P. M. General Longstreet advised me, if I wished to have a good view of the battle, to return to my tree of yesterday. I did so, and remained there with Lawley and Captain Schreibert during the rest of the afternoon. But until 4.45 P. M. all was profoundly still, and we began to doubt whether a fight was coming off to-day at all. At that time, however, Longstreet suddenly commenced a heavy cannonade on the right. Ewell immediately took it up on the left. The enemy replied with at least equal fury, and in a few moments the firing along the whole line was as heavy as it is possible to conceive. A dense smoke arose for six miles; there was little wind to drive it away, and the air seemed full of shells—each of which appeared to have a different style of going, and to make a different noise from the others. The ordnance on both sides is of a very varied description. Every now and then a caisson would blow up—if a Federal one, a Confederate yell would immediately follow. The Southern troops, when charging, or to express their delight, always yell in a manner peculiar to themselves. The Yankee cheer is much more like ours; but the Confederate officers declare that the rebel yell has a particular merit, and always produces a salutary and useful effect upon their adversaries. A corps is sometimes spoken of as a "good yelling regiment."

So soon as the firing began, General Lee joined

Hill just below our tree, and he remained there nearly all the time, looking through his field-glass— sometimes talking to Hill and sometimes to Colonel Long of his Staff. But generally he sat quite alone on the stump of a tree. What I remarked especially was, that during the whole time the firing continued, he only sent one message, and only received one report. It is evidently his system to arrange the plan thoroughly with the three corps commanders, and then leave to them the duty of modifying and carrying it out to the best of their abilities.

When the cannonade was at its height, a Confederate band of music, between the cemetery and ourselves, began to play polkas and waltzes, which sounded very curious, accompanied by the hissing and bursting of the shells.

At 5.45 all became comparatively quiet on our left and in the cemetery; but volleys of musketry on the right told us that Longstreet's infantry were advancing, and the onward progress of the smoke showed that he was progressing favorably; but about 6.30 there seemed to be a check, and even a slight retrograde movement. Soon after 7, General Lee got a report by signal from Longstreet to say " *we are doing well.*" A little before dark the firing dropped off in every direction, and soon ceased altogether. We then received intelligence that Longstreet had carried every thing before him for some time, capturing several batteries, and driving the enemy from his positions; but when Hill's Florida brigade and some other troops gave way, he was forced to abandon a small portion of the ground he had won, together with all the captured guns, except three. His troops, however, bivouacked during the night on ground occupied by the enemy this morning.

Every one deplores that Longstreet *will* expose himself in such a reckless manner. To-day he led a Georgian regiment in a charge against a battery, hat in hand, and in front of everybody. General Barksdale was killed and Semmes mortally wounded; but the most serious loss was that of General Hood, who was badly wounded in the arm early in the day. I heard that his Texans are in despair. Lawley and I rode back to the General's camp, which had been moved to within a mile of the scene of action. Longstreet, however, with most of his Staff, bivouacked on the field.

Major Fairfax arrived at about 10 P. M. in a very bad humor. He had under his charge about 1,000 to 1,500 Yankee prisoners who had been taken to-day; among them a general, whom I heard one of his men accusing of having been " so G—d d—d drunk that he had turned his guns upon his own men." But, on the other hand, the accuser was such a thundering blackguard, and proposed taking such a variety of oaths in order to escape from the U. S. army, that he is not worthy of much credit. A large train of horses and mules, &c., arrived to-day, sent in by General Stuart, and captured, it is understood, by his cavalry, which had penetrated to within 6 miles of Washington.

3d July (Friday).—At 6 A. M. I rode to the field with Colonel Manning, and went over that portion of the ground which, after a fierce contest, had been won from the enemy yesterday evening. The dead were being buried, but great numbers were still lying about; also many mortally wounded, for whom nothing could be done. Amongst the latter were a number of Yankees dressed in bad imitations of the Zouave costume. They opened their glazed eyes as I rode past in a painfully imploring manner.

We joined Generals Lee and Longstreet's Staff: they were reconnoitring and making preparations for renewing the attack. As we formed a pretty large party, we often drew upon ourselves the attention of the hostile sharpshooters, and were two or three times favored with a shell. One of these shells set a brick building on fire which was situated between the lines. This building was filled with wounded, principally Yankees, who, I am afraid, must have perished miserably in the flames. Colonel Sorrell had been slightly wounded yesterday, but still did duty. Major Walton's horse was killed, but there were no other casualties amongst my particular friends.

The plan of yesterday's attack seems to have been very simple—first a heavy cannonade all along the line, followed by an advance of Longstreet's two divisions and part of Hill's corps. In consequence of the enemy's having been driven back some distance, Longstreet's corps (part of it) was in a much more forward situation than yesterday. But the range of heights to be gained was still most formidable, and evidently strongly intrenched.

The distance between the Confederate guns and the Yankee position—*i. e.*, between the woods crowning the opposite ridges—was at least a mile—quite open, gently undulating, and exposed to artillery the whole distance. This was the ground which had to be crossed in to-day's attack. Pickett's division, which had just come up, was to bear the brunt in Longstreet's attack, together with Heth and Pettigrew in Hill's corps. Pickett's division was a weak one (under 5,000), owing to the absence of two brigades.

At noon all Longstreet's dispositions were made; his troops for attack were deployed into line, and lying down in the woods; his batteries were ready to open. The general then dismounted and went to sleep for a short time. The Austrian officer and I now rode off to get, if possible, into some commanding position from whence we could see the whole thing without being exposed to the tremendous fire which was about to commence. After riding about for half an hour without being able to discover so desirable a situation, we determined to make for the cupola, near Gettysburg, Ewell's headquarters. Just before we reached the entrance to the town, the cannonade opened with a fury which surpassed even that of yesterday.

Soon after passing through the toll-gate at the entrance of Gettysburg, we found that we had got into a heavy cross-fire; shells both Federal and Confederate passing over our heads with great frequency. At length two shrapnel shells burst quite close to us, and a ball from one of them hit the officer who was conducting us. We then turned round and changed our views with regard to the cupola—the fire of one side being bad enough, but preferable to that of both sides. A small boy of twelve years was riding with us at the time: this urchin took a diabolical interest in the bursting of the shells, and screamed with delight when he saw them take effect. I never saw this boy again, or found out who he was.

The road at Gettysburg was lined with Yankee dead, and as they had been killed on the 1st, the poor fellows had already begun to be very offensive. We then returned to the hill I was on yesterday. But finding that, to see the actual fighting, it was absolutely necessary to go into the thick of the thing, I determined to make my way to General Longstreet. It was then about 2.30. After passing General Lee

and his Staff, I rode on through the woods in the
direction in which I had left Longstreet. I soon began to meet many wounded men returning from the
front; many of them asked in piteous tones the way
to a doctor or an ambulance. The further I got, the
greater became the number of the wounded. At last
I came to a perfect stream of them flocking through
the woods in numbers as great as the crowd in Ox-
ford-street in the middle of the day. Some were
walking alone on crutches composed of two rifles,
others were supported by men less badly wounded
than themselves, and others were carried on stretchers by the ambulance corps; but in no case did I see
a sound man helping the wounded to the rear, unless
he carried the red badge of the ambulance corps.
They were still under a heavy fire; the shells were
continually bringing down great limbs of trees, and
carrying further destruction amongst this melancholy
procession. I saw all this in much less time than it
takes to write it, and although astonished to meet
such vast numbers of wounded, I had not seen *enough*
to give me any idea of the real extent of the mischief.

When I got close up to General Longstreet, I saw
one of his regiments advancing through the woods in
good order; so, thinking I was just in time to see the
attack, I remarked to the General that "*I wouldn't
have missed this for any thing.*" Longstreet was
seated at the top of a snake fence at the edge of the

wood, and looking perfectly calm and imperturbed. He replied, laughing, "*The devil you wouldn't! I would like to have missed it very much; we've attacked and been repulsed: look there!*"

For the first time I then had a view of the open space between the two positions, and saw it covered with Confederates slowly and sulkily returning towards us in small broken parties, under a heavy fire of artillery. But the fire where we were was not so bad as further to the rear; for although the air seemed alive with shell, yet the greater number burst behind us.

The General told me that Pickett's division had succeeded in carrying the enemy's position and capturing his guns, but after remaining there twenty minutes, it had been forced to retire, on the retreat of Heth and Pettigrew on its left. No person could have been more calm or self-possessed than General Longstreet under these trying circumstances, aggravated as they now were by the movements of the enemy, who began to show a strong disposition to advance. I could now thoroughly appreciate the term bulldog, which I had heard applied to him by the soldiers. Difficulties seem to make no other impression upon him than to make him a little more savage.

Major Walton was the only officer with him when I came up—all the rest had been put into the charge.

In a few minutes Major Latrobe arrived on foot, carrying his saddle, having just had his horse killed. Colonel Sorrell was also in the same predicament, and Captain Goree's horse was wounded in the mouth.

The General was making the best arrangements in his power to resist the threatened advance, by advancing some artillery, rallying the stragglers, &c. I remember seeing a General (Pettigrew, I think it was)* come up to him, and report that "he was unable to bring his men up again." Longstreet turned upon him and replied with some sarcasm: "*Very well; never mind, then, General; just let them remain where they are : the enemy's going to advance, and will spare you the trouble.*"

He asked for something to drink : I gave him some rum out of my silver flask, which I begged he would keep in remembrance of the occasion; he smiled, and, to my great satisfaction, accepted the memorial. He then went off to give some orders to M'Laws's division. Soon afterwards I joined General Lee, who had in the mean while come to that part of the field on becoming aware of the disaster. If Longstreet's conduct was admirable, that of General Lee was perfectly sublime. He was engaged in rallying and in encouraging the broken troops, and was riding about a little in front of the wood, quite alone—the whole of his

---

* This officer was afterwards killed at the passage of the Potomac.

Staff being engaged in a similar manner further to
the rear.   His face, which is always placid and cheer-
ful, did not show signs of the slightest disappointment,
care, or annoyance; and he was addressing to every
soldier he met a few words of encouragement, such
as, "All this will come right in the end: we'll talk
it over afterwards; but, in the mean time, all good
men must rally. We want all good and true men
just now," &c. He spoke to all the wounded men
that passed him, and the slightly wounded he ex-
horted "to bind up their hurts and take up a musket" in this emergency. Very few failed to answer
his appeal, and I saw many badly wounded men take
off their hats and cheer him. He said to me, "This
has been a sad day for us, Colonel—a sad day; but
we can't expect always to gain victories." He was
also kind enough to advise me to get into some more
sheltered position, as the shells were bursting round
us with considerable frequency.

Notwithstanding the misfortune which had so suddenly befallen him, General Lee seemed to observe
every thing, however trivial. When a mounted officer began licking his horse for shying at the bursting
of a shell, he called out, "Don't whip him, Captain;
don't whip him. I've got just such another foolish
horse myself, and whipping does no good."

I happened to see a man lying flat on his face in a
small ditch, and I remarked that I didn't think he

seemed dead; this drew General Lee's attention to the man, who commenced groaning dismally. Finding .appeals to his patriotism of no avail, General Lee had him ignominiously set on his legs by some neighboring gunners.

I saw General Willcox (an officer who wears a short round jacket and a battered straw hat) come up to him, and explain, almost crying, the state of his brigade. General Lee immediately shook hands with him and said cheerfully, "Never mind, General, *all this has been* MY *fault*—it is *I* that have lost this fight, and you must help me out of it in the best way you can." In this manner I saw General Lee encourage and reanimate his somewhat dispirited troops, and magnanimously take upon his own shoulders the whole weight of the repulse. It was impossible to look at him or to listen to him without feeling the strongest admiration, and I never saw any man fail him except the man in the ditch.

It is difficult to exaggerate the critical state of affairs as they appeared about this time. If the enemy or their general had shown any enterprise, there is no saying what might have happened. General Lee and his officers were evidently fully impressed with a sense of the situation; yet there was much less noise, fuss, or confusion of orders than at an ordinary field-day; the men, as they were rallied in the wood, were brought up in detachments, and lay down quietly and coolly in the positions assigned to them.

We heard that Generals Garnett and Armistead were killed, and General Kemper mortally wounded; also, that Pickett's division had only one field-officer unhurt. Nearly all this slaughter took place in an open space about one mile square, and within one hour.

At 6 P. M. we heard a long and continuous Yankee cheer, which we at first imagined was an indication of an advance; but it turned out to be their reception of a general officer, whom we saw riding· down the line, followed by about thirty horsemen. Soon afterwards I rode to the extreme front, where there were four pieces of rifled cannon almost without any infantry support. To the non-withdrawal of these guns is to be attributed the otherwise surprising inactivity of the enemy. I was immediately surrounded by a sergeant and about half-a-dozen gunners, who seemed in excellent spirits and full of confidence, in spite of their exposed situation. The sergeant expressed his ardent hope that the Yankees might have spirit enough to advance and receive the dose he had in readiness for them. They spoke in admiration of the advance of Pickett's division, and of the manner in which Pickett himself had led it. When they observed General Lee they said, "We've not lost confidence in the old man : this day's work won't do him no harm. ' Uncle Robert' will get us into Washington yet ; you bet he will !" &c. Whilst we were talking, the enemy's skirmishers began to advance slowly, and several ominous sounds in quick succession told us that we were attracting their attention, and that it was necessary to break up the conclave. I therefore turned round and took leave of these cheery and plucky gunners.

At 7 P. M., General Lee received a report that Johnson's division of Ewell's corps had been successful on the left, and had gained important advantages there. Firing entirely ceased in our front about this time; but we now heard some brisk musketry on our right, which I afterwards learned proceeded from Hood's Texans, who had managed to surround some enterprising Yankee cavalry, and were slaughtering them with great satisfaction. Only eighteen out of four hundred are said to have escaped.

At 7.30, all idea of a Yankee attack being over, I rode back to Moses's tent, and found that worthy commissary in very low spirits, all sorts of exaggerated rumors having reached him. On my way I met a great many wounded men, most anxious to inquire after Longstreet, who was reported killed; when I assured them he was quite well, they seemed to forget their own pain in the evident pleasure they felt in the safety of their chief. No words that I can use will adequately express the extraordinary patience and fortitude with which the wounded Confederates bore their sufferings.

I got something to eat with the doctors at 10 P. M., the first for fifteen hours.

I gave up my horse to-day to his owner, as from death and exhaustion the Staff are almost without horses.

4th July (Saturday).—I was awoke at daylight by Moses complaining that his valuable trunk, containing much public money, had been stolen from our tent whilst we slept. After a search it was found in a wood hard by, broken open and minus the money. Dr. Barksdale had been robbed in the same manner exactly. This is evidently the work of those rascally stragglers, who shirk going under fire, plunder the natives, and will hereafter swagger as the heroes of Gettysburg.

Lawley, the Austrian, and I, walked up to the front about eight o'clock, and on our way we met General Longstreet, who was in a high state of amusement and good humor. A flag of truce had just come over from the enemy, and its bearer announced among other things that "General Longstreet was wounded, and a prisoner, but would be taken care of." General Longstreet sent back word that he was extremely grateful, but that, being neither wounded nor a prisoner, he was quite able to take care of himself. The iron endurance of General Longstreet is most extraordinary: he seems to require neither food nor sleep. Most of his Staff now fall fast asleep directly they get off their horses, they are so exhausted from the last three days' work.

Whilst Lawley went to headquarters on business, I sat down and had a long talk with General Pendleton (the parson), chief of artillery. He told me the exact number of guns in action yesterday. He said that the universal opinion is in favor of the 12-pounder Napoleon guns as the best and simplest sort of ordnance for field purposes.* Nearly all the artillery with this army has either been captured from the enemy or cast from old 6-pounders taken at the early part of the war.

At 10 A. M. Lawley returned from headquarters, bringing the news that the army is to commence moving in the direction of Virginia this evening. This step is imperative from want of ammunition. But it was hoped that the enemy might attack during the day, especially as this is the 4th of July, and it was calculated that there was still ammunition for one day's fighting. The ordnance train had already commenced moving back towards Cashtown, and

---

* The Napoleon 12-pounders are smooth-bore brass guns, with chambers, very light, and with long range. They were invented or recommended by Louis Napoleon years ago. A large number are being cast at Augusta and elsewhere.

Ewell's immense train of plunder had been proceeding towards Hagerstown by the Fairfield road ever since an early hour this morning.

Johnson's division had evacuated during the night the position it had gained yesterday. It appears that for a time it was actually in possession of the cemetery, but had been forced to retire from thence from want of support by Pender's division, which had been retarded by that officer's wound. The whole of our left was therefore thrown back considerably.

At 1 P. M. the rain began to descend in torrents, and we took refuge in the hovel of an ignorant Pennsylvanian boor. The cottage was full of soldiers, none of whom had the slightest idea of the contemplated retreat, and all were talking of Washington and Baltimore with the greatest confidence.

At 2 P. M. we walked to General Longstreet's camp, which had been removed to a place three miles distant, on the Fairfield road. General Longstreet talked to me for a long time about the battle. He said the mistake they had made was in not concentrating the army more, and making the attack yesterday with 30,000 men instead of 15,000. The advance had been in three lines, and the troops of Hill's corps who gave way were young soldiers, who had never been under fire before. He thought the enemy would have attacked had the guns been withdrawn. Had they done so at that particular moment immediately after the repulse, it would have been awkward; but in that case he had given orders for the advance of Hood's division and M'Laws's on the right. I think, after all, that General Meade was right not to advance—his men would never have stood the tremendous fire of artillery they would have been exposed to.

Rather over 7,000 Yankees were captured during the three days; 3,500 took the parole; the remainder were now being marched to Richmond, escorted by the remains of Pickett's division. It is impossible to avoid seeing that the cause of this check to the Confederates lies in the utter contempt felt for the enemy by all ranks.

Wagons, horses, mules, and cattle captured in Pennsylvania, the solid advantages of this campaign, have been passing slowly along this road (Fairfield) all day: those taken by Ewell are particularly admired. So interminable was this train that it soon became evident that we should not be able to start till late at night. As soon as it became dark we all lay round a big fire, and I heard reports coming in from the different generals that the enemy was *retiring*, and had been doing so all day long. M'Laws reported nothing in his front but cavalry videttes. But this, of course, could make no difference to General Lee's plan: ammunition he must have—he had failed to capture it from the enemy (according to precedent); and as his communications with Virginia were intercepted, he was compelled to fall back towards Winchester, and draw his supplies from thence. General Milroy had kindly left an ample stock at that town when he made his precipitate exit some weeks ago. The army was also incumbered with an enormous wagon-train, the spoils of Pennsylvania, which it is highly desirable to get safely over the Potomac.

Shortly after 9 P. M. the rain began to descend in torrents. Lawley and I luckily got into the doctors' covered buggy, and began to get slowly under way a little after midnight.

5th July (Sunday).—The night was very bad— thunder and lightning, torrents of rain—the road knee-deep in mud and water, and often blocked up with wagons " come to grief." I pitied the wretched plight of the unfortunate soldiers who were to follow us. Our progress was naturally very slow indeed, and we took eight hours to go as many miles.

At 8 A. M. we halted a little beyond the village of Fairfield, near the entrance to a mountain-pass. No sooner had we done so, and lit a fire, than an alarm was spread that Yankee cavalry were upon us. Several shots flew over our heads, but we never could discover from whence they came. News also arrived of the capture of the whole of Ewell's beautiful wagons.* These reports created a regular stampede amongst the wagoners, and Longstreet's drivers started off as fast as they could go. Our medical trio, however, firmly declined to budge, and came to this wise conclusion, partly urged by the pangs of hunger, and partly from the consideration that, if the Yankee cavalry did come, the crowded state or the road in our rear would prevent our escape. Soon afterwards, some Confederate cavalry were pushed to the front, who cleared the pass after a slight skirmish.

At noon, Generals Lee and Longstreet arrived, and halted close to us. Soon afterwards Ewell came up. This is the first time I ever saw him. He is rather a remarkable-looking old soldier, with a bald head, a prominent nose, and rather a haggard, sickly face: having so lately lost his leg above the knee, he is still a complete cripple, and falls off his horse occasionally. Directly he dismounts he has to be put on crutches. He was Stonewall Jackson's coadjutor during the celebrated Valley campaigns, and he used to be a great swearer—in fact, he is said to have been the only person who was unable to restrain that propensity before Jackson; but since his late (rather romantic) marriage, he has (to use the American expression) "*joined the Church.*" When I saw him he was in a great state of disgust in consequence of the supposed

---

* It afterwards turned out that all escaped but thirty-eight.

loss of his wagons, and refused to be comforted by General Lee.

I joined Longstreet again, and, mounted on Lawley's venerable horse, started at 3 P. M. to ride through the pass. At 4 P. M. we stopped at a place where the roads fork, one leading to Emmetsburg, and the other to Hagerstown. Major Moses and I entered a farm-house, in which we found several women, two wounded Yankees, and one dead one, the result of this morning's skirmish. One of the sufferers was frightfully wounded in the head; the other was hit in the knee: the latter told me he was an Irishman, and had served in the Bengal Europeans during the Indian Mutiny. He now belonged to a Michigan cavalry regiment, and had already imbibed American ideas of Ireland's wrongs, and all that sort of trash. He told me that his officers were very bad, and that the idea in the army was that M'Clellan had assumed the chief command.

The women in this house were great Abolitionists. When Major Fairfax rode up, he inquired of one of them whether the corpse was that of a Confederate or Yankee (the body was in the veranda, covered with a white sheet). The woman made a gesture with her foot, and replied, " If it was a rebel, do you think it would be here long?" Fairfax then said, "Is it a woman who speaks in such a manner of a dead body which can do no one any harm?" She thereupon

colored up, and said she wasn't in earnest. At
6 o'clock we rode on again (by the Hagerstown
road), and came up with General Longstreet at 7.30.
The road was full of soldiers marching in a particularly lively manner—the wet and mud seemed to have
produced no effect whatever on their spirits, which
were as boisterous as ever. They had got hold of
colored prints of Mr. Lincoln, which they were passing about from company to company with many
remarks upon the personal beauty of Uncle Abe.
The same old chaff was going on of " Come out of
that hat—I know you're in it—I sees your legs a-
dangling down," &c. When we halted for the night,
skirmishing was going on in front and rear—Stuart
in front and Ewell in rear. Our bivouac being near
a large tavern, General Longstreet had ordered some
supper there for himself and his Staff; but when we
went to devour it, we discovered General M'Laws
and his officers rapidly finishing it. We, however,
soon got more, the Pennsylvanian proprietors being
particularly anxious to propitiate the General, in
hopes that he would spare their live stock, which had
been condemned to death by the ruthless Moses.

During supper, women came rushing in at intervals, saying—" Oh, good heavens, now they're killing
our fat hogs. Which is the General? which is the
Great Officer? Our milch cows are now going." To
all which expressions Longstreet replied, shaking his

head in a melancholy manner—"Yes, madam, it's very sad—very sad; and this sort of thing has been going on in Virginia more than two years—very sad." We all slept in the open, and the heavy rain produced no effect upon our slumbers.

I understand it is impossible to cross the lines by flag of truce. I therefore find myself in a dilemma about the expiration of my leave.

6th July (Monday).—Several horses were stolen last night, mine nearly so. It is necessary to be very careful, in order to prevent this misfortune. We started at 6.30, but got on very slowly, so blocked up was the road with wagons, some of which had been captured and burnt by the enemy yesterday. It now turned out that all Ewell's wagons escaped except thirty-eight, although, at one time, they had been all in the enemy's hands.

At 8.30 we halted for a couple of hours, and Generals Lee, Longstreet, Hill, and Willcox, had a consultation. I spoke to —— about my difficulties with regard to getting home, and the necessity of doing so, owing to the approaching expiration of my leave. He told me that the army had no intention at present of retreating for good, and advised me to stop with them and see what turned up. He also said that some of the enemy's dispatches had been intercepted, in which the following words occur :—" The noble but unfortunate army of the Potomac has again been obliged to retreat before superior numbers." I particularly observed the marching to-day of the 21st Mississippi, which was uncommonly good. This regiment all wear short round jackets, a most unusual circumstance, for they are generally unpopular in the South.

At 12 o'clock we halted again, and all set to work to eat cherries, which was the only food we got between 5 A. M. and 11 P. M.

I saw a most laughable spectacle this afternoon—viz., a negro dressed in full Yankee uniform, with a rifle at full cock, leading along a barefooted white man, with whom he had evidently changed clothes. General Longstreet stopped the pair, and asked the black man what it meant. He replied, " The two soldiers in charge of this here Yank have got drunk, so for fear he should escape I have took care of him, and brought him through that little town." The consequential manner of the negro, and the supreme contempt with which he spoke to his prisoner, were most amusing. This little episode of a Southern slave leading a white Yankee soldier through a Northern village, *alone and of his own accord*, would not have been gratifying to an abolitionist. Nor would the sympathizers both in England and in the North feel encouraged if they could hear the language of detestation and contempt with which the numerous negroes with the Southern armies speak of their liberators.*

I saw General Hood in his carriage; he looked rather bad, and has been suffering a good deal; the doctors seem to doubt whether they will be able to save his arm. I also saw General Hampton, of the cavalry, who has been shot in the hip, and has two sabre-cuts on the head, but he was in very good spirits.

A short time before we reached Hagerstown there was some firing in front, together with an alarm that the Yankee cavalry was upon us. The ambulances were sent back; but some of the wounded jumped out, and, producing the rifles which they had not parted with, they prepared to fight. After a good deal of desultory skirmishing, we seated ourselves upon a hill overlooking Hagerstown, and saw the

---

* From what I have seen of the Southern negroes, I am of opinion that the Confederates could, if they chose, convert a great number into soldiers; and from the affection which undoubtedly exists as a general rule between the slaves and their masters, I think that they would prove more efficient than black troops under any other circumstances. But I do not imagine that such an experiment will be tried, except as a very last resort, partly on account of the great value of the negroes, and partly because the Southerners consider it improper to introduce such an element on a large scale into civilized warfare. Any person who has seen negro features convulsed with rage, may form a slight estimate of what the result would be of arming a vast number of blacks, rousing their passions, and then allowing them free scope.

enemy's cavalry driven through the town pursued by
yelling Confederates. A good many Yankee prisoners now passed us; one of them who was smoking a
cigar, was a lieutenant of cavalry, dressed very smartly, and his hair brushed with the greatest care; he
formed rather a contrast to his ragged escort, and to
ourselves, who had not washed or shaved for ever so
long.

About 7 P.M. we rode through Hagerstown, in the
streets of which were several dead horses and a few
dead men. After proceeding about a mile beyond
the town we halted, and General Longstreet sent four
cavalrymen up a lane, with directions to report every
thing they saw. We then dismounted and lay down.
About ten minutes later (being nearly dark) we heard
a sudden rush—a panic—and then a regular stampede
commenced, in the midst of which I descried our four
cavalry heroes crossing a field as fast as they could
gallop. All was now complete confusion;—officers
mounting their horses, and pursuing those which had
got loose, and soldiers climbing over fences for protection against the supposed advancing Yankees. In
the middle of the din I heard an artillery officer shouting to his "cannoneers" to stand by him, and plant
the guns in a proper position for enfilading the lane.
I also distinguished Longstreet walking about, hus-
tled by the excited crowd, and remarking, in angry
tones, which could scarcely be heard, and to which

no attention was paid, " Now, you don't know what
it is—you don't know what it is." Whilst the row
and confusion were at their height, the object of all
this alarm at length emerged from the dark lane, in
the shape of a domestic four-wheel carriage, with a
harmless load of females. The stampede had, however, spread, increased in the rear, and caused much
harm and delay.

Cavalry skirmishing went on until quite dark, a
determined attack having been made by the enemy,
who did his best to prevent the trains from crossing
the Potomac at Williamsport. It resulted in the success of the Confederates; but every impartial man
confesses that these cavalry fights are miserable affairs.
Neither party has any idea of serious charging with
the sabre. They approach one another with considerable boldness, until they get to within about forty
yards, and then, at the very moment when a dash is
necessary, and the sword alone should be used, they
hesitate, halt, and commence a desultory fire with
carbines and revolvers. An Englishman, named
Winthrop, a captain in the Confederate army, and
formerly an officer in H. M.'s 22d regiment, although
not in the cavalry himself, seized the colors of one
of the regiments, and rode straight at the Yankees
in the most gallant manner, shouting to the men to
follow him. He continued to distinguish himself by
leading charges until his horse was unfortunately

killed. I heard his conduct on this occasion highly spoken of by all. Stuart's cavalry can hardly be called cavalry in the European sense of the word; but, on the other hand, the country in which they are accustomed to operate is not adapted for cavalry.

—— was forced at last to give up wearing even his Austrian forage-cap; for the last two days soldiers on the line of march had been visiting his ambulance in great numbers, under the impression (encouraged by the driver) that he was a Yankee general. The idea now was that the army would remain some days in or near its present position until the arrival of the ammunition from Winchester.

7th July (Tuesday).—Lawley, the Austrian, and I drove into Hagerstown this morning, and General Longstreet moved into a new position on the Williamsport road, which he was to occupy for the present. We got an excellent room in the Washington Hotel on producing greenbacks. Public opinion in Hagerstown seems to be pretty evenly divided between North and South, and probably accommodates itself to circumstances. For instance, yesterday the women waved their handkerchiefs when the Yankee cavalry were driven through the town, and to-day they went through the same compliment in honor of 3,500 Yankee (Gettysburg) prisoners whom I saw march through *en route* for Richmond. I overheard the conversation of some Confederate soldiers about these prisoners. One remarked, with respect to the Zouaves, of whom there were a few—"Those red-breeched fellows look as if they could fight, but they don't, though; no, not so well as the blue-bellies."

Lawley introduced me to General Stuart in the streets of Hagerstown to-day. He is commonly called Jeb Stuart, on account of his initials; he is a good-looking, jovial character, exactly like his photographs He has certainly accomplished wonders, and done excellent service in his peculiar style of warfare. He is a good and gallant soldier, though he sometimes incurs ridicule by his harmless affectation and pecu liarities. The other day he rode through a Virginian town, his horse covered with garlands of roses. He also departs considerably from the severe simplicity of dress adopted by other Confederate generals; but no one can deny that he is the right man in the right place. On a campaign, he seems to roam over the country according to his own discretion, and always gives a good account of himself, turning up at the right moment; and hitherto he has never got himself into any serious trouble.

I rode to General Longstreet's camp, which is about two miles in the direction of Williamsport, and consulted him about my difficulties with regard to my leave. He was most good-natured about it, and advised me under the circumstances to drive in the direc

tion of Hancock; and in the event of being ill-treated
on the way, to insist upon being taken before the
nearest U. S. officer of the highest rank, who would
probably protect me. I determined to take his advice
at once; so I took leave of him and of his officers.
Longstreet is generally a very taciturn and undemon-
strative man, but he was quite affectionate in his farewell. His last words were a hearty hope for the
speedy termination of the war. All his officers were
equally kind in their expressions on my taking leave,
though the last sentence uttered by Latrobe was not
entirely reassuring—viz., "You may take your oath
he'll be caught for a spy."

I then rode to General Lee's camp, and asked him
for a pass to get through his lines. We had a long
talk together, and he told me of the raid made by the
enemy, for the express purpose of arresting his badly
wounded son (a Confederate Brigadier-general), who
was lying in the house of a relation in Virginia.
They insisted upon carrying him off in a litter, though
he had never been out of bed, and had quite recently
been shot through the thigh. This seizure was
evidently made for purposes of retaliation. His
life has since been threatened, in the event of the
South retaliating for Burnside's alleged military mur-
ders in Kentucky. But few officers, however, speak
of the Northerners with so much moderation as General Lee; his extreme amiability seems to prevent

his speaking strongly against any one. I really felt quite sorry when I said good-by to so many gentlemen from whom I had received so much disinterested kindness.

I am now about to leave the Southern States, after travelling quite alone throughout their entire length and breadth, including Texas and the trans-Mississippi country, for nearly three months and a half, during which time I have been thrown amongst all classes of the population—the highest and lowest, and the most lawless. Although many were very sore about the conduct of England, I never received an uncivil word from anybody, but, on the contrary, I have been treated by all with more than kindness.* I have never met a man who was not anxious for a termination of the war; and I have never met a man, woman, or child who contemplated its termination as possible without an entire separation from the *now* detested Yankee. I have never been asked for alms or a gratuity by any man or woman, black or white. Every one knew who I was, and all spoke to me with the greatest confidence. I have rarely heard any person complain of the almost total ruin

---

* The only occasion on which I was roughly handled was when I had the misfortune to enter the city of Jackson, Mississippi, just as the Federals evacuated it. I do not complain of that affair, which, under the circumstances, was not to be wondered at.

which had befallen so many. All are prepared to undergo still greater sacrifices,—they contemplate and prepare to receive greater reverses which it is impossible to avert. They look to a successful termination of the war as certain, although few are sanguine enough to fix a speedy date for it, and nearly all bargain for its lasting at least all Lincoln's presidency. Although I have always been with the Confederates in the time of their misfortunes, yet I never heard any person use a desponding word as to the result of the struggle. When I was in Texas and Louisiana, Banks seemed to be carrying every thing before him, Grant was doing the same in Mississippi, and I certainly did not bring luck to my friends at Gettysburg. I have lived in bivouacs with all the Southern armies, which are as distinct from one another as the British is from the Austrian, and I have never once seen an instance of insubordination.

When I got back to Hagerstown, I endeavored to make arrangements for a horse and buggy to drive through the lines. With immense difficulty I secured the services of a Mr. ——, to take me to Hancock, and as much further as I chose to go, for a dollar a mile (greenbacks). I engaged also to pay him the value of his horse and buggy, in case they should be confiscated by either side. He was evidently extremely alarmed, and I was obliged to keep him up to the mark by assurances that his horse would in-

evitably be seized by the Confederates, unless protected by General Lee's pass in my possession.

8th July (Wednesday).—My conductor told me he
couldn't go to-day on account of a funeral, but he
promised faithfully to start to-morrow.   Every one
was full of forebodings as to my probable fate when
I fell into Yankee clutches.   In deference to their
advice I took off my gray shooting-jacket, in which
they said I was sure to be taken for a rebel, and I
put on a black coat; but I scouted all well-meant
advice as to endeavoring to disguise myself as an
" American citizen," or to conceal the exact truth
in any way.   I was aware that a great deal depended upon falling into the hands of a gentleman, and I
did not believe these were so rare in the Northern
army as the Confederates led me to suppose.

9th July (Thursday).—I left Hagerstown at 8 A.M.,
in my conductor's good buggy, after saying farewell
to Lawley, the Austrian, and the numerous Confederate officers who came to see me off, and wish me
good-luck.   We passed the Confederate advanced
post at about two miles from Hagerstown, and were
allowed to pass on the production of General Lee's
authority.   I was now fairly launched beyond the
Confederate lines for the first time since I had been
in America.   Immediately afterwards we began to

be asked all sorts of inquisitive questions about the rebels, which I left to my driver to answer. It became perfectly evident that this narrow strip of Maryland is entirely Unionist.

At about 12 o'clock we reached the top of a high hill, and halted to bait our horse at an inn called Fairview. No sooner had we descended from the buggy than about twenty rampageous Unionists appeared, who told us they had come up to get a good view of the big fight in which the G—d d—d rebels were to be all captured, or drowned in the Potomac.

My appearance evidently did not please them from the very first. With alarm I observed them talking to one another, and pointing at me. At length a particularly truculent-looking individual, with an enormous mustache, approached me, and, fixing his eyes long and steadfastly upon my trousers, he remarked, in the surliest possible tones, " *Them breeches is a d—d bad color.*" This he said in allusion, not to their dirty state, but to the fact of their being gray, the rebel color. I replied to this very disagreeable assertion in as conciliating a way as I possibly could; and in answer to his question as to who I was, I said that I was an English traveller. He then said that his wife was an English lady from Preston. I next expressed my pride of being a countryman of his wife's. He then told me in tones that admitted of no contradiction, that Preston was just forty-five

miles east of London; and he afterwards launched
into torrents of invectives against the rebels, who had
run him out of Virginia; and he stated his intention
of killing them in great numbers to gratify his taste.
With some difficulty I prevailed upon him and his
rabid brethren to drink, which pacified them slightly for a time; but when the horse was brought out
to be harnessed, it became evident I was not to be
allowed to proceed without a row. I therefore addressed the crowd, and asked them quietly who
among them wished to detain me; and I told them
at the same time, that I would not answer any questions put by those who were not persons in authority,
but that I should be most happy to explain myself
to any officer of the United States army. At length
they allowed me to proceed, on the understanding
that my buggy-driver should hand me over to General Kelly, at Hancock. The driver was provided
with a letter for the general, in which I afterwards
discovered that I was denounced as a spy, and
"handed over to the General *to be dealt with as justice to our cause demands.*" We were then allowed
to start, the driver being threatened with condign
vengeance if he let me escape.

After we had proceeded about six miles we fell
in with some Yankee cavalry, by whom we were immediately captured, and the responsibility of my
custody was thus removed from my conductor's

shoulders. A cavalry soldier was put in charge of us, and we passed through the numerous Yankee outposts under the title of "*Prisoners.*"

The hills near Hancock were white with Yankee tents, and there were, I believe, from 8,000 to 10,000 Federals there. I did not think much of the appearance of the Northern troops; they are certainly dressed in proper uniform, but their clothes are badly fitted, and they are often round-shouldered, dirty, and slovenly in appearance; in fact, bad imitations of soldiers. Now, the Confederate has no ambition to imitate the regular soldier at all; he looks the genuine rebel; but in spite of his bare feet, his ragged clothes, his old rug, and tooth-brush stuck like a rose in his button-hole,* he has a sort of devil-may-care, reckless, self-confident look, which is decidedly taking.

At 5 P.M. we drove up in front of the door of General Kelly's quarters, and to my immense relief I soon discovered that he was a gentleman. I then explained to him the whole truth, concealing nothing. I said I was a British officer on leave of absence, travelling for my own instruction; that I had been all the way to Mexico, and entered the Southern States by the Rio Grande, for the express purpose of not breaking any legally established blockade. I told him I had visited all the Southern armies in Missis-

---

* This tooth-brush in the button-hole is a very common custom, and has a most quaint effect.

sippi, Tennessee, Charleston, and Virginia, and seen
the late campaign as General Longstreet's guest, but
had in no way entered the Confederate service. I
also gave him my word that I had not got in my possession any letters, either public or private, from any
person in the South to any person anywhere else. I
showed him my British passport and General Lee's
pass as a British officer; and I explained that my
only object in coming North was to return to England in time for the expiration of my leave; and I
ended by expressing a hope that he would make my
detention as short as possible.

After considering a short time, he said that he
would certainly allow me to go on, but that he could
not allow my driver to go back. I felt immensely
relieved at the decision, but the countenance of my
companion lengthened considerably. It was, however, settled that he should take me on to Cumberland, and General Kelly good-naturedly promised to
do what he could for him on his return.

General Kelly then asked me in an off-hand manner
whether all General Lee's army was at Hagerstown;
but I replied, laughing, "You of course understand,
General, that, having got that pass from General Lee,
I am bound by every principle of honor not to give
you any information which can be of advantage to
you." He laughed and promised not to ask me any
more questions of that sort. He then sent his aid-

de-camp with me to the provost-marshal, who immediately gave me a pass for Cumberland. On my return to the General's, I discovered the perfidious driver (that zealous Southerner a few hours previous) hard at work communicating to General Kelly all he knew, and a great deal more besides; but, from what I heard, I don't think his information was very valuable.

I was treated by General Kelly and all his officers with the greatest good-nature and courtesy, although I had certainly come among them under circumstances suspicious, to say the least. I felt quite sorry that they should be opposed to my Southern friends, and I regretted still more that they should be obliged to serve with or under a Butler, a Milroy, or even a Hooker. I took leave of them at six o'clock; and I can truly say that the only Federal officers I have ever come in contact with were gentlemen.

We had got four miles beyond Hancock, when the tire of one of our wheels came off, and we had to stop for a night at a farm-house. I had supper with the farmer and his laborers, who had just come in from the fields, and the supper was much superior to that which can be procured at the first hotel at Richmond. All were violent Unionists, and perfectly under the impression that the rebels were totally demoralized, and about to lay down their arms. Of course I held my tongue, and gave no one reason to suppose that I had ever been in rebeldom.

10th July (Friday).—The drive from Hancock to Cumberland is a very mountainous forty-four miles—total distance from Hagerstown, sixty-six miles. We met with no further adventure on the road, although the people were very inquisitive, but I never opened my mouth. One woman in particular, who kept a toll-bar, thrust her ugly old head out of an upper window, and yelled out, "Air they a-fixin' for another battle out there?" jerking her head in the direction of Hagerstown. The driver replied that, although the bunch of rebels there was pretty big, yet he could not answer for their fixing arrangements, which he afterwards explained to me meant digging fortifications.

We arrived at Cumberland at 7 P. M. This is a great coal place, and a few weeks ago it was touched up by "Imboden," who burnt a lot of coal barges, which has rendered the people rabid against the Rebs. I started by stage for Johnstown at 8.30 P. M.

11th July (Saturday).—I hope I may never for my sins be again condemned to travel for thirty hours in an American stage on a used-up plank-road. We changed carriages at Somerset. All my fellow-travellers were of course violent Unionists, and invariably spoke of my late friends as Rebels or Rebs. They had all got into their heads that their Potomac army, not having been thoroughly thrashed, as it always has been hitherto, had achieved a tremendous victory; and that its new chief, General Meade, who in reality was driven into a strong position, which he had sense enough to stick to, is a wonderful strategist. They all hope that the remnants of Lee's army will not be allowed to ESCAPE over the Potomac; whereas, when I left the army two days ago, no man in it had a thought of escaping over the Potomac, and certainly General Meade was not in a position to attempt to prevent the passage, if crossing had become necessary.

I reached Johnstown on the Pennsylvania Railway at 6 P.M., and found that town in a great state of excitement in consequence of the review of two militia companies, who were receiving garlands from the fair ladies of Johnstown in gratitude for their daring conduct in turning out to resist Lee's invasion. Most of the men seemed to be respectable mechanics, not at all adapted for an early interview with the rebels. The garlands supplied were as big and apparently as substantial as a ship's life-buoys, and the recipients looked particularly helpless after they had got them. Heaven help those Pennsylvanian braves if a score of Hood's Texans had caught sight of them!

Left Johnstown by train at 7.30 P.M., and by paying half a dollar, I secured a berth in a sleeping-car—a most admirable and ingenious Yankee notion.

12*th July* (Sunday).—The Pittsburg and Phila-

13*

delphia Railway is, I believe, accounted one of the
best in America, which did not prevent my spending
eight hours last night off the line; but, being asleep
at the time, I was unaware of the circumstance. Instead of arriving at Philadelphia at 6 A. M., we did not
get there till 3 P. M.   Passed Harrisburg at 9 A.M.   It
was full of Yankee soldiers, and has evidently not
recovered from the excitement consequent upon the
late invasion, one effect of which has been to prevent
the cutting of the crops by the calling out of the
militia.

At Philadelphia I saw a train containing one hundred and fifty Confederate prisoners, who were being
stared at by a large number of the *beau monde* of
Philadelphia.   I mingled with the crowd which was
chaffing them. Most of the people were good-natured,
but I heard one suggestion to the effect that they
should be taken to the river, " and every mother's
son of them drowned there."

I arrived at New York at 10 P. M., and drove to
the Fifth Avenue Hotel.

13*th July* (Monday).—The luxury and comfort of
New York and Philadelphia strike one as extraordinary after having lately come from Charleston
and Richmond. The greenbacks seem to be nearly as
good as gold. The streets are as full as possible of
well-dressed people, and are crowded with able-bodied

civilians capable of bearing arms, who have evidently
no intention of doing so. They apparently *don't feel
the war at all* here; and until there is a grand smash
with their money, or some other catastrophe to make
them feel it, I can easily imagine that they will not
be anxious to make peace.

I walked the whole distance of Broadway to the
Consul's house, and nothing could exceed the apparent
prosperity; the street was covered with banners and
placards inviting people to enlist in various high-
sounding regiments. Bounties of $550 were offered,
and huge pictures hung across the street, on which
numbers of ragged *Graybacks,** terror depicted on
their features, were being pursued by the Federals.

On returning to the Fifth Avenue, I found all the
shopkeepers beginning to close their stores, and I perceived by degrees that there was great alarm about
the resistance to the draft which was going on this
morning. On reaching the hotel I perceived a whole
block of buildings on fire close by : engines were present, but were not allowed to play by the crowd. In
the hotel itself, universal consternation prevailed, and
an attack by the mob had been threatened. I walked
about in the neighborhood, and saw a company of
soldiers on the march, who were being jeered at and

* The Northerners call the Southerners "Graybacks," just as
the latter call the former "Bluebellies," on account of the color of
their dress.

hooted by small boys, and I saw a negro pursued by the crowd take refuge with the military; he was followed by loud cries of "Down with the b——y nigger! Kill all niggers!" &c. Never having been in New York before, and being totally ignorant of the state of feeling with regard to negroes, I inquired of a bystander what the negroes had done that they should want to kill them? He replied civilly enough—"Oh sir, they hate them here; they are the innocent cause of all these troubles." Shortly afterwards, I saw a troop of citizen cavalry come up; the troopers were very gorgeously attired, but evidently experienced so much difficulty in sitting their horses, that they were more likely to excite laughter than any other emotion.

14th July (Tuesday).—At breakfast this morning two Irish waiters, seeing I was a Britisher, came up to me one after another, and whispered at intervals in hoarse Hibernian accents—"It's disgraceful, sir. I've been drafted, sir. I'm a Briton. I love my country. I love the Union Jack, sir." I suggested an interview with Mr. Archibald, but neither of them seemed to care about going to the *Counsel* just yet. These rascals have probably been hard at work for years, voting as free and enlightened American citizens, and abusing England to their hearts' content.

I heard every one talking of the total demoralization of the Rebels as a certain fact, and all seemed to anticipate their approaching destruction. All this sounded very absurd to me, who had left Lee's army four days previously as full of fight as ever—much stronger in numbers, and ten times more efficient in every military point of view, than it was *when it crossed the Potomac to invade Maryland a year ago.* In its own opinion, Lee's army has not lost any of its prestige at the battle of Gettysburg, in which it most gallantly stormed strong intrenchments defended by the whole army of the Potomac, which never ventured outside its works, or approached in force within half a mile of the Confederate artillery.

The result of the battle of Gettysburg, together with the fall of Vicksburg and Port Hudson, seems to have turned everybody's head completely, and has deluded them with the idea of the speedy and complete subjugation of the South. I was filled with astonishment to hear the people speaking in this confident manner, when one of their most prosperous States had been so recently laid under contribution as far as Harrisburg; and Washington, their capital itself, having just been saved by a fortunate turn of luck. Four-fifths of the Pennsylvanian spoil had safely crossed the Potomac before I left Hagerstown.

The consternation in the streets seemed to be on the increase; fires were going on in all directions, and the streets were being patrolled by large bodies of police followed by special constables, the latter bearing truncheons, but not looking very happy. I heard a British captain making a deposition before the Consul, to the effect that the mob had got on board his vessel, and cruelly beaten his colored crew. As no British man-of-war was present, the French Admiral was appealed to, who at once requested that all British ships with colored crews might be anchored under the guns of his frigate.

The reports of outrages, hangings, and murder, were now most alarming, the terror and anxiety were universal. All shops were shut: all carriages and omnibuses had ceased running. No colored man or woman was visible or safe in the streets, or even in his own dwelling. Telegraphs were cut, and railroad tracks torn up. The draft was suspended, and the mob evidently had the upper hand.

The people who can't pay $300 naturally hate being forced to fight in order to liberate the very race who they are most anxious should be slaves. It is their direct interest not only that all slaves should remain slaves, but that the free Northern negroes who compete with them for labor should be sent to the South also.

15*th July* (Wednesday).—The hotel this morning was occupied by military, or rather by creatures in uniform. One of the sentries stopped me; and on my remonstrating to his officer, the latter blew up

the sentry, and said, " You are only to stop persons
in military dress—don't you know what military
dress is ?" "No," responded this efficient sentry—and
I left the pair discussing the definition of a soldier.
I had the greatest difficulty in getting a conveyance
down to the water. I saw a stone barficade in the
distance, and heard firing going on—and I was not
at all sorry to find myself on board the China.

POSTSCRIPT.

DURING my voyage home in the China, I had an opportunity of discussing with many intelligent Northern gentlemen all that I had seen in my Southern travels. We did so in a very amicable spirit, and I think they rendered justice to my wish to explain to them without exaggeration the state of feeling amongst their enemies. Although these Northerners belonged to quite the upper classes, and were not likely to be led blindly by the absurd nonsense of the sensation press at New York, yet their ignorance of the state of the case in the South was very great.

The recent successes had given them the impression that the last card of the South was played. Charleston was about to fall; Mobile, Savannah, and Wilmington would quickly follow; Lee's army they thought, was a disheartened, disorganized mob; Bragg's army in a still worse condition, fleeing before Rosecrans, who would carry every thing before him. They felt confident that the fall of the Mississippian fortresses would prevent communication from one bank to the other, and that the great river would soon be open to peaceful commerce.

All these illusions have since been dispelled, but they probably still cling to the idea of the great exhaustion of the Southern *personnel*.

But this difficulty of recruiting the Southern armies is not so great as is generally supposed. As I have already stated, no Confederate soldier is given his discharge from the army, however badly he may be wounded; but he is employed at such labor in the public service as he may be capable of performing, and his place in the ranks is taken by a sound man hitherto exempted. The slightly wounded are cured as quickly as possible, and are sent back at once to their regiments. *The women take care of this.* The number actually killed, or who die of their wounds, are the only total losses to the State, and these form but a small proportion of the enormous butcher's bills which seem at first so very appalling.

I myself remember, with General Polk's corps, a fine-looking man who had had both his hands blown off at the wrists by unskilful artillery-practice in one of the early battles. A currycomb and brush were fitted into his stumps, and he was engaged in grooming artillery-horses with considerable skill. This man was called an hostler; and, as the war drags on, the number of these handless hostlers will increase. By degrees the clerks at the offices, the orderlies, the railway and post-office officials, and the stage-drivers, will be composed of maimed and mutilated soldiers. The number of exempted persons all over the South is still very large, and they can easily be exchanged for worn veterans. Besides this fund to draw upon, a calculation is made of the number of boys who arrive each year at the fighting age. These are all "panting for the rifle," but have been latterly wisely forbidden the ranks until they are fit to undergo the hardships of a military life. By these means, it is the opinion of the Confederates that they can keep their armies recruited up to their present strength for several years; and, if the worst comes to the worst, they can always fall back upon their negroes as the last resort; but I do not think they contemplate such a necessity as likely to arise for a considerable time.

With respect to the supply of arms, cannon, powder, and military stores, the Confederates are under no alarm whatever. Augusta furnishes more than sufficient gunpowder; Atlanta, copper caps, &c. The Tredegar works at Richmond, and other foundries, cast more cannon than is wanted; and the Federal generals have always hitherto proved themselves the most indefatigable purveyors of artillery to the Confederate Government, for even in those actions which they claim as drawn battles or as victories, such as Corinth, Murfreesborough, and Gettysburg, they have never failed to make over cannon to the Southerners without exacting any in return.

My Northern friends on board the China spoke much and earnestly about the determination of the North to crush out the Rebellion at any sacrifice. But they did not show any disposition to *fight themselves* in this cause, although many of them would have made most eligible recruits; and if they had been Southerners, their female relations would have made them enter the army whether their inclinations led them that way or not.

I do not mention this difference of spirit by way of making any odious comparisons between North and South in this respect, because I feel sure that these Northern gentlemen would emulate the example of their enemy if they could foresee any danger of a Southern Butler exercising his infamous sway over Philadelphia, or of a Confederate Milroy ruling with intolerable despotism in Boston, by withholding the necessaries of life from helpless women with one hand, whilst tendering them with the other a hated and absurd oath of allegiance to a detested Government.

But the mass of respectable Northerners, though they may be willing to pay, do not very naturally feel themselves called upon to give their blood in a war of aggression, ambition, and conquest. For this war is essentially a war of conquest. If ever a nation did wage such a war, the North is now engaged, with a determination worthy of a more hopeful cause, in endeavoring to conquer the South; but the more I think of all that I have seen in the Confederate States of the devotion of the whole population, the more I feel inclined to say with General Polk— "How can you subjugate such a people as this?" and even supposing that their extermination were a feasible plan, as some Northerners have suggested, I never can believe that in the nineteenth century the civilized world will be condemned to witness the destruction of such a gallant race.

THE END.

INDEX

Aaron (slave), 148, 172
Abdelkader, 149
Abe, Uncle. See Lincoln, Abraham
Abolitionists, 81. See also Northerners; Soldiers, Union
African-Americans. See Blacks
Alabama, 134. See also specific cities
Alexander, Edward Porter, xxvii n16
Alexandria, Louisiana: and Banks, 54, 61; fall of, 61, 87, 88. See also Virginia
Allegiance, oath of, 131, 229
Alleyton, Texas, 63. See also Texas
Alligators, 98
Ambulance corps, 234
Ambulances, defined, 10
Anaconda (blockade-runner), 190. See also Blockades and blockade-runners
Apostle of Liberty. See Vallandigham, Clement L.
Arizona (gunboat), 95. See also Gunboats
Armistead, Lewis A., 270
Aroyo del Colorado, 33
Atlanta, Georgia, 177, 307. See also Georgia
Atrato (steamer), 7. See also Steamers

Augusta, Georgia: cannon foundries in, 176–77, 273; characteristics of, 174, 176–77; Episcopal church in, 174; gunpowder factories in, 176–77, 307; weather in, 174. See also Georgia

Bagdad, Mexico, 8–9, 21
Baker's Creek, 112
Balls and dances, 22–23, 73–74
Bankhead, Colonel, 54, 56–57
Bankhead, Mrs., 55
Banks, Nathaniel Prentiss: and Alexandria, Virginia, 54, 61; and Jackson, 74, 125; and Louisiana, 82; and Pyron's regiment, 74; and slaves, 87; as soldier, 74, 125; and Walker's division, 87–88
Barksdale, General, 233, 261
Bates's battalion, 69–70
Battery (promenade), 186
Battery Bee, 184
Bayou City (cotton boat), 72
Bayous, 98. See also Louisiana
Beauregard, Pierre: background of, 193, 199; cartoons about, 199; characteristics of, 193; and Charleston, South Carolina, 191, 201; and Fremantle,

Beauregard, Pierre (*cont.*)
xvii; and ironclads, 218–20;
and Shiloh, Tennessee, 148;
as soldier, 194; and weapons, 198
Bee, General, 11, 21, 22
Beef, drying of, 42
Behnsen (merchant), 15, 16, 21
Belmont, Missouri, 145
Benjamin, Judah P.: back-
ground of, 207; confiscation
of property of, 209; and
Davis, 213; and England,
208–9, 210; and Fremantle,
xvii; as gambler, 210; and
Jackson, xvii–xviii, 209–10;
and Russell, 210; and secession, 207–8, 210; as secretary of state, 206; as
secretary of war, 207
Big Drunk. *See* Houston,
Samuel
Blacks, 300, 302. *See also*
Plantations; Slaves and
slavery; Soldiers, black
Blackwood's Magazine, xiii
Blake, Walter, 199–200
Blockades and blockade-runners: and Charleston, South
Carolina, 179; criticism of,
184–85; and England, 203;
and France, 203; goods carried by, 202–3; and Mississippi River, 88, 99, 155; of
Mobile, Alabama, 130, 132–
33; and Sennec, 197, 204;
and Vallandigham, 203–4
Bluebellies, defined, 80, 299.
See also Soldiers, Union
Blue-noses, defined, 21
Blue Ridge Mountains, 223,
228

Borcke, Heros von, vii–viii,
228
Bowmont House Hotel, 107–8,
113. *See also* Hotels
Bradley, Major, 176
Bragg, Braxton: baptism of,
162; characteristics of, 145;
and Cleburne, 153; and El-
liott, 162; and Fremantle,
xvii; and Grenfell, 149, 163,
164; and Murfreesboro,
Tennessee, 151–52; and
Polk, 162; regiment of, 135;
and Rosecrans, 152; and
Shelbyville, Tennessee, 136;
as soldier, 241; and Vallan-
digham, 137
Brazos River, 65
Breckinridge [Breckenridge],
John Cabell, 154
British, 131, 191–92. *See also*
England
Brook guns, 181, 219. *See
also* Weapons
Brownsville, Texas, 13, 23.
See also Texas
Buchel, Colonel, 17, 21, 22
Buggies, defined, 10
Bull-dogs, defined, 159
Bull Run, battle of, 83
Burnside, Ambrose E.: and
Fredericksburg, Virginia,
132, 135; and Kentucky,
219, 287
Bushwhackers, 237
Butler, Benjamin F., 228

Canada, 208–9
Cannons. *See* Foundries, cannon
Canton, Mississippi, 104, 112,
126. *See also* Mississippi

Capitals, state, 134. *See also* specific cities

Caps, percussion, 177, 307

Carlisle, Pennsylvania, 242, 250. *See also* Pennsylvania

Cartoons, 199

Castle Pinckney, 183

Cavalry: characteristics of, 158–59, 170; criticism of, 250–51; and Grenfell, 158–59; and Hagerstown, Maryland, 283–85; and Martin, 168, 169; and Morgan, 159; and New York City, 300; successes of, 262; and Wharton, 159; and Wheeler, 159. *See also* Fifty-First Alabama Cavalry

Chaffin's Bluff, 218

Chambers, General, 65

Chambersburg, Pennsylvania: characteristics of, 239; and Confederate soldiers, 245–46; and Ewell, 241; and Lee, 245; and Lincoln, 246; and Moses, 241, 242, 243–45; patriotism of, 246; whiskey in, destruction of, 249–50. *See also* Pennsylvania

Chancellorsville, Virginia, 89. *See also* Virginia

Chaparral, defined, 30

Charleston, South Carolina: and Beauregard, 191, 201; and blockade-runners, 179; characteristics of, 179, 180, 197; destruction of, 179–80; slaves in, 179

Chattanooga, Tennessee, 136. *See also* Tennessee

Chattanooga Rebel (newspaper), 154

Cheetham (officer), 171

Cherokees, 76. *See also* Indians

Chicken-wagons, 113

Chicora (ironclad), 185, 190, 192. *See also* Ironclads

China (ship), 303, 305

Chubb, Captain, 69

Civil War: characteristics of, 308–9; and England, 208, 211, 213, 216–17. *See also* specific headings

Cleburne, Patrick R., 152–53, 171

Coffee, Confederate, defined, 79

Columbiads, 181. *See also* Weapons

Colville (merchant), 13, 21

Combahee River, 178

Confederate Image, The (Neely, Holzer, and Boritt), xxviii n18

Confederate States regulars, 181. *See also* Soldiers, Confederate

Conolly, Thomas, vii

Conrad (congressman), 219–20

Conscription: and British, 131; criticism of, xx, 55–56, 58, 86, 99; enforcement of, 58; exceptions to, 176; and Germans, 55–56, 58; and Irish, 300; and New York City, xxi, 299–300, 302. *See also* Soldiers, Confederate; Soldiers, Union

Cook, Colonel, 72

Corinth, Mississippi. *See* Shiloh, Tennessee

Corn, Indian, 62, 65, 79
Cotton trade: characteristics of, 30; and Ituria, 27; and Magruder, 36; in Texas, 60, 62, 65
Coulter, E. Merton, xv
Couriers, defined, 91, 171, 238
Creeks, defined, 46
Creoles, defined, 89
Crimean War, 149
Cumberland, Maryland, 296. See also Maryland
Currency, Confederate, 29

Dahlgrens, 181. See also Weapons
Dances, 22–23, 73–74
Davis (renegado), 11
Davis, Jefferson: background of, 213–14; and Benjamin, 213; cartoons about, 199; characteristics of, xvii, 211, 213, 214; and Confederate officers, 212; and Confederate soldiers, 212–13; and England, 211, 213; and Fremantle, xvii; and Grenfell, 212; and Maine, 211–12; and Massachusetts, 211; and Mexican War, 214; and Rains, 175; and Russell, 213; as secretary of war, 213–14; as soldier, 213
Debray, Colonel, 70–71, 72, 73
Deer, 32
Deserters, 89, 157. See also Soldiers, Confederate; Soldiers, Union
Destroying Angels, 142–43
Dickens, Charles, 84

Doctors, 119, 135
Don Pablo. See Zorn
Drewry's Bluff, 217–18
Duff, Colonel, 9–10, 12, 25. See also Partisan Rangers
Dupont, Samuel F., 200
Dutch cavalry, defined, 81

Elections, 68, 157
Elliott, Bishop: baptism performed by, 162; and Bragg, 162; as clergyman, 141, 154; and Hardee, 137; and Polk, 140; speech by, 157
Enfield rifles, 113, 156, 225. See also Weapons
England: and Benjamin, 208–9, 210; and blockades and blockade-runners, 203; and Civil War, 208, 211, 213, 216–17; and Confederate soldiers, 59; and Davis, 211, 213; and Hebert, 90; and Southerners, 216–17; and Union soldiers, 208–9. See also British
Episcopal church, 174, 232
Evans, General, 126
Ewell, Richard S.: and Carlisle, Pennsylvania, 242, 250; and Chambersburg, Pennsylvania, 241; characteristics of, 277; and Gettysburg, Pennsylvania, 251, 255, 257–58, 259, 271, 273–74; and Jackson, 125, 231, 277; and Lee, 278; marriage of, 277; and Pennsylvania, 233, 238, 242; religious beliefs of, 277; as soldier, 224, 231, 249; and weapons, 276–78, 280; and

Winchester, Virginia, 214, 221, 228; and York, Pennsylvania, 250

Factories, 110, 175–77, 307
Fairfax, Major, 261
Fair Oaks, Virginia, 125. See also Virginia
Fandangos, 15, 19–20
Farms, 102, 238. See also Plantations
Fergusson, James, 201
Fifty-First Alabama Cavalry, 160, 162. Sec also Cavalry
Fitzgerald, Jack, 128
Fitzgerald, Thomas, 128
Flag, Confederate, 184, 226
Fleas, 31, 34
Florida brigade, 257–58, 261. See also Soldiers, Confederate
Folly Island, 184, 188, 200
Foote, Andrew Hull, 200
Forrest, Nathan B., 152
Fort Apalache, 130. See also Mobile, Alabama
Fort Bankhead, 72
Fort Beauregard, 94–95, 96, 184. See also Harrisonburg, Louisiana
Fort Blakeley, 130. See also Mobile, Alabama
Fort Cummins, 184
Fort Gaines, 130. See also Mobile, Alabama
Fort Johnson, 184
Fort Magruder, 72
Fort Morgan, 130. See also Mobile, Alabama
Fort Moultrie, 184
Fort Pinto, 130. See also Mobile, Alabama

Fort Point, 72
Fort Ripley, 183
Fort Scurry, 72
Fort Spanish River, 130. See also Mobile, Alabama
Fort Sumter: characteristics of, 180–82, 189, 198; fighting at, 181–83, 187; and Monitors, 192–93, 195; weapons at, 181, 182
Fort Wagner, 184, 186
Forty-two pounders, 181. See also Weapons
Foundries, cannon, 176–77, 273, 307. See also Weapons
France, 203
Fredericksburg, Virginia, 132, 135. See also Virginia
Freeman, Douglas Southall, xiv–xv
Fremantle, Arthur James Lyon: and Beauregard, xvii; and Benjamin, xvii; and Bragg, xvii; characteristics of, x, xi, xii–xiii, xxvi n10; and Coulter, xv; and Davis, xvii; diary of, publication of, xiii–xiv, xxvi n12; disguise of, 290; and Freeman, xiv–xv; and Germans, xxii; and Gettysburg, Pennsylvania, xxiv n5; and Grenfell, xix; and Harrison, xiv; and Harwell, xv; and Hood, xxiv n5; and Houston, xvi; and Irish, xxii; and Jackson, xvii, xviii; and J. Johnston, xvii; and judges in Texas, x–xi; and Lee, xvi, xviii–xix; and Longstreet, x–xi, xv–xvi, xviii, xix; and Magruder, xvii; and Mexi-

Fremantle (*cont.*)
cans, xxii; and Otey, xii;
and Poles, xxii; and Polk,
xvii; as prisoner, 292–94;
and Quintard, xii; return to
England of, xiii, 280, 286–
87, 288–90, 294, 303, 305–
9; and Robertson, xv; and
Ross, x, xi, xiii; and Sargent, xvi–xvii; and Scheibert, ix–x, xxiv n5; and
Semmes, viii–ix; and
slaves, viii, xx–xxi; as soldier, viii, xi, xxv n8; and
Sorrel, xi, xii–xiii, xiv; as
spy, 108, 109, 292. *See also
specific headings*
Fremont, John C., 125
Front Royal, Virginia, 223–
24. *See also* Virginia

Galena (ironclad), 217, 218.
See also Ironclads
Galveston, Texas: characteris-
tics of, 71; and Cook, 72;
dances in, 73–74; and De-
bray, 70–71, 72; and Ma-
gruder, 36, 71–72;
recapture of, 72. *See also*
Texas
Galveston Bay, 70, 71
Gambling, 19, 20
Garnett, General, 270
General Price (gunboat), 95.
See also Gunboats
Georgia (state), 136, 173. *See
also specific cities*
Georgia (steamer), 131. *See
also* Steamers
Germans: and conscription,
55–56, 58; and Fremantle,
xxii; and Partisan Rangers,

55–56; and renegadoes, 25;
in San Antonio, Texas, 55–
56; and Union soldiers, 168,
209. *See also* Pennsylvania
Dutch
Gettysburg, Pennsylvania:
and Barksdale, 233, 261;
and Ewell, 251, 255, 257–
58, 259, 271, 273–74; and
Fairfax, 261; fighting at,
253–56, 257–75; and Fre-
mantle, xxiv n5; and Heth,
263, 266; and Hill, 251,
254–55, 257, 258, 259–60,
261, 263, 274; and Hood,
257, 258, 261, 271, 275; and
Johnson, 271, 274; and Lee,
248, 254, 256, 257, 259–60,
264–65, 267–69, 270–71,
275–76, 301; and Long-
street, 251, 256, 257, 258,
259, 260–61, 263, 265–66,
267, 271, 272–73, 274–75;
and M'Laws, 258, 275; and
Meade, 275; and Pender,
274; and Pendleton, 273;
and Pettigrew, 263, 266,
267; and Pickett, 258, 263,
266, 270; and Semmes, 261;
and weapons, 273. *See also*
Pennsylvania
Girard, Charles F., viii
Gist, General "State Rights":
background of, 114; breakfast for, 113; characteristics
of, 114; marriage of, 114–
15; regiment of, 113; as soldier, 112; and Yerger, 111
Gold, value of, 191
Grant, Ulysses S.: and Jackson, Mississippi, 110–11,
123, 135; and J. Johnston,

120, 123–24, 138; and Mississippi, 163; and Pemberton, 112; and Rosecrans, 163; as soldier, 194; and Vicksburg, Mississippi, 112, 118, 123–24

Graybacks, defined, 80, 299. *See also* Soldiers, Confederate

Greencastle, Pennsylvania, 238–39. *See also* Pennsylvania

Grenfell, George St. Leger: arrest of, 163, 164; background of, 148; and Bragg, 149, 163, 164; and cavalry, 158–59; characteristics of, 149–50, 159, 163–64; and Davis, 212; and Fremantle, xix; and Kentucky, 165; and Morgan, 149, 150; political beliefs of, 152; and Polk, 149, 150, 164; and slaves, 163–64; as soldier, 149–50, 212

Grierson's raid, 85, 103

Gunboats, 200. *See also* specific gunboats

Gunpowder, 175–77, 307. *See also* Weapons

Guns, Brook, 181, 219. *See also* Weapons

Guy's Gap, 160, 171

Hagerstown, Maryland: and cavalry, 283–85; divided loyalties in, 236, 285; fighting at, 282–86; and Longstreet, 283–84, 285; and Stuart, 286; and Winthrop, 284–85. *See also* Maryland

Hampton, Wade, 282

Hancock, Captain, 7, 9–10, 17

Hanley (congressman), 157

Hardee, William J.: as author, 138; characteristics of, 138–39; and Cleburne, 153; and Elliott, 137; and Liddell, 157; and Mason, 155; and Morgan, 155; and Murfreesboro, Tennessee, 138, 163, 165; and Polk, 137, 138, 139; and Shiloh, Tennessee, 138; as soldier, 138, 241; and Vallandigham, 137–38

Harney, General, 247

Harriet Lane (steamer): and *Bayou City,* 72; capture of, 28, 72, 77; dismantling of, 78; and *Neptune,* 71; and L. Smith, 28. *See also* Steamers

Harrisburg, Pennsylvania, 298. *See also* Pennsylvania

Harrison, Constance Cary, xiv

Harrisonburg, Louisiana: fighting at, 91–92, 94, 95, 96; fortifications of, 90, 93. *See also* Fort Beauregard; Louisiana

Harwell, Richard B., xv

Havana, Cuba, 7–8

Hay, Drummond, 149

Hebert, General, 89–90

Helena, Arkansas, 147

Heth, General, 257, 263, 266

Hill, A. P.: and Carlisle, Pennsylvania, 242; and Gettysburg, Pennsylvania, 251, 254–55, 257, 258, 259–60, 261, 263, 274; and weapons, 248

Hogs, 31

Hood, John B.: characteristics

Hood (*cont.*)
of, 242; and Fremantle, xxiv n5; and Gettysburg, Pennsylvania, 257, 258, 261, 271, 275; regiment of, 239, 243; as soldier, 242–43, 247; wounding of, 261, 282
Hooker, Joseph, 36, 209–10, 250
Hotels: in Louisiana, 96, 99; in Texas, 78, 79. *See also* specific hotels
Houston, Samuel (a.k.a. Big Drunk, Raven): background of, 68–69; characteristics of, xvi, 69; and Cherokees, 76; death of, 69; and Fremantle, xvi; marriage of, 76; nicknames of, 76; and Pyron's regiment, 75; and San Jacinto, battle of, 68; and Texas, secession of, 69
Houston, Texas, 66. *See also* Texas

"Imboden," 296
"I'm Bound to be a Soldier in the Army of the South" (song), 57
Immortalité (frigate), 7–8
Indiana regiment, 165–67
Indian corn, 62, 65, 79
Indian Mutiny, 149
Indians, 24–25, 56. *See also* Cherokees
Irish: and Confederate soldiers, 232; and conscription, 300; and Fremantle, xxii; and Union soldiers, 167–68, 209, 278

"Irish patriot," 183
Ironclads, 218–20. *See also* specific ironclads
Ironsides (frigate), 190, 198
Irrigation, 55
Ituria (merchant), 27

Jackson, Mississippi: characteristics of, 110; destruction of, 104, 106, 107, 108, 109–11, 113; and Evans, 126; factories in, 110; fall of, 101, 103, 104, 106, 118, 288; and Grant, 110–11, 123, 135; and J. Johnston, 106, 112, 123; journey to, 105; and Loring, 126; and Maxey, 126; and Union soldiers, 104; and Walker, 118. *See also* Mississippi
Jackson, Thomas J. "Stonewall": and Banks, 74, 125; and Benjamin, xvii–xviii, 209–10; and Chancellorsville, Virginia, 89; characteristics of, xvii, 125, 132; death of, 231, 249; and Ewell, 125, 231, 277; and Fremantle, xvii, xviii; and Fremont, 125; and Hooker, 209–10; and J. Johnston, 125; and Lee, 209–10; and Pope, 209–10; as professor, 151; reactions to, 225, 231; religious beliefs of, 249; and Slaughter, 132; as soldier, xvii–xviii, 125, 132, 209–10, 249; and Valley campaigns, 125; and Winchester, Virginia, 228; wounding of, 89
Jamaica, 191–92

James Island, 195–96
Java (ship), 69
Jews: characteristics of, 41,
43, 45; in Matamoros, Mexico, 14
John (slave), 68, 76
"John Brown" (song), 57
Johnson, Edward "Alle-
gheny," 271, 274
Johnston, Albert Sidney, 54,
148, 215
Johnston, Joseph E.: and
Breckenridge, 154; and
Canton, Mississippi, 104,
112, 126; characteristics of,
117, 121; and Fair Oaks,
Virginia, 125; flag designed
by, 226; and Fremantle,
xvii; and Grant, 120, 123–
24, 138; and Jackson, 125;
and Jackson, Mississippi,
106, 112, 123; as soldier,
101–2, 112, 117–18, 122,
194, 241; and Vicksburg,
Mississippi, 118, 123–24,
207, 220; wounding of, 124–
25
Johnstown, Pennsylvania,
297. *See also* Pennsylvania
Judge, the: characteristics of,
29, 30, 40, 48; drinking
habits of, 32, 40, 42, 47, 52;
and Longstreet, x, 51; as
mule driver, 29–30, 39, 42,
43; as senator, 32, 42; and
slaves, 52
Judges, in Texas, x–xi, 29–30

Kate (steamer), 184. *See also*
Steamers
Kelly, General, 293, 294, 295
Kemper, General, 270

Kentucky: and Burnside, 219,
287; destruction in, 287;
and Grenfell, 165; and
Wheeler, 158. *See also spe-
cific cities*
Keokuk (ironclad), wreck of,
181, 182–83, 187, 189, 198.
See also Ironclads
Killer Angels, The (Shaara),
xxvi n10
King, Butler, 216, 219
King's Ranch, 44
Knowles, H. A., 128

Ladies' cars, on railroads,
129, 136, 202
Lamar, Colonel, 196
Lawley, Francis Charles: as
author, vii, 227; illness of,
232, 235, 237, 238, 241,
243, 256; and Stuart, 286
Lee, Robert E.: and Borcke,
vii; and Chambersburg,
Pennsylvania, 245; and
Chancellorsville, Virginia,
89; characteristics of, xvi,
xviii, 248, 249, 287–88; and
Ewell, 278; and Fremantle,
xvi, xviii–xix; and Gettysburg, Pennsylvania, 248,
254, 256, 257, 259–60, 264–
65, 267–69, 270–71, 275–
76, 301; and Jackson, 209–
10; and Longstreet, 237,
249; and Magruder, 36; reactions to, 248; religious
beliefs of, 249; and Scheibert, 227; as soldier, xvi,
xviii–xix, 209–10, 241, 249,
260, 267–69; and weapons,
225–26, 248; and Wilcox,
xvi

Liddell, General, 155, 156–57, 166

Lincoln, Abraham (a.k.a. Uncle Abe): and Chambersburg, Pennsylvania, 246; criticism of, 121, 216, 246, 279; and Sargent, 51

Little Folly, 188

Liverpool, England, 203. *See also* England

Locomotives. *See* Railroads

Logan, Colonel, 94–95

Longstreet, James: background of, 237; and Carlisle, Pennsylvania, 242; characteristics of, 237, 246, 249, 287; and Fremantle, x–xi, xv–xvi, xviii, xix; and Gettysburg, Pennsylvania, 251, 256, 257, 258, 259, 260–61, 263, 265–66, 267, 271, 272–73, 274–75; and Hagerstown, Maryland, 283–84, 285; and Hooker, 250; and the Judge, x–xi, 51; and Lee, 237, 249; and Magruder, 36; and Meade, 250; nicknames of, 258, 266; and Northern women, 279–80; reactions to, 252, 253; and Ross, xi; and Sargent, 51; as soldier, xviii, xix, 237–38, 241, 261; and weapons, 248

Loring, General, 105, 112, 126

Louisiana: and Banks, 82; hotels in, 96, 99; landscape of, 86, 94, 98; roads in, 87; weather in, 99. *See also* specific cities

Louis-Napoleon. *See* Napoleon III

Lynchings: characteristics of, 11; criticism of, 58; of Montgomery, 11, 12, 19, 25, 28, 79; of spies, 108; in Texas, 24

M'Carthy (merchant), 53

M'Clellan, George Brinton, 35–36, 84, 278

M'Laws, General: and Gettysburg, Pennsylvania, 258, 275; regiment of, 233–34, 235, 238; as soldier, 247

Magruder, John Bankhead: characteristics of, 34–35, 37; and cotton trade, 36; and Fremantle, xvii; and Galveston, Texas, 36, 71–72; and Hooker, 36; and Lee, 36; and Longstreet, 36; and M'Clellan, 35–36; and Northerners, 35; and Sabine Pass, 36; as soldier, 36

Maine, 211–12

Maloney (merchant): house of, 17; as merchant, 13, 19; prosperity of, 17, 19; and robberies, 15, 19; wife of, 17

Manassas, battle of, 83

Marble Man, The (Connelly), xxviii n18

Marlborough, Duke of, 121

Martin, General, 168, 169

Maryland, 291, 296. *See also* specific cities

Mason, James M.: and cannon foundries, 176; and Hardee, 155; house of, 230; as

Southern commissioner in London, 206
Mason-Slidell affair, 209
Massachusetts, 211
Matamoros, Mexico, 14, 22–23
Maury, General, 129, 130–31
Maxey, General, 112, 126
Meade, George G., 250, 275, 297
Menger's hotel, 52, 53–54
Merrimac (ironclad), 217, 218. *See also* Ironclads
Methodist chapel, 104
Mexicans: and animals, 15; characteristics of, 14, 20, 23; derogatory terms for, 48; and Fremantle, xxii; and Texans, 48
Mexican War, 214
Mexico. *See* Mexicans; *specific cities*
Meyers (arrested at Gibraltar), 195
Military titles, 116, 121
Milroy, General: escape of, 214, 229; and Winchester, Virginia, 214, 228, 230, 276
Missions, 56
Mississippi (state): effects of war on, 212; farms in, 102; and Grant, 163; landscape of, 100, 114; railroads in, 100, 105, 106, 110, 125, 127; and Rosecrans, 163. *See also* Mississippians; *specific cities*
Mississippians, 109. *See also* Mississippi
Mississippi River: blockade of, 88, 99, 155; flooding of, 97; width of, 100

Missouri (ironclad), 79. *See also* Ironclads
Missouri (state). *See specific cities*
Mitchell, Captain, 183, 188, 200
Mitchell, Ormsby M., 142–43
Mobile, Alabama: blockade of, 130, 132–33; characteristics of, 129, 130; journey to, 127–29; and Maury, 129. *See also* Alabama
Mobile Register (newspaper), 164
Mobs, 299–300, 302
Money, Confederate, value of, 29
Mongomery (renegado): and Bee, 11; characteristics of, 11–12; lynching of, 11, 12, 19, 25, 28, 79
Monitors (ironclads): characteristics of, 198; defeat of, 57, 186; and Fort Sumter, 192–93, 195; and *Merrimac,* 217, 218. *See also* Ironclads
Monté, 20. *See also* Fandangos
Montgomery, Alabama, 134. *See also* Alabama
Moore (British consul), 215
Morgan, John H.: and cavalry, 159; and Grenfell, 149, 150; as guerrilla, 152; and Hardee, 155; marriage of, 150
Morris Island, 187–88
Moses, Major: and Chambersburg, Pennsylvania, 241, 242, 243–45; characteristics of, 240

Mosquite-trees, 10
Moultrieville, South Carolina, 183–84. *See also* South Carolina
Munroe, Louisiana, 89–90. *See also* Louisiana
Murfreesboro, Tennessee: and Bragg, 151–52; fighting at, 148, 151–52, 171; and Hardee, 138, 163, 165; and Polk, 145, 148, 163; and Rosecrans, 145, 152. *See also* Tennessee

Napoleon guns, 113, 273. *See also* Weapons
Napoleon I, 121
Napoleon III, viii, 273
Natchez, Mississippi, 100. *See also* Mississippi
Nelson (slave), 101
Neptune (steamer), 71. *See also* Steamers
New Orleans, Louisiana, 131. *See also* Louisiana
Newspapers, Southern, 154, 201, 220
New York City: and blacks, 300, 302; and cavalry, 300; characteristics of, 298–99; and conscription, xxi, 299–300, 302; mobs in, 299–300, 302
Niblitt's Bluff, 74
Norris, Major, 204
Norris, Sergeant, 222
North Carolina, 205. *See also* specific cities
Northerners: and Magruder, 35; and Maury, 130–31; and slaves, 93, 133, 281–82; and Southern women, 140–

43, 154; and universal suffrage, 68. *See also* Abolitionists; Soldiers, Union; Women, Northern; *specific headings*
Nueces River, 48–49

Oakville, Texas, 49. *See also* Texas
Oath of allegiance, 131, 229
Oetling (Prussian consul), 15, 16
Officers, Confederate: characteristics of, xix, 172, 212; and Davis, 212; election of, 59. *See also* Soldiers, Confederate; *specific officers*
Officers, Union, 295. *See also* Soldiers, Union; *specific officers*
Orlando (ship), 8
Otey, W. N. Mercer, and Fremantle, xii

Pablo, Don. *See* Zorn
Palmetto State (ironclad), 185, 190. *See also* Ironclads
Parrot guns, 181. *See also* Weapons
Partisan Rangers, 9, 24–25, 55–56. *See also* Duff, Colonel
Passports, 127, 134–35, 136
Patrick Henry (gunboat), 217–18. *See also* Gunboats
"Peculiar institution." *See* Slaves and slavery
Pemberton, General, 105, 112, 116–17
Peñaloso, Captain, 58
Pender (officer), 224–25, 226, 274

Pendleton, General, 247, 273
Pennsylvania: characteristics of, 238; and Ewell, 233, 238, 242; farms in, 238; landscape of, 252; weather in, 276, 280. *See also specific cities*
Pennsylvania Dutch, 246. *See also* Germans
Percussion caps, 177, 307
Perryville, Kentucky, 145, 166–67. *See also* Kentucky
Pettigrew, James J., 263, 266, 267
Philadelphia, Pennsylvania, 298–99. *See also* Pennsylvania
Phillipps's regiment, 78
Physicians, 119, 135
Pickett, George E.: characteristics of, 247; and Gettysburg, Pennsylvania, 258, 263, 266, 270; and San Juan Island, 247; as soldier, 247
Pirates, 149
Pittsburg (ironclad), 95, 96. *See also* Ironclads
Pittsburg and Philadelphia Railway, 297–98. *See also* Railroads
Pittsburg Landing, Tennessee. *See* Shiloh, Tennessee
Plantations, 91. *See also* Blacks; Farms; Slaves
Poles, xxii
Polignac (officer), 153
Polk, Leonidas: and Alexander, xxvii n16; background of, 140; and Belmont, Missouri, 145; as bishop, xxvii n16, 139, 140, 144–45, 146; bodyguards of, 171; and Bragg, 162; characteristics of, xvii, 124, 139, 171–72; and Cheetham, 171; and Elliott, 140; and Fremantle, xvii; and Grenfell, 149, 150, 164; and Hardee, 137, 138, 139; and Indiana regiment, 165–67; and Liddell, 166; and Murfreesboro, Tennessee, 145, 148, 163; and Perryville, Kentucky, 145, 166–67; and Shiloh, Tennessee, 145; as soldier, 241
Pope, John, 209–10
Potomac River, 236
Powhatan (sloop of war), 190
Prickly pears, 30
Prisoners, Union soldiers as, 135–36, 177, 253, 254, 255, 256, 258, 261, 275, 283, 285–86
Puebla, Mexico, 17
Pyron's regiment, 74–75. *See also* Soldiers, Confederate

Quintard, Charles Todd, xii, 141, 148

Rabbits, 45, 60
Racoon (blockade-runner), 190. *See also* Blockades and blockade-runners
Railroads: characteristics of, 64, 65, 202, 205; destruction of, 100, 106, 110, 125, 127, 152, 173; in Georgia, 173; ladies' cars on, 129, 136, 202; in Mississippi, 100, 105, 106, 110, 125, 127; and passports, 127,

Railroads (*cont.*)
134–35, 136; shootings on, 128; sleeping cars on, 297–98; spies on, 134; in Texas, 64, 65; and tobacco-chewing, 137; in Virginia, 205–6
Rains, Colonel, 175–76
Randolph, General, 219
Rat ranches, defined, 32
Rats, 32
Rattlesnakes, in Texas, 34, 46, 48
Raven. *See* Houston, Samuel
Renegadoes, 21, 25
Renshaw, Commodore, 28, 72
Reynolds, General, 255
Rhett, Colonel, 181, 183
Richmond (ironclad), 218, 219. *See also* Ironclads
Richmond, Colonel, 170, 172
Richmond, Texas, 64–65. *See also* Texas
Richmond, Virginia: cannon foundries in, 307; capitol building in, 215–16; characteristics of, 206–7; fighting at, 215; newspapers in, 220; and Stoneman, 221; weather in, 207. *See also* Virginia
Ricks, William F., 141–43
Rifle and Light Infantry Tactics (Hardee), 138
Rifles, Enfield, 113, 156, 225. *See also* Weapons
Rio Grande River, 8–9
Ripley, General, 177–78, 198, 200
River-gropers, 200. *See also* specific gunboats
Roads: in Louisiana, 87; in Tennessee, 144; in Texas,

45–46, 59, 61, 78
Robertson (merchant), 178
Robertson, James I., Jr., xv
Rocky, Texas, 50. *See also* Texas
Rosecrans, William S.: and Bragg, 152; and Grant, 163; and Mississippi, 163; and Murfreesboro, Tennessee, 145, 152; as soldier, 81; and Vallandigham, 137
Ross, Fitzgerald: as author, viii; and Fremantle, x, xi, xiii; and Longstreet, xi
Royal Yacht (steamer), 69. *See also* Steamers
Ruby (blockade-runner), 188, 190. *See also* Blockades and blockade-runners
Russell, Dr., 108–10, 126
Russell, William Howard, vii, 210, 213

Sabine Pass, 36
Saddles, Mexican, 24
St. Michael's Church, 197
San Antonio, Texas, 53, 55–56. *See also* Texas
San Antonio River, 52, 55, 56
"Sands, The," 38
San Jacinto, battle of, 68
San José, mission of, 56
San Juan, mission of, 56
San Juan Island, 247
San Luis Potosi, Mexico, 16
San Pedro River, 56
Sargent (mule driver): characteristics of, xvi–xvii, 30, 32, 33, 49; drinking habits of, 32, 42, 43, 47–48, 52; and Fremantle, xvi–xvii; and Lincoln, 51; and Long-

street, 51; as mule driver, 33, 39–40, 42, 47, 50, 52; and slaves, xx–xxi, 40, 52

Scheibert, Justus: and Fremantle, ix–x, xxiv n5; and Lee, 227; and Stuart, vii–viii, 227

Schreibert, Justus. *See* Scheibert, Justus

Scorpions, 45

Scouts, 119, 161

Scurry, General, 67, 68

Secession: and Benjamin, 207–8, 210; of Texas, 25, 69

"Secessionville," 195, 196–97

Sedden (secretary of war), 214–15

Seguin, Texas, 59. *See also* Texas

Semmes, Raphael, viii–ix, 233, 261

Sennec (officer), 197, 204

Seven Pines, Virginia, 125. *See also* Virginia

Shelbyville, Tennessee, 136, 146. *See also* Tennessee

Shellings, 72–73, 93

Shenandoah River, 224

Shenandoah Valley, 223

Sherman, William T., 55

Shiloh, Tennessee: and Beauregard, 148; fighting at, 148; and Hardee, 138; and A. Johnston, 54, 215; and Polk, 145

Shootings, on railroads, 128

Shreveport, Louisiana, 84, 85. *See also* Louisiana

Signal corps, 141, 165

Slaughter, General, 132

Slaves and slavery: and Banks, 87; and British, 191–92; buying and selling of, 179, 191; characteristics of, 97, 133, 282; in Charleston, South Carolina, 179; and Chubb, 69; clothing of, 56, 75, 186, 223; criticism of, 120, 191; and Duff, 25; effects of war on, 120, 133; emancipation of, 191–92; and Fremantle, viii, xx–xxi; and Grenfell, 163–64; housing of, 86, 91, 120; ill-treatment of, 52, 81–82; in Jamaica, 191–92; and the Judge, 52; and M'Carthy, 53; and M'Laws's division, 238; and Northerners, 93, 133, 281–82; and Partisan Rangers, 25; and Sargent, xx–xxi, 40, 52; and shellings, 72–73, 93; as soldiers, xxi, 282, 307; and Southerners, 52, 76, 81–82, 102, 120, 191–92; value of, 62, 282; well-being of, xx–xxi, 52, 56, 66–67, 75–76, 86, 92, 120, 191, 223. *See also* Blacks

Sleeping cars, on railroads, 297–98

Slidell, John, 119

Smith, Kirby, 83, 84

Smith, Leon, 28

Smythe (detains Fremantle), 107–8, 109, 126

Snakes, 98

Snuff, 49

Soldiers, black: destruction by, 178; hanging of, 147; slaves as, xxi, 282, 307. *See also* Blacks

Soldiers, Confederate: and

Soldiers, Confederate (*cont.*)
Chambersburg, Pennsylvania, 245–46; characteristics of, 122–23, 133–34, 231–32; clothing of, 21, 113, 155–56, 163, 223, 231–32, 293, 299; and Davis, 212–13; as deserters, 157; destruction by, 238, 246, 272; discipline of, 21, 59, 122, 123, 157, 194, 289; drinking habits of, 122; and election of officers, 59; and England, 59; flags of, 226; foreigners as, 181, 232; horses of, 226; as horse thieves, 235; nicknames of, 80, 210, 299; number of, 158, 208; patriotism of, 122–23, 133–34, 135; politeness of, 57; poverty of, 19; slaves as, xxi, 282, 307; weapons of, 113, 156, 162, 225–26, 231–32, 307; women as, 173; wounding of, 86, 133–34, 306–7. *See also* Conscription; Officers, Confederate; *specific regiments and soldiers*

Soldiers, Union: and Canada, 208–9; clothing of, 293, 299; as deserters, 89; destruction by, 141–43, 272; and England, 208–9; foreigners as, 167–68, 209, 278; graves of, 232–33; and Jackson, Mississippi, 104; nicknames of, 80, 299; number of, 208; as prisoners, 135–36, 177, 253, 254, 255, 256, 258, 261, 275, 283, 285–86. *See also*

Abolitionists; Conscription; Northerners; Officers, Union; *specific regiments and soldiers*

Sorrel, Gilbert Moxley, xi, xii–xiii, xiv

South Carolina, 178. *See also specific cities*

Southerners: characteristics of, 308–9; and England, 216–17; and slaves, 52, 76, 81–82, 102, 120, 191–92; and universal suffrage, 68, 157; and weapons, 129. *See also* Women, Southern; *specific headings*

Southern History of the War (Pollard), xiv

Spies: execution of, 157; Fremantle as, 108, 109, 292; lynching of, 108; on railroads, 134

Stagecoaches: characteristics of, 58–59, 60, 61–62, 77, 82–83, 87, 296; defined, 58; and mealtime, 63, 87; and tobacco-chewing, 59, 60, 87

State capitals, 134. *See also specific cities*

Steamers, 9, 90, 184. *See also specific steamers*

Stockdale, Judge, 65

Stoneman, George, 221

"Stonewall" Brigade, 252. *See also* Soldiers, Confederate

Stono (steamer), 200. *See also* Steamers

Stuart, James E. "Jeb": and Borcke, vii–viii, 228; characteristics of, 286; and Hagerstown, Maryland, 286; and Lawley, 286; regiment of, 251; and Scheibert, vii–viii, 227; as soldier, 286; and Washington, D.C., 262

Styles, Colonel, 157–58

Submarines, 192–93

Suffrage, universal, 68, 157

Sugar, 65

Sulokowski, Colonel, 72

Sumner, Charles, 210

Sumter (gunboat), viii. *See also* Gunboats

Swamp Angels, 69–70

Swamps, 98

Tailing, defined, 26

Tennessee: divided loyalties in, 145–46, 172; landscape of, 136–37, 155, 160, 172; roads in, 144; weather in, 158, 163, 168. *See also specific cities*

Tennessee River, 137

Texans: characteristics of, 60–61, 92; derogatory terms for, 48; drinking habits of, 26–27, 33, 42, 47–48; horsemanship of, 26; and Mexicans, 48; and snuff, 49; and tobacco-chewing, 59, 60. *See also* Texas

Texas: crops in, 60, 62, 65, 79; and Duff, 25; hotels in, 78, 79; and Houston, 69; insects in, 31, 34, 45; irrigation of, 55; judges in, x–xi, 29–30; landscape of, 29, 30, 32, 38, 39, 44–45, 47, 50, 51, 55, 60, 62, 63, 65, 66, 78, 79, 82; lawlessness of, 23–24; lynchings in, 24; railroads in, 64, 65; roads in, 45–46, 59, 61, 78; secession of, 25, 69; towns in, 63; weather in, 45–46, 47, 49, 51, 59; wildlife in, 31, 32, 34, 45, 46, 48, 60. *See also* Texans; *specific cities*

Texas Rangers, 33–34, 46, 78

Texas Unionists, 21, 25

Ticks, 34

Titles, military, 116, 121

Tobacco-chewing: and railroads, 137; and stagecoaches, 59, 60, 87; and Texans, 59, 60

Torpedo-rams, 199

Trains. *See* Railroads

Tredegar works, 307. *See also* Foundries, cannon

Tucker (slave), 97, 98, 101

Tucker, Captain, 190

Turkish lanterns, defined, 34

Twenty-First Mississippi Regiment, 281. *See also* Soldiers, Confederate

Uncle Abe. *See* Lincoln, Abraham

Universal suffrage, 68, 157

Vallandigham, Clement L. (a.k.a. Apostle of Liberty): and blockade-runners, 203–4; and Bragg, 137; "dumping down" of, 160, 161; and Hardee, 137–38; letter about, 160; and Norris, 204; as Ohio governor-nominee, 204; and Rosecrans, 137

Valley campaigns, 125

Van Dorn, Earl, 24, 146–47

Vicksburg, Mississippi: fall of, 111, 207, 220; fighting at, 100, 112, 115, 116, 122,

Vicksburg (*cont.*)
207; and Grant, 112, 118,
123–24; and J. Johnston,
118, 123–24, 207, 220; and
Pemberton, 112, 116–17.
See also Mississippi
Virginia: divided loyalties in,
234, 235; effects of war on,
223; Episcopal church in,
232; landscape of, 206, 221,
223; railroads in, 205–6;
weather in, 206, 221, 233,
235. *See also specific cities*
Voting, 68, 157

Wachita River, 88, 90, 96
Walker, General, 87–88, 118
Wartrace, Tennessee, 157,
171. *See also* Tennessee
Washington, D.C., 262
Weapons: and Beauregard,
198; of Confederate sol-
diers, 113, 156, 162, 225–
26, 231–32, 307; and Ewell,
276–78, 280; at Fort Sum-
ter, 181, 182; and Gettysburg, Pennsylvania, 273;
and Hill, 248; and Lee,
225–26, 248; and Long-
street, 248; of Pyron's regiment, 74–75; and Ripley,
198; and Southerners, 129.
See also specific weapons
Webb, Colonel: characteristics
of, 160, 161, 170; regiment
of, 161, 162, 169, 170
Weitzel (officer), 74
"We'll Hang Jeff Davis on a
Sour-Apple Tree" (song), 57
Wellington, Duke of, 121
Westfield (steamer), 71. *See
also* Steamers

Wharton (officer), 159
Wheeler, Joseph, 158, 159
Whiskey, 249–50
Whitworth, 188. *See also*
Weapons
Wilcox, Cadmus, xvi
Wilmington, North Carolina,
205
Winchester, Virginia: and
Butler, 228; capture of,
227–28, 229; characteristics
of, 230–31; effects of war
on, 229, 231; and Ewell,
214, 221, 228; and Jackson,
228; and Milroy, 214, 228,
230, 276; and oath of allegiance, 229. *See also* Virginia
Winthrop, Captain, 284–85
Withers, General, 171
Wolseley, Garnot, vii
Women, Northern: divided
loyalties of, 285; effects of
war on, 279–80; and Long-
street, 279–80; patriotism
of, 239–40, 243, 244, 278–
79. *See also* Northerners
Women, Southern: characteristics of, 103, 143–44; divided loyalties of, 234;
effects of war on, xx, 102,
131–32, 212, 229–30, 231;
hospital work of, 231, 306;
and Northerners, 140–43,
154; patriotism of, xx, 147,
174, 224, 308; and rail-
roads, 129, 136, 202; as soldiers, 173. *See also*
Southerners
Woodford, Commodore, 95
Wood's regiment, 33–34, 46,
78

Yankee Commodore (steamer), 71. *See also* Steamers

"Yankee Devil," 187

Yankees. *See* Northerners

Yeatman, Colonel, 172

Yerger, Captain, 109, 111

York, Pennsylvania, 250. *See also* Pennsylvania

Yorktown (gunboat), 217–18. *See also* Gunboats

Zorn (acting British vice-consul, a.k.a. Don Pablo), 15, 20–21

Zouaves, 286